The Road
I Have Travelled

The Road
I Have Travelled

Altina Schinasi Miranda

Apodaca Hill
Press

Photo Restoration & Layout by Algar Vandal Thagne
Book Design by Colleen Mariah Rae
Logo, Cover, & Title Page Designs by Algar Vandal Thagne

To Celestino, my husband, whose love surrounds
me like a warm river in which I bathe daily

1

Sometimes it seems even to me this story should begin: *Once upon a time in a land far away.* It all starts the year I was eight in a village about thirty miles north of New York City in a Victorian house situated on four acres surrounded by a white marble wall. At least it started as a Victorian house until my father, a Turkish Sephardic Jew with millions of dollars at his disposal, got hold of it and began to transform it, as he transformed anything he touched, into an image of himself. The fifteen rooms in our summer house became thirty-five, which was the amount of rooms he felt a house should have. On what he called the sun porch, he had a large copper dome constructed, and when the sun shone on it, it could be seen for miles around and became a focus for finger-pointing visitors to the village—"the dome of that crazy Turk."

"Crazy like a fox," someone would usually reply. "I'd like to be crazy like that and crazy rich."

My father had been poor, poor, poor, and he became rich, rich, rich. There was nothing so expensive that Moussa Schinasi wouldn't buy it. He was extremely extravagant, and he had

Father

exquisite taste. He gloried in being surrounded by the richest and most expensive fabrics. The carpets were all red and the walls brocaded silks and satins.

My father left his childhood home in Manisa at the age of fifteen, penniless and barefoot. He shipped out on a cattle boat to Alexandria, Egypt, where he worked on the docks loading and unloading boats and learning about the tobacco business. There was a rich Greek there named Garaffolo, who took a fancy to my father. He took him into his home, and he kept him as a son, his own son having died. My father meant a great deal to Garaffolo; he taught him manners and social graces. My father stayed with Garaffolo until he was almost thirty. And then one day Garaffolo said, "It's time for you to go to the United States of America because that's where the opportunity is." And so with money that Garaffollo gave him, my father was able to come to the U.S. without going through Ellis Island.

In 1893, my father showed up at the Chicago Exposition with a pack of ready-rolled cigarettes. This was novel because in those days, everyone rolled cigarettes by hand. His patented machine was a revolutionary innovation.

After the Exposition, my father returned to New York, and he had his brother Solomon Schinasi join him. They started a little factory on 120th Street and Broadway, brought over workers from Turkey, and they started making ready-made cigarettes. These were sold by salesman, and my father and his brother were soon very successful.

Within five or six years, they were millionaires, which was rather striking. But, said my father, in those days if you had brains and if you worked hard, you couldn't help but do well.

Because he'd made a fortune importing Turkish tobacco to the United States, Abdul Hamid, the last Sultan of Turkey, "knighted" him. My father was a member of the young Turks that followed the Sultan and supported Kemal Pasha who ruled Turkey for many years. Hanging on my wall today is a curious photograph of the Sultan that accompanied the medal and the citation that my father received. The photograph shows a small man seated on a chair, and the image occupies only a small area in the total frame. It's surrounded by elaborately embroidered design in bronze and gold on a beige material that's now yellowed with age. On the citation I read that in the month of Rabiil-Awwaal, in the year 1324 of the Mohammedan calendar, my father received the Medjidiya Medal of fourth degree "for his excellent efforts in promoting this industry which won for him His Majesty's commendation."

Around the turn of the century, after seven years alone in the U.S., my father decided it was time to find a wife. He was already fifty, and he thought his days as a playboy were over.

He returned to Turkey to ask for a friend's help. There he happened to see a photo of the man's granddaughter, who was then only sixteen and away at school. "She is beautiful," my father said. "Would she like to marry me?"

Joseph Ben Rubi laughed. "Moussa, you are an

Mother

old man, Laurette is a child."

But my father pushed on. "When she comes back from school, would you ask her?"

Surprisingly, when my mother came back from school and met my father, she fell in love. But he was a very handsome and dashing man, and he was also very wealthy by then and could buy anything he wanted or needed. And he was an important man in Turkey. She said yes to his proposal.

They married in Turkey, and he brought her to the United States, where he built for her a big marble house on Riverside Drive in New York City, the house in which I was born on August 4, 1907.

I always thought one of the reasons my mother accepted my father was partly the idea of going to America, a new country; Mama was full of a sense of adventure. She couldn't have known that the new country, where she would have to follow the rules that my father laid down, would be like a prison.

My father's jealousy dominated him. Although he was completely unfaithful to her—something he thought was his prerogative—he would not let Mama out of the house without a companion. And very often when he was out, he'd draw the shades so she couldn't look out of the windows.

Each of them had their own car and their own chauffeur. Sometimes when her chauffeur drove her into the city to shop, he'd later report back to Papa who questioned him closely as to where she had been. In my parents early years together, she was allowed no money of her own, but she could go to any store in New York, buy anything that she wanted and charge it to my father.

I remember one night when they were going to the opera. My mother had a dress that was cut down a little bit in the front. My father said he wouldn't go out if she wore that dress. So she had to call the seamstress to sew a little piece on the bodice so that nothing would be seen. That's the sort of thing that she endured.

My mother was everything that my father wasn't. She was timid where he was bold. She was romantic where he was pragmatic. She spent time dreaming; he spent his time in action. In my early memories of Mama, I see her lying on a chaise lounge, intently reading a French novel. Novels to be read were piled up on the floor beside her. She, also, lay a good deal in bed and cried and read French novels and cried and read some more. Her room was usually dim, and there were all kinds of medicine and bottles on the table. She was always gentle with us but seemed to cut us off, barricaded as she was by her books and bottles. But sometimes she would call us to her and read aloud to us in French; sometimes she would tell us about the days that were for her the happiest, those two years in a French boarding school in Lausanne, Switzerland, before she met my father.

Life in America was hard for my mother. We were Sephardic Jews, and so the German Jews of that time didn't accept us. For my father, this wasn't a problem. He was a very independent man, and he didn't really care about being in society or not being in society. It mattered very little to him.

But it mattered to my mother, who'd been raised in a much more middle-class way than my father who had really brought himself up. People's opinion mattered greatly to my mother, and she was always saying, "What will people say?"

My father was an immigrant—a never-to-be-assimilated immigrant. To try and rid him of his old superstitions was like trying to tear feathers from a duck. And his list of superstitions was long. Nuns were very bad luck, black cats and funerals, hats on the bed, Friday, the 13th of every month, Tuesday was not good but not as bad as Friday. You never opened an umbrella in the house. People who flattered usually possessed the evil eye. If a picture fell from the wall, death was hovering close by. You always got out of bed with your right foot. People who were pale had tuberculosis, were, contagious and should be kept out of the house.

My mother wasn't superstitious, but she was religious—in her own fashion. Each year she became enamored of a different religion—Bahai, Persian, Buddhist, Christian Science, Yoga, diet religions. She was always in search for a solution, an explanation.

My father, however, was not interested in speculating as to whether there was or was not a God, but he gave substantial donations to the temple each year just in case there was.

The ideas my parents shared in common were ethical ideas. You did not lie, or cheat, or steal, or bear false witness against your neighbor. You never refused to help someone who needed help if you were able to give it. Beyond that, they had little if anything in common—except the three of us.

There was Victoria, four years older than I, and at twelve, proud and beautiful with a long neck; Juliette, two years older than I, timid and shy and attached to Victoria, following her every footstep; and then me, Altina, like some afterthought, tagging along several feet behind.

The household contained members of many nationalities, but not any Americans with whom my father did not feel at home. Inside the house, there were only women. There was Jackson, our English nurse, who always wore a gray pseudo-silk dress under which she wore a corset. Every morning, she laced herself up tightly so that there was no place on her body that was soft to the touch. It went from her hips to way up under her breasts and gave her a hard, welded shape. At night she would take off her corset and heave a great sigh of relief. It was like seeing the dismantling of a battleship in His Majesty's navy.

Also in our household was Loff, a roly-poly Irish lady who mended everything that needed mending in the house. Sometimes when she had extra time she would make me a dress, and it was always my favorite dress. With her pink full face, soft gray eyes, and button nose, Loff looked to me like a pin cushion. I loved her. Hers was my favorite room, and I always felt happy there with her. She kept a sewing basket for me in the corner of the room, and when things got too confusing in the house, I would go up there and sew.

Then there was Mary, the Irish girl who was our

chambermaid. Very funny and jolly, her way of talking was different from Jackson. Mary had a boyfriend who used to take her out once a week, and I would watch her as she dressed up and made herself pretty to go out with him. I saw that if you were a woman, you had to make yourself pretty to go out with a man.

There was Anna, another chambermaid. Her hair was white and wavy. She loved my mother, and would say to me, "Be good to your mother because she is very sad."

"Why?" I would ask.

"Because of the things your father does."

"What does he do?

"I can't tell you. You are too young to know." This would leave me troubled. What could my beloved father do that was bad?

We had for a time a Moroccan chef with an extraordinary talent for cooking and an evil and violent temper. He once chased the kitchen maid around the village brandishing a butcher's knife so that even my father had to agree to fire him and forego his wonderful meals. He was replaced by an Egyptian cook called Minna who weighed 300 pounds and needed a lot of assistance because of her great weight, but she too was an extraordinary cook. I would help her in the kitchen, and that's how I learned to cook. On Sundays, which was ice cream day, she enlisted me to turn the mixture of cream in a large wooden barrel for hours until it became ice cream. She would tell me about Egypt, about the people who dressed in black and moved like shadows along the streets, and about how outside the city in the desert were big constructions called pyramids that people would come to visit. She told me about the food they ate, and the kind of houses they lived in, and how the English were ruling over them. "Why, if you don't like the English, don't you tell them to go away?" I would ask.

She would laugh, "Because my little child, they have guns, and people with guns always have things their way."

There was Celia, the German waitress, who walked with heavy steps and did everything according to the rules. She made me do things over and over again until I did them right.

She said that in her country she was very poor and that she had come to the United States so she could send money home to her family so they would have enough to eat. She was very plain, quite ugly and too fat, and she didn't smile very often. I decided I didn't want to go to Germany.

Then we had a French governess, whom we called Mademoiselle. Anytime she would mention Celia, she would say, "Sale Boche."

"What's that?" I asked my mother.

"Dirty German," my mother answered. "The French always hated the Germans. They have had so many wars and the Germans usually win."

Mademoiselle looked down on all the servants; she said they were lower class, and I should not forget that.

Outside the house there were Patrick and Michael, the two gardeners. They lived in the gardener's cottages with their wives. Michael was an exceedingly cheery fellow, but Patrick was so shy that when you spoke to him his face would get all red and he would put his head down.

Patrick's wife died. The next morning, Michael came running over just as my father was getting into his car. "Patrick, Patrick," he said, but he could hardly get the words out. "Patrick has hanged himself. I took him down, I think he is dead, but we had best get the doctor." He was indeed dead, and we all missed him. I cried for a full half day. Michael was never the same after that, and his cheeriness turned to gloom.

George Stobie was the groom who took care of the horses. We had a pretty mare and a large chestnut-colored pony named Victor, who pulled our pony cart. We went out almost every afternoon in the pony cart with George. We went for two hours, each of us having a turn at driving. The roads around were all dirt, so it was easy for us to drive. George was our most favorite person, and he let us tickle and squeeze him and put wild flowers in the head band of his hat.

The children of the village, who looked at us with the same look they would use if they saw freaks in the circus, would sometimes run after the cart yelling "rich kids, rich kids," and George would beat them off with his whip. One thing we knew, being rich was bad, bad, bad—otherwise why would kids yell at us as though they hated us?

There was, also, Jaco, the big Turkish watchman who patrolled the house and garden accompanied by his dog Togo. "He will warn me," Jaco said, "if anything goes wrong." Jaco was a beautiful old man with white hair. He was enormous and strong with an almost toothless grin. He was always sweet and kind and welcoming of us children. Jaco stayed up all night long, walking from room to room. In each room there was a punch clock, and it was his duty to go into each room every hour and punch the clock. In the morning he would bring the tapes to my father to prove that he had been in every room and not sleeping.

I sometimes wonder where my father got all his ideas and how he developed all these routines. He was very orderly and if even an ashtray was out of place, he knew it and he wanted to know who had moved it and why.

He liked every object in the house. Whatever he collected he did so because he was attracted to it and not for its value.

My mother was completely indifferent to all the furniture and all the objects. She would have liked to give them away, throw them away, have a tidal wave come and sweep away the whole immense collection of things. She would often say, "I don't need all this. All I want are two rooms and a kitchenette."

My sisters were not overly fond of me. We had a playground for our exercise, and they would always get on the seesaw and leave no room for me.

"I want to go," I would yell. "It's my turn now." They would turn their faces toward me: "You want a turn?"

"Yes, yes." Then they would put me on   the

Victoria, Altina & Juliette

seesaw and begin turning it rapidly faster and faster until I was screaming and falling off.

"That will teach you," they'd say, and they would collapse with laughter.

Our nurse would appear, and full of pity she'd pick me up off the ground, saying to my sisters, "What are you children doing?" I was her pet, which did not increase my sisters' already meager love for me.

I was the youngest and the smallest, and I was my father's favorite. His face would light up when he would see me. "Come here, 'Tunchy,'" he would say and pick me up to sit on his lap. Papa's coming home at night was always a time for great celebration because he always brought little gifts—a box of candy, a little statue, a bunch of flowers, a little dress. Then he would hold me and tell me stories about his day at the factory. At Christmas, he used to take us to visit his factory, and we carried little containers in which we collected change from the workers to give to sick children in the city. The workers in the factory made a great fuss over us and said how cute we were, so we liked going there.

There were no unions in those days, so the workers in the factory all thought that my father was like the president of the country or the mayor. It was a paternal relationship he had with his workers. On Sundays there was a long line of workers who would come to the house, and my father would listen to their problems and try to help them. If they were sick—there was a lot of tuberculosis at the time—he would send them for a cure and pay for it. And none of the families was allowed to starve. My father was a very benevolent man in his way. He was also a rough man.

I knew my father very well, not in a close or intimate way, but I never doubted for a moment that he loved me. He was always my court of last appeal. But as I grew older, my feelings for him rather changed. I began to compare him to the Americans and the modern world into which I was thrust at school. Then it began to appear that it was my world that was strange and the outside world normal, with things as they should be. This struggle to reconcile the two worlds has always been with me, and even now I sometimes look around at the people I am with and think, "What am I doing here with all these strange creatures?"

2

As a child, mine was a circumscribed world—a monastery or nunnery—with only essential communication with the world that existed outside. But I wanted more. I would look through the windows and watch people walking down the street. I wondered who they were and if they felt about things the way I did. My knowledge of people came, besides from my family, from the servants and from the few visitors who entered the walls.

The visitor I dreaded most was the little Black Rabbi. He came once a year, in the fall, just before we left our summer home to return to our house in New York City. The little Black Rabbi wasn't really black, but he dressed in black. His hat was black, his suit was black, his beard was black, and his shoes were black. I don't remember if his socks were black, but they must have been, or I would have noticed.

It was always fall when he came, and he would walk around the garden holding a small black book in his hands. It was open, and he would follow the lines with one long finger, sensitive and graceful, and he would be singing and chanting as he read. It wasn't English that he was reading; I knew that.

It was Hebrew, and his voice was singsong and low.

I would follow him around. He'd walk down the gravel path and past the big apple tree. The apples were just beginning to get red. There were some apples lying on the ground. He'd bend over and pick up one and put it in the pocket of his jacket. It would make a bulge. I'd wonder when he would eat it.

He'd walk on to the stables where the rich smell of horses came through the air. Then past the houses where the gardeners lived and back into the orchard.

There was no use in trying to talk to him because I knew he only spoke Hebrew. The grand Rabbi of the Temple sent him once a year, as he was too old and important to come himself. The little Black Rabbi looked very young and poor, as though the suit he had on was the only one he owned.

I would continue to follow him around. I was hoping the sun wouldn't go down. This part of his coming was all right, but when the sun would go down, the awful part would begin. The sun was beginning to set.

The little Rabbi was turning back, and his steps were directed towards the house. He slipped his book into the pocket of his jacket. Now his steps were firm, as though a straight line was pulling him. He no longer had the pensive slow quality that his steps had had as he walked around the garden. He got to the house and walked down the steps that led into the basement. He knocked on the iron door. The door opened and Jaco let him in . . . and then the door shut and they both disappeared.

I stood outside feeling trembling rising in my throat. I remembered what happened the year before, and I knew that it would happen again. The little Black Rabbi had stood in the basement, a crate of all-white chickens beside him on the ground, the cover half closed. He'd taken off his hat and put a shawl over his shoulders. Then he'd opened the crate and leaned over and taken a chicken out and with his hands that looked like claws; he'd twisted the chicken's wings into a knot so that it couldn't move, and he'd begun to swing it in circles. The basement smelled bad and the chickens squawked and cried and he cut their throats and then the blood spattered. All eyes had been fixed on the little Rabbi; all watched in silence.

Then my father's voice rang out, cutting the silence. "Children, we are making a gift to God, and each of you will have a chicken sacrificed for you and this will protect you and keep you from harm during the year." My father, my beloved father, had stood stern and unsmiling with my mother next to him, her hands clasped in front of her, while we three children nestled against her, lifting our eyes occasionally to rest on her face, hoping for a signal from her that would say "Stop, stop."

My older sister had been the first to go and stand by the Rabbi. Her eyes black with fear. The Rabbi's face seemed unnaturally white as he swung the chicken above her head. Then I'd seen him cut the chicken's neck and seen the blood spurt out.

I had run out of the basement and went upstairs to find Loff in the sewing room, and that's where my father had found me. He'd stood outside the door and called me. I'd gone over and looked up at him.

"I'm ashamed of you," he'd said. "You ran away like a coward. But you are young and next year you will be older and stronger, and I expect you to stand there like a soldier. I am doing this to protect you. You will do this for me if you love me."

"I will. I will," I had said.

Now I was older but still scared, but since I loved my father above everyone else, I knew I would have to do it this year.

Pretty soon I heard Nurse Jackson's voice calling: "Children, it's time now, to go down to the basement for the ceremony." She said 'ceremony' in the way the English say it, running over it fast that made it sound beautiful and exciting. But there were a lot of other things about Jackson that were not beautiful or exciting. Her corset was one; her principles another. She lived by two: that the English way was the *right* way and that no matter how much anything hurt, you never cried but kept a stiff upper lip.

The little Rabbi was standing in the middle of the room. "You will be the first," my father said, and he gave me a little push with his hand. I went and stood by the Rabbi. I could smell his sweat. He turned towards me with the chicken in his

Nurse Jackson

hand. I shut my eyes. I could feel him raising his arm and beginning the slow swing over my head. And then the chanting began, singsong up and down, now strong, now reedy and thin. I began praying silently. "Please God, if you are up there and watching this, don't let the feathers fall on me, don't let the blood splash on me, and don't let the chicken suffer. I will promise to be good. I will do everything my nurse tells me to do, I will not fight with my sisters, I will not refuse to eat the food on my plate, I will not smudge up the ink on my homework. I will be good good good if only you will not let the feathers fall on me and the blood splash on me, and make it all end soon, as soon as possible."

Finally it was over. I opened my eyes and the Rabbi's back was towards me and he was leaning over. I looked for my father, and he had a strange smile on his lips. He nodded and I knew I could go. I wouldn't have to stay and watch the other killings. I ran out the door and up the basement stairs, then up to the first floor, then up to the second and to the third, and raced down the hall to the sewing room where I knew Loff would be and where when I could see her face all the bad things would disappear. When I saw her I wanted to throw myself at her, but I didn't. She looked up from her sewing and her soft rosy face and soft gleaming eyes made me want to cry, but I didn't.

"What's the matter, dearie?" she said. She always called me dearie.

"Nothing," I answered. "I just came up here to sew on the pillow I am making for Mama."

"You're looking a little peaked." She used words like that. I went over to my corner of the sewing room where I kept my sewing basket. I pulled out my cross-stitch pillow. The blue sky was almost done. Soon I would be doing the green lawn and then the most fun part, the flowers in pinks, yellows, and reds. "Do you think Mama will like this, Loff?"

"I'm sure she will, dearie." We sewed in silence for a while, and my insides stopped jumping around.

"I know you're not Jewish, Loff. What are you?"

"No, I'm not," and she looked up from her sewing. "I'm Catholic."

"Is that why you wear that gold cross around your neck?"

"Yes. It's pretty, isn't it? And the Lord keeps me safe with it."

"Do you have the ceremony too?"

Loff looked startled. "You mean the chickens? No, that's not in my religion." We were both silent for a while.

"Loff, when I grow up I think I want to be a Catholic . . . "

"You'll see, when you grow up. You'll see."

The summer passed, and we put on our annual play in the playhouse, a play for which we wrote the script and designed the set and made the costumes. Victoria was always the heroine. She wore a white dress embroidered with daffodils. Julie played the witch and had a long black gown with a pointed witch's hat. As usual, I played the hero in a striped linen suit, and I rescued the heroine from the witch.

Each year, we had two showings, one for our parents and their friends and the second showing for the servants. It was always termed a great success. We charged twenty-five cents per person, and that way collected some money for our next year's production. We'd put the money into a tin bank, which we'd give to our mother to keep for us.

3

Every fall we'd return to the place where I was born, our thirty-five-room white marble mansion at 107th Street and Riverside Drive in New York City. My father had built the house in 1907 with marble he'd had brought over from Italy. When the sightseeing buses that went on Riverside Drive would pass, the driver would point to our house and say, "That's a swell joint"; when they'd pass my uncle's house on 89th Street and Riverside, he would say, "That's a sweller joint," and when they passed the Schwab house on 72nd Street, he would say, "That's the swellest joint." Mr. Schwab was the head of U.S. Steel. The happiest time in my life was spent in this house full of its treasures of paintings and sculpture. I loved it.

From the upstairs window we could see the Hudson River and beyond it to New Jersey. It was great to see the yachts of the rich sailing up the river and, best of all, an occasional battleship would majestically come by and anchor there.

There was a wide flight of stairs leading up to the front door. On either side was a large sleeping lion, and every morning on my way to school, I would pat and then kiss the lion goodbye.

New York House, Riverside Drive

I remember one morning going downstairs and looking out the window and seeing black hand prints all over the front steps. This worried my father, who thought it meant the Mafia was after him. He took it so seriously that he hired a bodyguard—a tall young man who sat downstairs in the front hall when my father was at home. He was a pleasant fellow who would play with us.

The house at 107 Riverside Drive was not easily penetrated. When I'd come in from school, I would first open the door to a small white wooden shelter built in front of the main entrance to shield a person from the cold winter winds.

From there, I'd ring the bell that would bring the maid to open the first iron door. In case she was letting in someone she didn't know, she would leave him standing there between the first and second iron door, securely locked between the two. That second door opened to a twelve by fifteen foot rectangular vestibule, which was marble from floor to ceiling with mosaics on the walls. It was lit by a hanging Tiffany lamp, and it all felt very oriental.

Beyond, there was an archway that led into the main hall and reception room, which was rarely used except by people who were relatively strange to us. The room gave the impression that everything was deep rose red including the staircase. The balustrade on the staircase was carved mahogany as was the ceiling. The fifteen-foot-high walls were covered with rose damask with small lines of gold decoration.

Against the walls stood furniture—a couch and chairs—of carved mahogany which were also upholstered in rose-colored velvet. Next to the couch, a Louis XIV clock stood on a long table with ashtrays and sculptures and carved small sculptures surrounding them. On the opposite side of the room against the wall below the staircase was a player piano. The music was on a roller inside, and you could peddle the piano with your feet and the music would play. On the opposite side of the room sat a record player made of dark carved wood, containing Turkish records. My father would sit and listen to them, but the rest of us found them boring and without melody.

To the left of the entrance was a delicately painted drawing room used on special occasions for special people. Around the walls were placed six locked glass-doored cabinets containing precious objects in china and silver. Occasionally my mother would open the cabinets and let us take out the objects and examine them.

The furniture in this room was all Louis XIV in style and upholstered in handwoven tapestries. An Aubusson carpet in delicate shades of blue and ochre covered the floor. On the ceiling surrounded by white molding was a painting reminiscent of Fragonard.

Each room had a special and different character. Our favorite was our family room, which was next to the drawing room, two steps up from the entry hall. It was rather small, with walls of carved teak wood and ceiling of mosaic with a skylight in light blue glass. Tiffany lamps were on each of the tables, and arounu the fireplace at the end of the room was a wall of marble and mosaics.

After dinner, we would go to the family room and sit and talk until about ten o'clock. My father had a chair reserved for him, and no one else would ever sit in it. We sat on the blue-velvet upholstered couches built into the walls on either side of the room. I'd usually sit on the Turkish rugs on the floor, either reading a book or sketching in my sketch book. We'd stay in the family room until we were told on the chiming of the clock that it was time to go to bed.

My father led all the conversation. My mother was more passive and usually was embroidering a teacloth or luncheon napkins. When they were having a fight, there was either silence or sporadic bursts of fire, and then a warning from my mother: "Don't forget that the children are here."

Leading out from the entrance hall was the dining room. It was a large square room with a big round carved mahogany table, where we children had dinner with our parents every night. I loved being underneath that table because there were two lions holding up the table. I liked to kiss their feet, but once a maid came in and laughed and laughed when she saw me. After that, I didn't kiss the lions anymore.

The dining room walls were covered in dark green damask and satin. Around the ceiling was carved a wooden decoration and the ceiling was painted with white clouds and a few girl and boy angels. It was a strong and pleasant room.

One night a month, my father had a poker game at the big round table in the dining room. The men were Greek, French, Armenian, German occasionally, but never American. A true-blooded American was a strange bird in that house, and I always observed him carefully.

While the men played poker, the women sat in a little parlor, drinking coffee and eating sweets, and talking in whispers and very low tones about how bad their husbands were. I would sit on the floor and listen. The men all seemed nice to me. They would pinch my cheeks and bounce me up and down on their laps. Perhaps, I thought, it was only as husbands that they were so bad.

Through a little passage was the pantry and a dumb waiter used to bring up the food from the kitchen below. To the left was a large coat closet and beyond that a barber shop with a real barber's chair where my father went every morning and had a barber from the outside shave him or cut his hair.

Up from this small passageway was the back staircase leading to the servants quarters, where there were seven rooms and a bathroom. The stairs were dark at night, and sometimes my father would send me upstairs on an errand and I'd feel very fearful until I reached the top where there was a light.

On the second floor from the front staircase was a long hall. On the walls were large oil paintings that my father had bought at auctions. I would spend a lot of time looking at them, and when I got married, my father let me choose the one I wanted. I still have it. It's two Dutch children, by a painter called Albert Cuijp. I copied it once. It took me three weeks, and I learned more about painting and underpainting and glazing than I ever learned in any school.

At the end of the second-floor hall was a large room where my parents spent much of their time. It had a very large window out of which one could see the park below, the Hudson river, and the coast of New Jersey. The furniture was painted Venetian. There was a dressing table where my father put on his stiff collars which had to be fastened onto his shirt. Sometimes he would break the collars and with a cry of rage, dash them to the floor.

Beyond this room and leading to the bathroom was a small dressing room where my mother kept her clothes. Against the wall stood a safe where she kept her jewelry. The bathroom in white and gold was enormous. It had an enclosed toilet, a separate shower, a large bathtub, and two sinks at the end.

Off the main room was a bedroom which my mother used. My father had separate quarters at the other end of the hall. He had a bedroom and a sitting room and his own bathroom two steps up from his bedroom. None of us dared to go into his quarters because he had such a keen eye for seeing if anything had been disturbed. If an over-zealous maid moved something from one place to another anywhere in the huge house, my father would notice it. He'd let out a loud bellow, and when she came creeping in, he'd make her put the object back *exactly* where it had been. My father also had a complete inventory of every object in the house, including every small ashtray, whether valuable or not. Once a year, his secretary would arrive with a long list and check off every piece one by one. We three sisters would follow her silently around, nodding our heads with each check that she made on the paper.

In my father's bedroom there was a deep blue carpet on the floor and a large double bed in the corner; the whole room was blue and tan and very peaceful in tone. The bathroom was fairly small, in marble with only the necessities—toilet, wash basin, bathtub, a full-length mirror, and towel racks to heat the towels.

I think he rarely used the sitting room. There was a couch against the wall with pillows, and he occasionally went there for a private talk with someone.

Above on the third floor were another two bedrooms and a bathroom. Miss Jackson slept in the front room with my two sisters, since it was large and spacious with bookcases and desks for studying. I slept in the small bedroom which had a large closet with mirrored doors that held all our toys. I didn't mind sleeping there alone. It was nice and peaceful. It was the room where we had our Christmas celebration, when my father had a bell put up that hung from the ceiling. He felt a bell was less Christian than a tree.

Down in the basement was the kitchen, the laundry, and several working rooms. Outside there was a garden with a few benches.

My mother and father used to have "little fights" and then they had "big fights." For the big fights they would always send us away from wherever they were so that we wouldn't hear. We usually went up to the third floor and sat in a circle playing cards—usually casino. Although we were too far away to hear their words, we still listened to their voices. We could hear the up and down of their tones, and we felt very scared when their voices were loud and relieved when they were down. Every time they went down, we hoped that it was the end, but they usually started up again. Victoria had a wristwatch, and we used to ask her, "How long have they been at it?" Finally after three-quarters of an hour or so there'd be silence.

We really didn't take sides. We only used to want it to stop. My mother cried a lot after the fights, and she'd skip having dinner and have something sent to her room. My father would sometimes go out and not come back until the next day. We'd have our dinner with Jackson. Everyone would seem very nervous and act like people during a thunderstorm, expecting the unpredictable.

It happened once that my father came down the front steps immaculately dressed, his gray fedora set slightly at an angle on his head. His face was set in stern lines. The house maids followed him out onto the porch and stood waiting. Whenever he left or arrived the servants formed a sort of committee on the steps. They usually stood with their hands folded across their aprons and their eyes fixed on his face. When he smiled they smiled, when he frowned they became still and apprehensive. At the last moment before leaving he

would usually tell them for the sixth time what time
he expected to be back for dinner. They all stood
about this day waiting for Mother to come down.
Father began to twitch impatiently and was just
about to let out a bellow when she came down. She
looked radiantly beautiful in a hat made of small
sapphire blue feathers in the middle of which was
a little diamond pin shaped like a question mark. It
was the first time that any of us had seen the hat.
It was new and it was wonderful. Father pressed
his lips together and his eyes became hot with
rage. He motioned the servants inside. I could feel
them gluing their ears to the windows. "Go
upstairs," he said to my mother, "and put on a hat
that a respectable woman would wear. Do you
expect me to have a wife who looks like a
prostitute? Do you expect to see a lot of men down
in the city? Bah!" His face twisted in anger.

Mother's face fell, grew rosy red, and her eyes
filled with tears. "Please, not in front of the
children." She tried a small, a very small measure
of defiance: "This is a lovely hat. It's only you and
your . . . your hideous jealousy."

Father raised his hand as though he would
strike her. She turned quickly and went into the
house.

We children stood awkwardly on the porch. We
leaned over and with an extraordinary excess of
interest began to examine the shrubbery. With all
the acute understanding of children, we knew that
our father must not be made consciously aware of
the fact that we had been aware of the scene. The
minutes dragged by. Victoria began hopping up

and down first on one foot and then on the other, and I followed suit. We pretended to be playing a kind of hopscotch.

Father turned towards me. "Go upstairs and get me a handkerchief and put some eau de cologne on it. Victoria, come and walk through the garden with me while we wait for your mother." They walked slowly down the garden path towards the white marble fountain where the fat fish were spewing streams of sparkling water. I quickly did as he asked.

In a little while, Mother came down again. This time she wore a small black inconspicuous hat. Her radiance and beauty had disappeared. She looked pale and tortured, and her eyes were jet black against her face. She climbed into the car and waited for Father to come. He came slowly up the drive and climbed in beside her. They drove off in silence and the atmosphere of the morning which had been rather happily excited had become ominous and fearful.

Usually we'd never discuss the scenes between our father and mother. This day, though, I could bear it no longer. "Victoria," I burst out. "Why does Papa always scold Mother?"

Victoria didn't answer for a long time, and then she said, "Cook says it's because he's IN LOVE with her, and he's afraid that she'll go off and marry someone else and leave him."

"But she wouldn't, would she?" I asked, fear rising in me.

"Of course not," said Victoria. "Cook says he thinks that because he's IN LOVE with her."

I played quietly and absentmindedly for the next few minutes and then full of the perplexing scene of the morning and Victoria's mysterious explanation, I decided to go to my thinking place in the garden. My thinking place was a large apple tree that had a circle of shade under it. I lay down and put my cheek against the cool grass. My thoughts weren't at all clear and seemed to wave to and fro among the leaves above me. Soon I was fast asleep. I dreamed that I was in a beautiful deep green garden with a high white wall all around it. Flowers in exquisite colors were growing in abundance against the wall. At either end were two high iron gates with "5 Green Gage Avenue" written in curling wrought iron letters. There was a big white sign on the gate which said, "Beware of the Dog." My father suddenly appeared before me. He was dressed in a gleaming white satin suit and a white turban was twisted around his head. There was a ruby pin shaped like a question mark shining in its folds. On his feet he wore paisley-colored shoes with the ends turned up very high. In his hand he carried a whip that was long and curled on the ground like a snake. He fixed his eyes on me, and they were cold and green. He spoke in a deep sing-song voice. "You may wander all over the garden, you may pick the flowers, and you may eat the dark red cherries that hang on that tree over there, you may play on the swings, but do not,"—and here he raised his arm high—"do not attempt to leave the garden or something dreadful will happen to you, for I am in love, see, I am in love." I woke up.

That night I had another dream. As I ran, the grass felt sleek and soft under my feet. I saw my mother sitting by a white fountain that looked something like the one in our own garden save that bright-colored birds were flying in and out of the spray. My mother was weeping and in her hands she held a long white paper on which she was writing hurriedly, hurriedly. She was wearing the little black hat pulled low over her face, and she was chained to her chair. Bright red rambler roses grew over the chains. The servants stood around her, their eyes fixed and stony, and they chanted over and over again, "No one must come near her, or see her, or speak to her; no one must come near her, or see her, or speak to her—."

"Mother," I cried. "Please speak to me." I ran forward, but an arm like an iron bar hit me across the chest and held me there. Sobs shook me. I turned my head and saw my father standing with his lips curling. I looked down at my feet and saw a white envelope and written on it in my mother's handwriting was her sister Rachel's name and address. I picked it up and hid it under my skirt. I ran as fast as I could. I knew my father must not see what was in it and that I must send it: my mother wanted me to. I felt the envelope with my fingers. It was thin, awfully thin; it felt like tissue paper. Maybe it was empty, but I would write the message. I knew what my mother wanted to say; she would write, "Come, Rachel, come quickly and save me." I picked up a twig and broke it and with the wet green part under the bark, I wrote on the outside of the envelope. The letters were faint; you could hardly see them. But I couldn't worry about that. I must send it. I ran to the gate. It was high, high, high, and there was no handle on it. Suddenly through the bars I saw fat jolly Mrs. Simpson who lived in the house next door. I called, I reached out, my hand struck something, and a sharp pain ran up my arm. I awoke to find Nurse standing over me shaking me by the arm.

I think my father patterned his idea of how children should be brought up on the images of British royalty. We travelled to Europe every year. At first, my sisters and I were tutored at home in their bedroom. Every morning from nine to one teachers gave the three of us classes in French, math, science, geography, and music history. Twice we had examinations which were handed to the heads of City Education.

One day, my father's lawyer came to visit us. He had a profile like a parrot and the body of a seal. He shook his finger at my father. "You cannot live here as you would have in Turkey. These children are American, born here. They must go to school like other children."

This was the first time I saw or heard anyone telling my father what he should do. Overnight, everything changed. My mother became happy; she took us to stores to buy us school clothes. They were dark blue and looked like uniforms.

The next day we were driven the thirteen blocks from our house to our new school, Horace Mann, a private school—not fancy, but academically very good. When we arrived, the children all stared at us, first because of the chauffeur-driven limousine and second because we were all three dressed alike in our dark blue serge dresses and white collars. I think they thought we came from a prison or somewhere strange. All the kids were dressed in their usual everyday clothes. I knew we looked odd to them.

I was ten years old, and I was put in the fourth grade in a class of about twenty-five children. They looked at me as though I were a freak, and I looked back at them, half in fear, and half in hope that they would like me.

My teacher's name was Miss Robins, and by coincidence her hair seemed to be the color of a robin's breast. She wore it in a bun on top of her head. She was nice, and I liked her. She put her arm around me and put me at a desk with a girl named Mabel.

My desk mate was a small fat little girl with blue eyes. She seemed quite friendly. During recess, she offered me half her sandwich. It was peanut butter and jelly. I gave her half of mine, chicken and mayonnaise, and we sat on a bench, eating and smiling. I began to think I would like school. It was fun having kids to play with and to study with, so different from being alone with a tutor.

As soon as we got home, we told our mother that we could not wear those dresses. My mother agreed, and after that we wore our regular clothes and began to fit in more at the school.

The mayor's son also went to that school, and he would arrive in a limousine with lights flashing. But that was all right because he was the mayor's son; we weren't that important to arrive in a limousine. Sometimes we could talk William, the driver, into letting us off five blocks before the school so that we could walk to school like the other kids.

Although we made some friends at Horace Mann, we rarely if ever invited them to the house. Once I invited a girl to visit, and she happened to come on the day that the man from Tiffany came to wind up all the clocks and see if they were in order. He was a very nice, serious man with white hair and spectacles. As there were at least two clocks in every room, there were over seventy clocks to be wound, including two grandfather clocks, so it took him all day.

The next day at school, she told all our classmates about the clock winder and about what a big weird house we lived in. It took a long time for that story to wear itself out, and I never invited anyone again. But my sisters did.

4

Occasionally someone from the outside world could come to visit, and we three girls would give the visitor the same kind of concentrated attention that we sometimes gave to an unexpected white mushroom that suddenly appeared on the green lawn. We would give the visitor a period of trial and observation, after which Victoria would call us together and give us her opinion and tell us what the future treatment of the visitor would be. The visitor on this occasion was Eunice Schneiderman, who was twelve. She had come to our summer house to stay two weeks. Her mother brought her and left her standing on the porch as their car drove off.

We surveyed her carefully. Our eyes travelled from her hair tied neatly in a white bow at the back of her head to her shiny black shoes and white socks. Being the eldest and eleven, Victoria stepped forward and shook her hand. In turn we followed. Eunice's hand was sticky and wet. I leaned forward and looked intently into her face. She wore eyeglasses and they gleamed and acted like a wall of separation. She gave me a feeling of being neat, but imperceptibly soiled.

We took her on a tour of the garden. We introduced her to Togo the dog and Victor the pony. We let her feed Victor a bit of sugar, showing her how to hold her palm flat so that he wouldn't hurt her but at the same time be able to get it easily.

We introduced her to our archenemy, Jackson, who if you touched her felt hard and armored like a battleship. We introduced her to George Stobie who took care of our pony, but we didn't tell her how we called him "The Devil Stobie" and loved to pretend that he was an evil man who had us all in his power, and whom we constantly had to cajole and charm to mitigate his evilness, or that we would sometimes stop by the road and pick flowers and put them all around his hat and then insist on driving through the village to show the people that we had him in our power. Nor did we tell her when the village children ran after the cart yelling, "Rich kids, rich kids," George would stand up, his face red and angry yelling back, "Get off there, ye dirty brats." Or how we would sit there still and frightened and ashamed, feeling that the world was hostile and it was better back in the garden.

We didn't initiate her into any of our secrets, but waited expectantly for her reactions; and we always watched Victoria's face for a signal, a clue as to what the verdict would be. I never knew how Victoria arrived at her conclusions, but I felt the formation of them running like waves over Victoria, and whatever the conclusion was, just or unjust, right or wrong, it became the law for Julie and me.

It was on the afternoon of the third day of

Eunice's visit that Victoria invited her to go for a walk. She linked her arm through Eunice's, and we understood that it was to be a private walk. Our eyes followed the two figures until they were out of sight. For the rest of the afternoon we played in a desultory fashion, waiting for their return. They came back an hour or so before dinner, and Eunice went to her room. Victoria indicated to us that we were to go to the secret meeting place. The secret meeting place was in the attic up on the third floor of the house. It could only be reached by rickety staircase, so steep that no one but us dared to climb it and the closest we ever came to being disturbed was by the harsh voice of Jackson shouting up from the bottom of the staircase. We sat there, now crosslegged in a circle. Julie's and my eyes were fixed on Victoria's face.

Victoria spoke, "I don't like her, she smells bad, her hands are sticky, and she's a goody-goody, too."

Julie made no reply. My heart took a fast beat. I opened my mouth. "I don't think she's so bad really. I think she's trying, she just doesn't understand, she's not like us, she's different."

Victoria fixed her eyes on me. "Besides being a goody-goody, I think she's a tattletale. I don't like her. We've got to get rid of her." Victoria picked up her riding whip, which in crucial times she always carried with her. She walked over to the small attic window and looked out.

I felt a rising tide of excitement. In capital letters I saw, SOMETHING IS GOING TO HAPPEN.

NOW. SOON. Nothing was formulated, but the impulse was started. Somehow, in some way, Eunice would go. I knew it would happen.

Victoria turned to Julie and said, "Come, Julie, let's go." And lacing their arms about each other's waists they went off leaving me standing alone.

I walked soberly down the rickety staircase, my heart continued to beat fast and full of fear. I wanted to warn Eunice and still not betray my sisters. I went to Eunice's room and timidly knocked on the door. Eunice opened it and stood there looking as usual, slightly moist and damp. I searched my mind quick and fast, for some in-between act that would not constitute a betrayal and still be a warning.

"I thought you might like to come with me and feed the rabbits." I hung on Eunice's answer.

"No, thanks. I am going to write to my mother." And the sentence dropped like a stone between us.

I turned and ran down the stairs into the garden. I leaned against the apple tree and looked up into a sky crisscrossed by apple branches. I felt sad and helpless.

At dinner that night, Victoria and Julie seemed to be sitting like two halves of a whole thought, and I felt cut off from them lost in a deep quiet. I looked down at my salad plate finding some dim comfort in drawing designs with my fork through the salad dressing. "What are you thinking?" my father asked, and he pinched my cheek hard, but since I loved him I didn't mind that it hurt. Why was it that what you were thinking was always impossible to explain and if ever you did try it would only lead to endless trouble?

I knew I couldn't tell him what I was thinking, so I had to make up something real fast.

"I was thinking that maybe tomorrow, if it is warm, you could come swimming with me. It is always so much more fun when you are there."

My father looked pleased. "I'll see," he said. "If I get back in time from the city, I will. Wait for me."

"Yes, yes, I will." And I went back to my salad and my troubled thoughts.

Victoria broke in suddenly and said, "Let's play with the Ouiji Board tonight." And a gleam flashed from her face to Julie's.

I had never been sure about my feelings for the Ouiji Board. I knew that Jackson's minister had told her that she was not to use it, that it would be a sin if she did. Were there really spirits in the other world who could see and know everything you were doing? Who could send you messages, and maybe evil ones? Who could make you do things you didn't want to do? Was Victoria going to call on these spirits? Or was it all a fake and people pushed the board around to make it spell out what they wanted it to? My mother and father thought it was just a silly game, but Jackson thought it was sin.

"Eunice has never played with the Ouiji Board," said Victoria and inclined her graceful neck towards Eunice.

Dinner over, they went quickly into the study. I lagged behind. I felt a little giggly as I always did when I felt uncertain. Arriving in the room I found Victoria, Julie, and Eunice standing around the table looking down at the Ouiji Board. It shone like a polished bone against the green of the table.

"Who's first?" Julie asked.

"Eunice, let's you and I," said Victoria.

They sat down facing each other, their fingers placed lightly on the board.

"You mustn't push, Eunice," Victoria went on. "It will move all by itself." Victoria closed her eyes and waited. Eunice opened and closed hers intermittently. The others brought up their chairs and stared expectantly at the board. A few seconds passed. Nothing happened. The silence began to ring in my ears. Suddenly Eunice jumped to her feet. "I don't want to play," she said. "I think it's a silly game."

The pupils of Victoria's eyes darkened. She looked offended. She got up slowly and gracefully and shrugged her shoulders. There was a long, uncomfortable silence.

"Julie, let's you and I do it," I said. "It usually works for us."

We sat down. I could feel my fingers trembling on the slippery wood. The Board began moving almost instantly. It began spelling out slowly in a wobbly fashion and then with a sudden increased tempo T-O-N-I-G-H-T — E-U-N-I-C-E — W-I-L-L —D-I-E.

My attention was riveted to my hands. I looked at them with sudden disbelief. And next came the horrifying thought. Tonight at midnight is tomorrow. I looked up at the clock. It was nine-fifteen, two hours and forty-five minutes to midnight. I was suddenly seized with a desire to laugh. I looked up at the others. They all looked uneasy, disbelieving and yet believing. Eunice stood quiet and pale. Her voice came thin and small. "I think it's silly, I think it's silly."

"Jackson, Jackson," Julie cried. "Did you hear what the Ouiji Board said?" Jackson listened, a slight flush crept up her cheek.

"What nonsense," she answered and she picked up the board and carried it to the closet and put it firmly on the shelf. Victoria moved over to the piano and idly began to play. I got out my drawing things and began drawing Togo. Julie and Eunice got out a box of dominoes and sat on the floor playing.

My mind kept spinning around the message from the Ouiji Board. Dear God, don't let Eunice die. I looked up at the clock. The hands pointed to nine-thirty. Two hours and a half more to go. That wasn't very much. I glanced over at Eunice. She and Julie were playing solemnly. I thought, "Hard to draw when your mind's elsewhere, but Togo, you are a beautiful dog."

Jackson's voice broke in with its sharp, barking bite. "Time for bed, children."

I carefully began putting my things away. Fine to be going to bed. In the morning I would wake up, the sun would be shining, Eunice would be alive, and the whole nightmare would be over.

"Miss Jackson," Eunice said, "I don't want to sleep alone." At first I expected Jackson's usual "What nonsense," but instead Jackson was silent for a moment and then said, "Well, perhaps one of the children can sleep with you." I didn't need to hear the next three words. Victoria would disdain to sleep with anyone, Julie was too timid to be of any assistance in a crisis.

"How about you?" Jackson thumped me lightly on the head. Looking at Eunice's white and frightened face, I knew there could only be one answer.

"All right," I said.

I went to my room and undressed as slowly as possible. I brushed my teeth with infinite care. I combed my hair getting all the knots out. There didn't seem to be anything more to do. I decided to take a book along. I climbed the stairs to Eunice's room and found her already in bed.

"Hello," I said wanly. "I brought a book along to read." Eunice nodded.

"Eunice," I persisted. "I don't believe in that old Ouiji Board. I think it's silly. Only ignorant people believe in ghosts and things. It was just an accident."

"I don't feel well," Eunice said. "I think I am going to vomit."

"I'd better get Jackson." And I got out of bed and ran down the stairs and hall to Jackson's room. Back in Eunice's room we found her white and shaking, hanging over the basin in the bathroom, seized by a paroxysm of vomiting.

"Go and tell your mother," Jackson said. "She'd better call the doctor." The clock's hands pointed to ten-fifteen. Again I went down the stairs and down the hall, and I pounded on my mother's door. I stayed and listened while my mother called the doctor and then waited in the front hall for him to arrive. When he came he went straight up to Eunice's room. I had wanted to stop him and tell him about the Ouiji Board, but I didn't dare. It was a bad thing, I knew he wouldn't like it.

I followed him up and stood outside the door, but I couldn't hear much but the mumbling of voices. I felt cold there standing in my nightgown, my teeth began chattering. I walked down the hall and looked out of the window. The lawn rolled away from the house in the dim moonlight. I placed my hands together.

"Please, God, don't let Eunice die, and I will promise always to be a good girl." I felt a qualm even as I said it, and added, "If possible." I knew God didn't like liars.

The door opened, and my mother and the doctor came out together.

"You'll catch cold, standing there," my mother said. "Go to your room, now. Miss Jackson will stay with Eunice." I tried to read their faces. Was Eunice dead? Would they bury her tomorrow? My mother proceeded down the hall and went to her room. She picked up the telephone and shut the door.

I went to my room and climbed into bed still feeling cold and chilly. I heard the clock strike twelve, but I finally fell asleep. When I awakened, I heard movement and voices in the hall. I ran and opened the door but the hall was empty. I quickly crossed over to Victoria and Julie's room. I found them leaning out of the window looking down at the car in the driveway. My mother and Mrs. Schneiderman and Eunice were standing on the porch. Eunice had a blanket wrapped around her. The two women shook hands politely, and Eunice was bundled into the car.

We watched as the car turned the corner at the end of the driveway. What a relief. Eunice was still alive, and nothing terrible had really happened.

Victoria looked at Juliette. Juliette looked at me. I looked back at Victoria. I heard a little giggle come out of Victoria, and then simultaneously we burst into gales of laughter.

5

Our best times were when we went out riding on horseback. Victoria always got the best horse. His name was Jack, and he was a single footer, which meant that you didn't have to post but could sit firmly on his back and be carried along effortlessly. Victoria always looked like a queen when she rode him. I knew I could never look like that but I longed to ride him anyway. Julie had a mare called Ginger whose neck stretched out and always seemed to be too near the ground. She was also lazy and had to be prodded to keep up with the other horses. I, being the youngest and the smallest, rode a large pony called Spottie. He was very willful and would take the bit between his teeth when he wanted to run and there was no stopping him.

There was a piece of road that we always crossed that was known as "the track," and here we let our horses out to run full speed and race each other. I often won, not because I wanted to, but because Spottie wanted to beat the big ones. I was always pretty scared at the speed and the lack of control I had over Spottie, but when it was over, I felt okay again.

"Scared, weren't you?" Victoria would yell at me.

"No, no, not at all."

"Liar," she'd say, but she'd let it go at that.

My father always liked to watch us as we rode away. Once I heard someone say to him, "I saw your two girls and your son on horseback the other day." I knew that they thought I was a boy and that that pleased my father; he did not contradict them. If only I could have been a boy to please my beloved father. He was the idol of my young years. But in my eighth year, that began to change.

It was in the late summer, and the country house was in a general state of excitement. We were going to have visitors—people to come and stay and actually live in the house. No one before, it seemed, ever came to the house and stayed. They always seemed to do something or say something that displeased my father, and they would go away and never come back.

We were lonely for people from the outside world, and we would live for a long time on the memory of words or laughs or some physical idiosyncrasy that they might have had. Now at last, someone was really going to come and stay.

Our mother's sister, Rachel, whose photograph was on my mother's dressing table and to whom she always seemed to be writing letters—she was coming with her husband and their two little boys. Their house in Salonica, Greece, and the whole Jewish quarter had been burned to the ground although it was not clear by whom it had been burned. It would be the first time in fourteen years that the sisters would be reunited; they had not seen each other since my mother had married my father and left Salonica, which was then still part of Turkey.

Two cars had been ordered and were standing long and black under the portal. The boat was expected at three o'clock. It was now only twelve o'clock in the morning, but it was a long drive to the city and the docks. My mother and father went in the first car, the second following them, and we watched them until they were out of sight.

Children and dogs always seem to hear the sounds of arrivals long before anyone else is aware of them, and so, many hours later, we heard the hum of the returning motors and ran to tell our Nurse. We stood then and waited on the stoop hardly able to stand still, quivering up and down on the balls of our feet.

The first car rolled up with my father and Aunt Rachel. The car was piled high with bags that were covered with bright-colored, gaudy hotel labels—Hotel Regina, Victoria, Gloria Palast, Splendid, Majestic and other hyperbolized names. Aunt Rachel stepped out, tall, slender, and wreathed with smiles. She embraced us warmly and she smelled very good.

The next car drove up with my mother, Uncle David, little cousin Marcel, and a thin wispy old lady who sat holding my baby cousin Raymond on her lap. This old lady we knew must be the famous Miriam who had been nurse to both our mother and Aunt Rachel and who was now nurse for our little cousins.

We children thought our cousin Marcel was the

most beautiful child we had ever seen. We rushed him upstairs and washed his fat little hands while he chattered rapid French between his smiles. We were rather disappointed about the French part, for while we realized that he would speak French, we had somehow hoped that he would have an adequate supply of English sandwiched in somewhere. After washing his hands, we all hastened downstairs fearful that we might be missing some of the happenings. We found the new arrivals on the sun porch. They were drinking Turkish ouzo and eating small sandwiches. Everyone looked clean and shiny and they were all talking and laughing fast, and acting as though it would take them months and months before they would be through saying what they had to say. Aunt Rachel regaled them with stories about the passengers on the boat, and we children thought that we had never before heard of people funnier or more amazing.

The same spirit carried all through dinner. We had rarely seen our father in such high spirits. He and Aunt Rachel carried on the major part of the conversation. Between the streams of talk, we saw our father fix his eyes frequently and watchfully on Uncle David's face, but David seemed unaware of it, and spoke little and only occasionally laughed his deep and pleasant laugh.

"Now, David and Rachel," my father said at one point, "why don't you make up your minds to stay here? Forget all about Salonica—your place is here. David, I have plenty of room for you in my business, and I'm glad to have you." And with one of his spacious gestures he reached over and patted him patronizingly, but affectionately, on the back. Father always seemed bigger than anyone else, and the people around him always would look shrunken inside their clothes. It always seemed to me that when they first walked into the room, they and their clothes were the proper size; but after a few moments, their clothes remained the same size, but they would have become too small for them. This didn't always happen. That night Aunt Rachel was her own proper size, and it was definitely her evening. Hers and Father's. But then, of course, it was always Father's evening.

The night was warm, and after dinner they found their way to the screened porch. After the hilarity of the dinner, they were all a little subdued and conversation seemed to lag. The children sat around looking carefully from one person to the other and noticing all the physical details that stamp an adult so clearly into the mind of a child. Uncle David had such lovely long hands, and the few dark hairs on the backs of them made them all the more white and delicate. There was a deep cleft in his chin that made him look like a general of the Civil War. I sat on the floor at his feet, and as he ran his long fingers through my hair I felt very happy. Aunt Rachel seemed to be full of little electric waves—her hair waved crisply but with grace away from her head and settled in a coil on her head. Her dress with its collars and frills all seemed to be inclined the same way as her hair in moving little waves that came and left and used her as their sort of center.

The clock struck ten, and Father didn't yawn. It was his habit to yawn at ten for the first time, at ten fifteen for the second time, and then at ten-thirty he would get up, stretch and bid everyone good night. But tonight he seemed to be in an exalted mood, of high cheer. Our mother kept looking at him curiously. He ordered high balls. Everyone must drink a toast, a toast to Aunt Rachel, a toast to his children, to his success, to everything. His laughter seemed strained and his face looked a hard shade of red. He put his hand to his head. "Laurette," he said to his wife, "I am dizzy, I think I'll go upstairs."

We all sprang to our feet. "It's the heat, the long day, the excitement." He turned and walked towards the stairs. David suddenly put his arm in a comforting and protective gesture around our mother. My father turned at the stairs and saw my mother standing there with David's arm around her. His face suddenly became paralyzed, his features white and drawn. We children in a flash of understanding knew that something dreadful had happened. David should never have done that. David was doomed. Then moving slowly, my father went upstairs followed by my mother.

I thought about his being very jealous of my mother. "To bed now, children," said my mother as she came down. "It's been a long day." She went to the door and called for Nurse who appeared as always much too quickly to suit us children.

Nurse appeared to be in a softer mood that night and instead of scolding us for the inevitable, ever-recurring and abundant wrongs of which we always seemed to be guilty, she only hurried us through our washing and undressing and hastily tucked us into bed.

It felt good to lie straight and cool under the fresh clean sheets. My thoughts again reviewed the sight of my father's face at the foot of the stairs and his expression as he had looked at David. I thought of my father's jealousy and crossed my fingers hopefully under the sheets and whispered to myself, "Dear God, please don't let anything bad happen." And having done everything that I could to avert disaster, my thoughts wandered on to how I was going to show Marcel the house and garden. I knew every part of the house and garden with all of my senses and perceptions. I knew how every corner of the house felt to the touch of my hands and feet, and sometimes I would even rub my face against the walls. I loved the musty smell of long unopened books in the library and would always feel a rising tide of excitement in myself when I would sprawl on the ground with them and look at the huge steel engravings in them. I knew the garden, every rise and fall in the surface of the land, and the rhythm of its surface as I ran or walked on it. I knew its change of color and aspect with each changing hour of the day and each bit of knowledge was a sort of personal and precious secret. I would have liked to have shown it to David and Rachel too, but I knew that grownups were never interested in those kinds of discoveries, and I thought that their bodies must be different from children's bodies, encased, cut off and unresponsive to the delights of touching, smelling, and feeling deeply the place around them. I promised myself solemnly that I would never forget how it felt to be a child. I crept out of bed to kiss Victoria, crawled back and soon fell asleep.

When we awoke the next morning Victoria rushed into the bathroom first, and I had to wait for her. I ran down the hall to the servants' stairs and was about to call down to Cook to find out what there would be for breakfast when I was arrested by the unusual babble of voices in the kitchen. The interested and unexpected news of the house usually came floating up the well of the servants' stairs. This morning, I kept hearing the word "stroke."

"Then he probably won't last long," in Cook's voice. "Probably kick the bucket before the summer is out."

"Then again," the gardener broke in, "he might live for years. Depends on what kind of a life a man's led, and whether he's been careful about preserving his strength." And here they all laughed in a way that I knew that they had said something strictly not for children. I rushed back to tell Victoria: "Papa is ill. Papa's had a stroke."

The children became affected by the gloom that pervaded the house. Everyone talked in whispers, and doctors and nurses tiptoed in and out of the sickroom where our father was lying. He was paralyzed slightly on the left side of his body.

Facing my father's bed on the opposite wall was a large oil painting of his mother in a heavy gold frame. It had been painted from a photograph of her on her deathbed, since painting her during her life was considered a threat that might take her life from her. It showed her lying against a white pillow, her face large and pale, crowned by wavy dark hair. Her eyes were closed. My father used to boast that she didn't have a single white hair on her head.

On the fourth day after my father's illness, at eleven that night the painting crashed to the ground. It was so heavy that we heard it all over the house, and we came running to his room. My mother was already there and wouldn't let us in, but I caught a glimpse of my father's face looking white and frightened on his bed.

A picture falling off the wall, I knew, was an omen of death and would be counted as one more thing that happened that was bad since the arrival of my aunt and uncle.

A week after that the house was filled with smoke. My uncle was the first to discover it, and the fire department was called. The fire had started in the basement, in the laundry. Someone had forgotten to disconnect the iron. But this simple explanation did not satisfy my father. The fire was quickly extinguished, but now after this third happening, everyone in the house was alerted and waiting for the next possible ominous thing to happen.

A few nights later we were sitting at the table in the big round red dining room with its bay window looking out on the calm waters in the Sound. I saw the sailboats going by. I wished I could be on one of them away from the awfulness of the house which was so changed since my father's illness.

Now my aunt and mother rarely spoke or smiled and Uncle David usually nervous, would light a cigarette and walk out before dessert had been served.

Only my mother, and then we three children, were allowed to go into my father's room. He did not want to see Rachel or David or Marcel.

This night we were sitting at the table when we were startled to see my father standing at the doorway supported by his nurse. He was pale and trembling, his bathrobe loosely falling around him, his eyes starting out of his pale face and his voice came trembling and the fingers of his good hand pointing at Rachel and David.

My mother let out a small cry and ran towards him. He pushed her aside. He fixed his eyes on Rachel and David.

"I want you to leave this house before another night has passed. I have a premonition of danger and death. You have brought sickness to this house and you must go. It is the only way to stop more evil from happening." He pulled on the bell rope near the door, and when the maid came he ordered, "Have the car here within the hour. These people are leaving."

He turned and dragged himself back to his room.

Rachel, startled, was crying softly and my mother's face was red and burning.

"Remember, Rachel, he is ill and he doesn't know what he is saying." But even as she said this, we all realized its untruthfulness, and her hands, held up in appeal, dropped. "No, I know you must go. He is convinced that your arrival brought him this sickness and all these other things."

We followed my aunt and uncle to their room. We sat on the edge of the bed and watched Aunt Rachel pack. We watched her hands as they went from the drawers to the suitcases and back, and we felt uneasy and mute. There was nothing we could say or do. In a short time the trunks, bags, and suitcases were locked and closed.

Only Marcel was happy and excited at the idea of travelling at night, and he stood by the window, his sailor hat on the back of his head and his little coat sticking out wide all around him, ready to leave long before the time of departure.

My mother came into the room holding a white envelope and gave it to David. "This is all the money I have at the moment," she said, "but I will bring some more." David took it silently and put it into his pocket.

We went to see Miriam who after helping Rachel pack was sitting silently, waiting for the next order.

We went over to her.

"Why, Miriam, is everyone so unhappy? Why is Father so angry with Rachel and David and Marcel and the baby? What have they done?"

Miriam's tears fell gently down her face onto her brown hands folded in her lap. "Your father is a superstitious man. He comes from the Orient, he believes in the power of the 'evil eye.' He believes that your aunt and uncle brought it with them into this house and that it will destroy him and his whole family. That is why they must go. Nothing will change him or what he believes. It is very hard for all of us, but it must be our destiny. We will have to go. What can I tell you, my children?"

After that I never felt the same about my father. He was changed from the strong, noble image that he had been to a frail, threatening person who brought suffering to those around him. He no longer occupied his godlike position in my eyes. He was capable of doing wrong—of being sick, of being physically weak. I began to question what he did, no longer obeying him without examining what he was asking. I began to feel more sympathy for my mother and less impatience for her constant tears. I was nine years old, and I began thinking of how it would be to live elsewhere, with different people—American people I read about in books, people who didn't live by superstitions, who didn't believe in intangible omens like "evil eyes." Nobody had ever seen an evil eye. Perhaps one should only believe in things that you could touch and feel—everything else was imagined with a big question mark.

When my father looked at me, he didn't know that my feelings for him had changed. But I didn't want to go into his room anymore. My mother used to say to me, "Why don't you go in to see Papa? He has been asking for you."

And I had no answer. No answer at all. When I went to see my uncle and aunt and Marcel who were living in a small apartment in New York on Riverside Drive and I saw how unhappy they were and that they had done nothing to deserve being thrown out and exiled from the house, I felt angry and wanted to punish my father and to shake my finger at him and ask, "Why did you do this?" But no one in the house was allowed to mention their names. It was as though a wave had swept over them and washed them out to sea, never to be seen or heard from again.

But my mother went to see them twice a week, and when she took us, she made us swear not to tell my father where we had been; and so we entered in a conspiracy against my father, and that added to my feeling of estrangement.

My mother began to defy my father in other ways, and they would have loud quarrels. Their quarrels frightened me. What would become of us all? Once my father said, "I will close the houses, the children can go to boarding schools, and you can go back to Turkey to your father."

For us, Mama had always been more like a grownup sister than a mother—someone to hug and kiss and snuggle up to. As the years went by, though, she grew up and became for us like a mother. She began talking to us a lot, about being unhappy and wanting us to go away to school. I began asking my mother about when she went to boarding school. She would always brighten up when I asked her about her school, and she would ask me, "Would you like to go to boarding school." And I would answer, "Yes, yes I would."

She would say, "You will have to wait until you are twelve, and then you can go."

My sisters thought I was crazy to want to go to boarding school. "They are very strict and punish you if you do not do what they want."

But my longing to be away increased every day. My mother read American newspapers and magazines and wanted to become, and wanted us

to become, like American women—free,
independent. It wasn't easy for her; nothing could
be done unless my father consented. Her dream
for us was the antithesis of my father's dream for
us. Although he'd been in the U.S. longer, he'd
never lost his Old World ways. All my father
seemed to have in mind was to keep us virgins
until the day when dressed in white and under a
veil he would hand each of us over to a wealthy
husband. We were instructed that marriage was
the ultimate career for a woman. It gave her
everything she would need for a long and happy
life. Better a so-so husband than no husband.

One day my father's lawyer friend who looked
like a parrot said, "You know, you are not in
Turkey anymore. You are in the U.S.A.—under
American laws—and here women have rights that
they do not have in Turkey. Your wife is entitled to
a third of your fortune. She can divorce you, if she
is not happy."

This was news not only to my mother, but to all
of us. It meant that my mother was not a slave
having to do whatever my father told her.

Now, she walked with a firmer step. She didn't
seem to be so afraid anymore. She contradicted
my father, about almost everything. It was like
seeing the emergence of a new person.

I think children looked towards strength, and so
until I was twelve, I hadn't paid much attention to
what my mother said, but only had listened to my
father. But now the page was turning. Now my
mother began to have power, and now I began
listening to her.

6

During my mother's youth, it was customary for the girls from upper class families in Turkey to be sent to boarding schools in Switzerland, so she went to a school in Lausanne where she spent three years. Those had been the happiest times of her life, and she often told us all about it.

She already spoke French, but there her mastery of the language was much improved. She met girls from France, Germany, Belgium, and Russia. The atmosphere was stimulating. At holiday time the school would invite the boy's school in the town to come and dance, and my mother would describe these times as the most exquisitely enjoyable hours that she had ever known. The boys would be dressed in their dark blue uniforms of tight-fitting jackets and slim dark pants, their shining hair carefully combed. The girls would wear white with lace ruffles around their skirts so that when they danced the skirts would billow around them. They'd dance and dance while the faculty sat in rows observing them. My mother told how she fell in love with a different boy each time and how she always hoped there was some way to make that time last forever.

She also loved to talk about the walks up the mountains in the afternoon and how when they reached the top, they would be fed bread and chocolate, milk and honey.

My mother couldn't say enough nice things about boarding school, fueling my desire to go. Victoria and Julie never changed their minds about wanting to stay at home, but I wanted only to get away and live American style, in a different fashion. I imagined I would have wonderful friends who would love me and I would love them, and maybe I would never go home again. I would miss my mother and father, but they could come to see me.

The time arrived. I was twelve years old, and I was allowed to go to boarding school. But boarding school was a great shock to me. My parents had chosen Dana Hall, a New England Episcopalian boarding school, deeply rooted in Puritan ethics. It was located in Wellesley, Massachusetts, and had been established as a preparatory school for Wellesley College.

At Dana Hall, I learned that being comfortable was sinful and being uncomfortable was virtuous and would reap rewards. The furniture was all made of hard wood—backs and seats. The food was plain and wholesome. No scrap of food should be left on any plate: Think of the starving children in China. "How will that scrap of food I leave on my plate ever get to them?" I'd think. It was just another unreasonable fact that was never explained to me.

I was introduced to Jesus Christ who seemed to

be everywhere and to whom we prayed three times a day. He died to save me, I was told, another unexplainable statement. No use questioning— any Christian would understand. Since I was not a Christian, I couldn't be expected to understand; and since I was not only not a Christian but a token Jew in this school of Christians and since I didn't want to direct anyone's attention to that fact, I had better keep my mouth shut and my questions to myself.

Miss Cook was the head of the whole school. She was tiny and elegant with clear white skin, white hair that she wore in a coil around her head, and soft blue eyes. I never heard her laugh but there was always a suggestion of a smile on her lips.

Much unlike her was Miss Lees, the principal of the lower school, which was called Ten Acres. Miss Lees was a mountain of a woman, and when she prayed, the little white school house was filled with her sonorous voice as she called on God to punish those who were unclean and who sinned.

But at the school, there was a whole world whose stirrings were never discussed. Sex was an unmentionable word, but my roommate used to take a spoon to bed with her, which she applied to her private parts, and she would moan gently at night and say, "I can't stand it—I can't stand it—"

There was a Canadian girl called Grace Douglas. She was tall and heavyset like a man. She had pale smooth skin and emerald green eyes. She was the nearest thing to a boy in that female ghetto. Every girl in the school had a crush on her and longed to touch or be touched by her. "Has she ever kissed you," one girl would whisper to another.

There was a rule in the school that if a girl spent the night away from her own room in the room of another girl she would be expelled. It was an unwritten rule that homosexuality was forbidden.

While Miss Lees spoke, I'd look through the windows at the landscape—gray and bleak and in keeping with the ascetic bleakness of the little whitewashed New England school house. A giant oak tree with its black arms raised and twisted pointed up to the sky. It seemed to find an echo in the black towering monumental figure of the woman who stood inside on a raised platform. Miss Lees stood over the girls intoning the Lord's Prayer and her deep, booming resonant voice penetrated and permeated each word. From the Lord's Prayer, she would go on into improvisations of her own, and her voice became louder and stronger as she looked up to God and softer and more threatening as she would turn to look down at the girls seated before her on their hard wooden benches. "Let only those come to Me, who are pure in heart and who have clean hands."

I looked down at my hands folded in my lap. They looked brown and dirty against the pale blue of my uniform. I never could quite follow the sense or meaning of Miss Lees' words, but they combined to create in me a terror and sense of awe. As the words thundered through the air around me I sometimes felt that God must be right there in the room above us, coming down through some cleft in the ceiling, His Great Arms stretched out above us, and I was in His Grip and afraid. I wondered how this room that seemed no more than a fragile shell of white wood could contain such awesome presences.

Miss Lees turned over the pages of the Bible in the reader before her. In the semi-pause, I'd let my eyes travel to the other figure that was seated on the platform. This was Miss Van Orden, assistant to Miss Lees and teacher of English. She looked pale and young, her hair braided around her head in a shining coil. When her eyes were not fixed on Miss Lees they contemplated the ground around her feet with a lost and vague expression. She always made me think of a novice in a convent. She had the air of not belonging, of being in transit.

The girls bowed their heads once more in prayer, and then the class was dismissed. Miss Lees walked out strong and striding; Miss Van Orden followed meekly behind. Before they reached the door, Miss Lees turned and placed her hand on Miss Van Orden's shoulder.

I quickly sought my roommate, Dickie Folmer, seated at the end of the row. Dickie was Catholic, and was busy recovering her chewing gum which she had placed under the bench during prayers. She chewed with quiet satisfaction. It was lunchtime, and so we got our coats and overshoes and started walking towards the Main Building where we took our meals.

"Shooting off her mouth again," Dickie said, "and she and taut Miss Van Orden, always stuck together like glue."

I didn't answer; I somehow felt it would be sacrilegious to talk about Miss Lees. As I walked along the slippery boardwalk to the main house, I noticed the oak tree again and that its roots looked curiously eaten away.

The hall in front of the dining room was jammed with girls leaning against the walls, waiting to get in. Miss Lees and Miss Van Orden appeared and the girls opened up a respectful passageway to let them through.

I was at Miss Lees' table and bowed my head as Grace was said. "Oh, Lord, bless this food and us to Thy service." I wondered what we would have for lunch. I looked up and found myself staring into Miss Lees' black-brown eyes, enlarged and shining behind the thick lenses of her glasses. Grace over, she turned to me. "My dear, during Grace, your eyes must be lowered." Recalcitrant thoughts like, "What were you doing then, Miss Lees, looking up?" were quickly smothered, and I only answered, "I'm sorry, Miss Lees."

The food arrived and Miss Lees served us. I got a thin-looking piece of chicken with scraggly hairs on its skin and some watery lima beans. Miss Lees' plate was piled higher and fuller than anyone else's. I found myself watching Miss Lees eat, and suddenly from the strident awesome figure who a few minutes before had transfixed me on the platform, I saw her now as a great mound of human flesh, bones, veins, and sagging muscles. I watched her as she chewed her food, as her lips curled over the morsels and left little bits sticking to her teeth. I was aware that the food must be churning in her stomach, making inward noises, I saw her as a great mound of animalness, and then with a jerk of horror, I pulled my mind back.

I had lost my appetite by the time the farina pudding had arrived, and I knew I couldn't eat it. I left it sitting there, and when I looked around I saw that all the other plates were empty and only mine remained full and untouched. "May I be excused from eating the pudding, Miss Lees?"

Miss Lees looked displeased. "It's an extremely good pudding and wasting food is a sin. Remain at the table, and eat it."

The others rose to leave. I was left alone. I was filled with an unreasoning rage. I ate a spoonful and then got up.

It was Monday and classes were over for the day, but I had to go over to the schoolhouse to get my assignments for the week, which were posted on the bulletin board. Then I would be free the whole afternoon to do whatever I wanted to do. What would I do? For these were the days for me when childhood had vanished and in its place had come the uneasy times. Feelings of lightness and agility had been replaced by feelings of a skin too tight. I no longer found delight in the small things of the world. I could remember when I used to lie on the grass and poke down into the earth and turn over worms and observe their movements for long minutes, or pluck leaves off trees and smell them as deeply as I could. The visible world and its touchable joys no longer seemed important. What then was important? What then did matter?

The hours I spend alone now had taken on an internal and secretive shape. I liked to spend long times in front of the mirror, staring, staring at myself and gusts of high ecstatic joy would sweep over me. "Mirror, mirror, on the wall, mirror, mirror, tell me all." But then once rude interruptive knocks had come on the locked door and the unanswerable question "Hey, what are you doing in there?" and the gust of joy had vanished and a blush of shame took its place. Now as I walked on the boardwalk I pretended it was a tightrope and carefully placed one foot before the other.

Dickie and a few other girls were standing around the bulletin board and I went up to read the notices.

MISS LEES***BIBLE CLASS 1A—
EXAMINATION scheduled Tuesday morning.

Tuesday—that was tomorrow—that meant the whole afternoon was shot—that meant studying from now on—if you failed Bible it counted more against you than any other subject. And now rage came explosively from me.

"Goddamn her," I said, and my voice was loud and angry. "Scheduling an examination for tomorrow. I could slap her big ugly face." There was a queer silence around me. I turned and saw that Dickie was pointing to the room beyond, her lips forming the words, "She's in there, you idiot." My heart sank; I felt very ill. There wasn't a chance in the world that Miss Lees hadn't heard. I would be expelled. I turned quickly and left the schoolhouse.

I knew that my first problem was that I couldn't face Miss Lees at dinner that night. I decided to go over to the infirmary and ask Mrs. Brown, the school nurse, for an excuse slip from dinner. I felt some degree of comfort as I looked at Mrs. Brown. Everything about her seemed limited and comfortable. Problems here did not seem insoluble as they did with Miss Lees. A cold got drops in the nose; a sprained ankle, a tight strap bandage. All the terror and mystery evaporated here. I wished I could stay a little longer. Mrs. Brown wrote me out an excuse and measured out a careful dose of milk of magnesia for me to take. I hated milk of magnesia; still it was better than facing Miss Lees—yet.

I would have to go to my room and think it over. What would happen if I were expelled? When I got to my room I lay down on my bed. The minutes ticked by. I got up and went to my desk and took out my Bible books, but as I read, Miss Lees' face and figure seemed to be stamped on every page. I longed desperately to be home. I thought of my mother in her soft silk dresses, of the rich warm mingled smells that always pervaded the house, of the reassuring feel of the carpets under one's feet. I looked around my room: it was so cold, so clean, so barren, all straight lines, and the hardwood chairs seemed to push you out of them rather than to welcome you into them. This was a place of big words and small creature comforts; at home it was twisted around the other way.

I tried again to study, but always the persistent

question "What shall I do?" kept returning, circling round and round in my head, until finally my thoughts reached an area of quiet, a center of solution, a decision: I would wait until nine o'clock, until Miss Lees had returned to her room in the schoolhouse and would be alone, and then I would go over there and knock on the door and say, "Miss Lees, I'm sorry." Miss Lees would probably be sitting at her desk, austere and stern, papers piled high before her. "My labors," she often said, "are never done."

My mind made up, I began to feel better. I began to feel hungry and was sorry that I was going to miss dinner. I wondered if I could go to dinner and apologize afterwards. I turned this over in my mind and decided against it.

Dickie came rushing into the room. She was getting ready for dinner. "What are you going to do, Tina?" she asked.

I shook my head. "I don't know yet," I said.

The clock finally said nine. I looked out the window and saw a light burning in Miss Lees' room in the schoolhouse. I dressed quickly, put on my coat and overshoes and again made the walk to the schoolhouse. It was bitterly cold, and the wind bit into my face. My ears were unfeelable. They will probably drop off, I thought, as a punishment. The schoolhouse felt warm and good as I stepped inside. I walked across the hall and stood for a moment in front of Miss Lees' door. I heard a murmur of voices, a thin giggle and a deep laugh. I knew they were sex sounds. I suddenly felt out of place as though the nightmare were taking a wrong turn to an unknown place. I knocked and without waiting for an answer pushed the door open and walked in. The room was in a strange disarray. A pillow from the bed had dropped to the floor. Miss Van Orden was standing in a white gown, her hair down, a golden sheath around her. Miss Lees' face was flushed and seemed broken into pieces that didn't fit. Her voice came out slow and choked. "What do you want, Altina?"

I opened my mouth, no words seemed to come. Finally I heard my voice saying, "I'm sorry." It seemed pointless now. Miss Lees got up and moved forward, she pushed me out of the room.

"I'll speak to you tomorrow."

I walked slowly back to the main house. I wanted time to think before I looked into Dickie's questioning face. But of one thing I felt sure. There would be no punishment for me.

"You're lucky, kid," Dickie said when I told her. "She'll never have the nerve to punish you now. I always knew there was something fishy going on between her and Miss Van Orden."

After that, whenever I saw Miss Lees, she always seemed to be looking over my head. I seemed to have lost contact and communication with her. She never referred to that night, and she seemed more careful about putting her arm around Miss Van Orden's shoulders. Although it seemed impossible that Miss Lees, that powerful person, could be afraid of me, I think she was. She never corrected me again, nor did she praise me. It was more as though I didn't exist, as though I had become invisible.

I began thinking about the next year and the upper school that I would have to go to. I wrote a letter to my mother and said, "I think I want to come home."

She answered, "Just try it out for the first term, and then if by Christmas you are unhappy, you can come home." I agreed.

7

From the lower school that had been dominated by Miss Lees, I went to the upper school, for my last two years. From the countrified atmosphere of the first year, we moved to a very large building that dominated four acres of land.

The principal of the high school was a woman called Miss Waldo. She was quite masculine in appearance, very well liked and popular, but I never felt at ease with her, nor she with me.

My roommate was a girl called Frances Baker. She was very good looking and had an air of pride. But her breasts were very strange. They hung down like two bananas, and when she put on her bra, she would roll them up and fit them into the circle, so you couldn't tell from seeing her that she had funny bosoms. She was dark and had full voluptuous lips and dark eyes that looked almost Chinese. Her waist was very small and her hips swelled out around her waist. Later I used to see sculptures by La Chaise, and they always made me think of Frannie.

Her father was a lively man, and he would come weekends and with Miss Cook's permission take us to Boston to the Copley Plaza Hotel where we would spend the night. He would take us out to dinner and then to dance at a cabaret. He loved to dance and never seemed to have enough.

His wife seemed diametrically opposed to him. His first wife had died, and he married her nurse. She was very austere and religious and refused to sit in our room when she came because she said we used perfume, which to her mind was immoral. So we had to put a small chair for her in the corridor outside the room, and she would pass her time mending Frances' clothes.

She was not disagreeable, but she was very withdrawn and only had a tight little smile on her lips. She was Frances' stepmother, and Frances felt for her a combination of respect and contempt. "How could my father have married her?" she once said to me.

Mr. Baker liked me and I liked him. Still I felt self-conscious about being Jewish. I could not imagine my father and Mr. Baker together. Mr. Baker was so American and my father with his broken English would not have cut a good figure next to him.

Grades were never a problem for me, but they didn't help me wipe out the stigma of my being different, of having foreign parents and of being Jewish. I decided popularity would. I was voted the most popular girl in my class, and that was what I wanted to be. But I can't say that I was happy. I always felt under a strain. I was always trying to prove something. I was always alert and watchful that I might slip and make a mistake.

Frances and I lived in a small room with twin

beds at opposite ends. We had twenty minutes a day to clean them up. Clean sheets once a week. Room inspection everyday. We had a nice housemother who lived at the end of the hall.

We had a bath twice a week and were only allowed to fill the tub halfway up. We wore uniforms with sailor collars for school time, but at three o'clock we could change and wear whatever we liked. No makeup was allowed. I have very high color and once at inspection Miss Cook thought I had rouge and took a handkerchief and rubbed my cheeks. But I passed the test—no rouge!

Once I sat in chapel holding hands with a little friend of mine, Mabel Hopkins, but Miss Waldo passing by said, "None of that."

"None of what?" I thought, but I didn't ask.

We were changed to different tables every three weeks. The only table that was bad was "The Manners Table," where you went when you didn't handle your knife and fork properly or were sloppy with your food. I was there twice and my roommate, never.

I was two years younger than the girls in my class, having skipped several grades, so I seemed more unsophisticated and I had no boyfriend conversations.

I tried to make up a boyfriend that I could talk about, but he didn't seem real. One weekend I went home with a girl, and she invited two boys one evening, and I got along pretty well. His name was Jim and he seemed to like me and we held hands. I was always worried about whom I could invite for the prom each year, and that year I "thanked God" for Jim. I could ask him.

There was always something to worry about.

I was overweight and took a lot of teasing, but I went on a diet and lost my fat belly! Dieting was hard because I loved to eat; but the vision I kept before me of how I wanted to look at the senior prom steeled my resolution. I succeeded. I was not really good looking, but I was what in those days they called cute. I think it was a certain cherubic look.

I was elected to the elite sorority—T.K.D. You had to have a certain average in your grades and be popular. About a quarter of the class made it. Looking back, I think I am against these sororities that said, "I am better than you are."

I had one wonderful teacher in history who later became the head of Sarah Lawrence. She was very left wing and socialistic, and I became converted to her ideas. When I went home and told my father, he said, "If before twenty-one you are not socialistic, it's because you have no heart. If you are socialistic after twenty-one, it is because you have no head." I respected my father, but I did not think I would change.

I had another great teacher, an English teacher, and we spent the whole term studying *Hamlet*. I've always felt it was worth it since Hamlet has so many aspects: the psychology of the relationships between the characters, the historical perspective, and the beauty and poetry of its lines. We memorized large sections, and they have remained with all my life.

"To be or not to be . . . "

"Neither a borrower nor a lender be."

Etc.

So as not to appear different, I went to the Episcopalian church every Sunday. I could not go along with the prayers and recitations. The Nicene Creed—"I was born in sin." A big No!

The girls were not interested in the religious parts. They were all in love with the minister who was a widower with three small children, and I think it was in the heart of every girl to want to marry him. He had a pink-colored face, and we used to call him "Pinkie." After church he used to go to Miss Cook's house, and through the big bay window we used to see the minister and his children kneeling in prayer.

Miss Cook was very pretty. She had white curly hair, a peaches and cream complexion, a small graceful body clothed in rather tight pale blue clothes. I used to wonder what went on in her head. She seemed too perfect to be true.

When my father came up to my graduation, he put his arm around her. He was very fond of women and felt at ease with them. I thought, "God might strike him dead," but nothing happened, and Miss Cook, unbelievably, seemed to like it.

I was the President of the Junior class as well as most popular. But then came the senior class elections. I heard that in the discussion preceding the vote it was said that it could not be allowed for the senior president of an all-Christian school to be Jewish because I'd be representing the school at graduation.

I think that was the first sleepless night that I

experienced. My problems before had always found a solution, but there was no solution for this. It was something I could not change.

I think this Jewish problem has been threaded through all my life until it culminated in Hitler and the massacre of the Jews. Now, it is much less acute after the bloodletting of six million.

I was elected Vice-President and also class historian because of my ability to write. Lucille Tinian, an Irish girl, was elected President and her sister Pat was elected treasurer. They were both attractive and would walk into the dining room, their arms around each other's waist, and they made a good entrance.

Miss Waldo favored Lucille and her sister, and approached me about having Pat read my class history at the graduation. "Wouldn't it be nice," she said, "since Pat is the sister of the President, for her to read it?"

Luckily I stood my ground. "I wrote it," I said, "and I am entitled to read it."

Miss Waldo withdrew her request, and at graduation Miss Cook publicly thanked me and said it was one of the best histories she had ever heard.

It was a victory in the middle of my defeat.

At sixteen, being above average in intelligence if not in wisdom, I graduated. I felt sad when I left Dana Hall, and I remember crying on the train that took me home.

8

After graduation my mother took my sister and me to Europe on a big ocean liner. Life began to be fun. We went to Paris, golden beautiful Paris of the 20s. We were taken around by three French men, handsome and sophisticated. I was introduced to the splendors of Western Civilization and history, the architecture, the museums, the cathedrals. I had my first drink and my first cigarette, had my hair bobbed flapper style and wore high-heeled shoes. I went to the opera, the races. I danced at every possible occasion. I floated around in a daze of promised sex, but not fulfilled. I could hardly wait to wake up and start the day with its promise of delicious happenings.

The Champs Elysee stretched broad and wide and led to the Etoile with its arch and sculptured supports on either side. At night the lights went on—soft purple bathed the whole area. It was before cars were allowed to park on the Champs Elysee, and so it was still spacious and graceful. The big cafes with their canopies, small tables, and chairs crept out on the sides of the avenue, and the waiters in dark suits and white aprons served their customers. That was all on the Right

Bank—the fancy hotels, the shops, displaying their jewels and clothes. But what seduced and enraptured me was the Left Bank across the Seine from the Louvre. It had a gray, misty, romantic quality, little galleries tucked away on small side streets, restaurants, and shops with antiques and bric-a-brac.

I found my way to René's studio. He was Aunt Rachel's nephew by marriage, Turkish, but having lived in Paris for many years, now more French than Turkish. He was a fine artist. He made his living illustrating books for Andre Gidé, Julian Green, and other famous writers. He worked in woodblocks and etchings.

My auntie Rachel took me to meet him when I first arrived, told him I was a beginning artist, and asked if he could help me. He agreed—he would take me and teach me to do wood blocks, and in return I would wash his brushes and keep his studio clean and tidy.

René was small with dark eyes and a beautifully carved forehead, an aquiline nose, and a sensitive mouth with curving lips.

His studio smelt of turpentine and paint and was lit with kerosene lamps. There were a few working tables and chairs, a cot in the corner where René slept, and a coal stove for heating. The lighting made it seem like a Caravaggio painting, the light picking up folds and forms and letting the others disappear into the darkness. René's studio had at one time belonged to Modigliani, and I liked to think that his spirit still invaded the space.

I loved everything in the studio. The mirror with

the cracks in it and its worn gold frame. The furniture that all looked old and as though it had been used and touched by living hands. The paintings on the walls in dark rich colors that René had done.

My dream was to be able to draw and paint as well as René did.

Of all the painters he revered, in modern times Picasso was at the head. I still didn't understand Picasso and his distortions, but I gradually began to grasp their meaning under René's tutelage. Everything I learned about art started, I think, in René's studio in Paris.

A sort of ritual started. René would be painting, and I would sit over the table and do my wood blocks. We talked and exchanged ideas. The twentieth century disappeared. Harshness, loud noises, machine sounds—all were cloaked in gentleness and tenderness. René himself seemed to be carved out of the atmosphere. I would watch him sometimes as he would bend over his table to make an illustration. His dark hair framed his face, which seemed extremely pale. So did all the faces on the street in Paris.

Occasionally, he would look up and smile as I struggled with a drawing, and his eyes were soft as he looked at me. Our time together was happy.

When it came time for me to go home, he would lead me down the staircase, walk the short distance to the street, hail a taxi, stand at the street corner, and watch until the taxi was out of sight. By that, I knew that he loved me.

Back on the other side of the Seine, I felt like a chameleon slowly changing its color until once again I was the bright, accepted colors of the Right Bank, the chic women, the fancy hotels.

When I returned to the United States, the scenes and emotions I had experienced in René's studio sank deep into my unconscious until they left a space around it that was occupied by different standards of ambition, money, social ways of doing things, stylish ways of wearing clothes.

Snobbishness and respect for people who had money, people who had titles, status and position; clever conversation, witty sayings, going to the theater to see the latest play, reading the latest book, having people for whom I couldn't feel real respect pointed out to me by my sisters as examples that I should follow—it was like some sort of race, trying to stay ahead, not feeling any deep pleasure in any of the things I was doing.

I think I have always been torn between a materialistic kind of world that my family and all the surrounding people lived in and the artists' world of people that were different, but whom I really felt akin to and liked. But I let the world I had grown up in take hold—I thought, "This is the real world; this must be where I belong." I'm sorry that I didn't listen to the voices that were deep inside of me and that I went instead in search of the crude and obvious world that chattered around me.

The United States of America is a strong country—powerful—and France seemed graceful and beautiful, but far away.

When it came time to decide whether I was going to college or to art school, I chose art school. I always loved to draw. I used to take photographs and pictures and copy them carefully. That was my greatest pleasure. My parents wanted me to learn to play the piano, but I was a complete bust at that. But I always drew. And I would cut out dolls and make stages that I'd put them on. I'd feel really omnipotent. I'd think, "Here I'm really in charge. I can make these people do whatever I want them to do; they're my people." And I think I felt that about my artwork, too, that I was in charge, that I could make all these things that nobody had ever seen before, and that they would be just mine.

I've always had a mind of my own about art. When I went to boarding school, they gave me an art teacher who came from the Boston Museum. We didn't get along at all because I always wanted to draw what I wanted to draw. My first drawing for her was a garbage man and his horse pulling the garbage cart. My teacher said, "Oh, no. This will never do. You have to start at the beginning." For her, the beginning was to draw from casts of Greek and Roman sculptures. And I didn't like it. So I wrote home and said, "I don't like the art teacher. I don't want to take art." My parents said I didn't have to, but the principal of the school didn't like that at all because she knew I had a talent for art and she couldn't understand why I was not more submissive.

After working with René, though, I did decide to

study art. I think it was a mistake. You make certain wrong turns in your life, and that was one of the wrong turns in my life. I definitely should have gone to college because I was bright and talented in other ways besides drawing. But I decided on art school.

I went back to live with my parents, and I studied at the Roerich Museum on Riverside Drive and 103rd Street. It was named after a famous Russian painter who did the sets for the Diaghilev ballets and also painted very beautiful surrealistic landscapes. His two sons, who were also very gifted painters, started this art school. My teacher there, Samuel Halpert, was very uninspiring, but nevertheless I liked it. And I'll never forget something an older girl in the class said to me: "One thing you must remember—keep your art as a very important part of your life because no matter what else goes wrong, you have it and it'll be kind of a support and a standby for you."

And it really was.

9

For three years, we'd gone back and forth to Europe, spending several months there at a time. I had hundreds of boyfriends over the years, but my mother—and I do blame her for this—was very hellbent for me to get married because in those days a girl was supposed to get married and you were supposed to get married young because the bloom would be off the rose by the time you were twenty-one or twenty-two. So it was sort of stuck in my mind. I respected what my mother said, and if she said I should get married, I felt I should get married.

One of my Dana Hall classmates had invited me to visit her in Little Rock, Arkansas, at Christmas time. I went. Part of me liked it—the social whirl: the dances, the parties, the lunches, and the introductions to young men from Yale, Harvard, Antioch, Columbia—all filled with ambitious dreams of the future, success, money. My mother was in the background but her wishes were always present: Get married—get married. Damn! Is that all they wish for me? Can't I be an artist, a journalist, what is all this about getting married, having a man, living in an apartment or house, saying to all my classmates, "Look at me: I am married and I am going to have a baby." Words, words like a newspaper headline printed on paper with no substance. But look at the faces of all the parents, beaming happily when someone would announce, "I'm engaged. Look at my ring. Isn't it beautiful? And my fiancé is a lawyer . . . an architect . . . a doctor." We were all dancing to a rhythm that was established for us by our parents—our elders. Nice boy; nice girl; good family; they are bound to be happy—

And then came smashing down—the reality: Who is this stranger I am wedded to? Let me out of here. But no, it is too late, you are going to have a baby, you can't get away now it is too late—

It was on this Arkansas visit that I met my future husband, Morris Sanders. His friends called him Morrie or Bidge that Christmas vacation. He was a cousin of my classmate. He went to Yale; he was going to be an architect. The word "brilliant" was always used to describe him. He spoke well, with authority. He was very good looking. He did everything well. I did notice that he was not popular, that men—especially the men—felt resentment towards him. One small, rather unattractive man who liked me, said to me several times, "Don't think of marrying him. I have known him since we were both six years old, and I can tell you, he is a jerk."

I didn't pay much attention to what he said. I dismissed it in my mind. I thought, he's jealous, that's all. Besides, I liked Bidge a lot.

Mr. Sanders

Many other girls eyed me with envy when they saw that Bidge was paying a great deal of attention to me, and that added to my feeling of being attracted to him.

"When we are back East," he said, "I'll come to New York to see you. It's near New Haven. We can go to concerts, art galleries—see some wonderful things together."

He did come to New York—two or three times that year. We used to go tea dances and to art shows. I was very impressed by the fact that he was so bright and knew so much about art and architecture. I was sure I'd made a good match.

That summer, though, I went to France to study painting. There I met a Frenchman who was a lawyer and an alpinist. After a whirlwind courtship, he asked me to marry him.

Then Bidge showed up in Paris; he'd followed me there to propose.

So they both wanted to marry me, and I couldn't decide which one to marry. I would sit on the bed in my hotel room in Paris and throw coins: heads, it's Bidge; tails, it's this other guy. That didn't help me decide. Finally, though, what did was the fact that Bidge was an American. I didn't know if I wanted to marry a Frenchman and live in France.

Bidge went to Cartier and bought me a heavy gold ring with his initials "M.S." engraved inside. That was my engagement ring.

A year later, a week after his graduation, we were married.

I was married at our family's city house in the

delicate and gilded Louis XIV-style drawing room with its pale blue and pale gold Aubusson carpet. The windows opened to the river, and around the walls were the locked cabinets filled with all those wonderful, mysterious things. I would spend hours looking at the precious bits of porcelain and ivory, at the music boxes that when opened released feathered birds, rising up.

I remember I said I did not want to be married in a white dress with a veil and a train. So I had a gentle beige crepe de chine dress, ankle length.

I also remember going out with Bidge the night before and startling myself with the declaration that I really didn't want to get married—that I really wanted to be an artist or a journalist.

As soon as I said this, I tried to deny it. I always seemed to be in some kind of conflict with myself and with what I was doing. I think it was a struggle between what I wanted to do and what I thought my parents wanted me to do.

But I was nineteen, an absurd age for an unformed, unrealized person to get married.

Rabbi Stephen Wise arrived to marry us. He only stayed long enough to complete the ceremony. It all felt business-like and unromantic. He didn't know us; we didn't know him. But he was a prominent rabbi—he was the rabbi prominent people should have marry their children.

After the wedding ceremony, we walked back through the main hall with its heavy carved-oak Italian furniture and Renaissance rose red carpets and marble tables that held candelabras and clocks.

Surprisingly, my father sat down on a small chair in the hall and began to cry.

"Why are you crying, Papa?" I asked.

"Because you are my baby, and now I have lost you," he said.

I decided the marriage was no fun the first week. It was like standing in an empty circle, with He-him in the middle. That's how I thought about him—He-him. He was the subject and the object of every sentence. He said, he thought, he did—to him, about him, towards him.

A circle empty of my family, my sisters, my girlfriends, my boyfriends. Only He-him standing in the middle, his bushy eyebrows drawn together in a disapproving frown making a hairy black line across his face.

For three years, I'd been surrounded by boys ready to take me wherever I wanted to go—sailing, dancing, mountain climbing. To have all that end so abruptly, to have my sole companion be a person harsh, critical, seemingly never happy or pleased, neither with himself or me, was like living in a dark room with glimpses of sunlight through the drawn shades.

How do you know what people are capable of? What are the deep depths of them? The ambiance of a situation takes over—you are a man, I am a woman; the music playing as you dance, the feel of his arms around you, his face close to yours. That's all there is, that's all that's important . . . Wrong. You should have noticed the quick jerkiness of his gestures, the occasional times when he would bang his fist against his head. It said, "Oh woe is me, woe is me, a Shakespearean tragedy." Or when he would say, sounding desperate: "How can you love this ugly face, this ugly mug?"

"Why do you hate yourself? You are brilliant, first in your class, what more do you want?" I didn't say these words, I just pulled him to me.

I must have been a super virgin, impenetrable. My wedding night was spent in fruitless forays of his penis trying to penetrate me. It was painful, it was awful. I felt like a volcano on fire, and I thought of a female cat that I had had who was in heat and spent the night crying and hurling herself against the walls. There was no relief in sight.

I said, "I'm going to get dressed; I'm going out for a walk." We were staying in a country inn outside of New York.

He looked at me with fury. "You can't do that, go out and leave me on our wedding night."

If I had suggested murder or mutilation, he could not have been more horrified. So, I dropped the subject and turned over on my side, praying for sleep to release me.

Earlier in the night he had surveyed my body with what seemed to be both appetite and distaste. "You certainly are very female looking," he said. "Your breasts and you are very soft . . . On our trip I think you should get up early every morning and take a cold shower and then rub yourself vigorously and get into shape." Shape—shape? What kind of shape? I decided that was one thing I would not do. I who loved to snuggle in warm silky sheets and drift slowly and deliciously into a state of awakening.

The next day when we returned to the city, I went to see my girlfriend Adele Brandwen who was married and who was very careful and precise about everything she did. If anyone would have a solution she would.

"You could go to a doctor and he could surgically open you up so that it would no longer be painful."

"Oh, Bidge wouldn't like that and I'm not sure that I would either. I couldn't do that."

"Well, then, slowly, keep on trying and eventually, he'll be able to get it in."

"Do you think it's worth all this trouble and pain? What's this whole thing about sex being so great?"

"Later on you'll find out that it is great. Not the first few times when it seems so difficult and it's impossible for you to enjoy it, but when the pain and difficulty disappear, you'll see. So just be patient."

In those prehistoric days, everything about sex seemed to be unmentionable. When I was ten years old and saw the word "fuck" scrawled on the wall and my classmates pointing and giggling, I pointed and giggled, too, although I understood nothing at all. I went home and asked Loff, "What does 'fuck' mean?"

She said, "Never say that word again." Even with my marriage, my ignorance remained, compounded with a sense of wickedness and shame.

There seemed to be a conspiracy of silence when it came to sex. Books all seemed to end with "They kissed and got married and lived happily or unhappily ever after." It wasn't until D.H. Lawrence's *Lady Chatterley's Lover* hit the stands that any writer was talking graphically about sex. When I hear now about fourteen-year-old girls getting pregnant and about AIDS, it seems to me that we are galloping fast in the opposite and wrong direction.

Finally on our trip when we reached Rome, I had my first orgasm, and as I swirled high up in the sky and stars of sexual ecstasy, I understood something about sex and what all the talk was about.

Apart from sex, things weren't going so well. Bidge was a Yale man, graduated with honors from architectural school. He had an extraordinary mind. He only read classical and worthwhile books. Novels were trash. Of course, I read novels. I was in for a general overhaul—I could see that.

Bidge also had an extraordinary memory—he remembered every nursery rhyme that he had ever learned—and his memory served him well. When he was asked to come up with a design, he could forage through his closet of remembered images he had seen or read about or heard about and speedily come up with something daring and beautiful.

True, Bidge was a Yale graduate, but he had remnants of being a country boy from Little Rock, Arkansas, and when we got to Paris, it was "gay Paree" for him. On our second night there, he wanted to go out on the town alone, and I was to stay home with a good book. When I said I didn't want to stay home with a good book, but would call up some of my boyfriends that I had from previous trips whom I knew would be glad to take me out, he found this offensive. I was a poor sport and so forth. So we spent an unsatisfactory evening together, each wishing we were apart and elsewhere.

In Rome we hooked up with three Yale guys, also architectural school graduates, and things began to look brighter. They were all nice fellows.

Tony Lord was from the South and handsome in a lanky Gary Cooper style. He was very kind and easygoing. He had the least amount of money of any of us and had to be very thrifty about what he spent on food and drink, but he was very touchy about letting anybody pay any of his share.

Then there was Dale White, who was small, quick and witty, and always full of ideas about things that would be fun to do.

And there was Lou Gelders, who looked like a thin, freckled El Greco, frail and less talented than the others, but he understood my femaleness and what I liked to do.

We had a regular routine. Every morning we would get our stuff together and go out sketching. The churches, the houses, the domes, the cathedrals. Wherever you turned there was something to draw.

They were all skilled, well trained and talented. I was clumsy and ignorant. I always longed to do something different than theirs, something that would make them gasp in amazement at my talent, only it didn't happen. Their drawings were elegant and tasteful, and they were looking forward to having a show at the Architectural League when they got back to the states.

All these feelings of good fellowship, though, couldn't mask my growing feelings that there were strange, unexplained things about Bidge. His reactions were sometimes violent and ugly. It culminated when Lou Gelders said in a happy tone of voice, "Your wife has beautiful legs."

Bidge got up and said, "For that you'll get a punch in the nose." Wham, and poor Lou was blasted to the floor. He lay there looking crumpled and pathetic, and blood started to ooze from his nose. He opened his eyes, startled and bewildered.

I bent over him and pressed his hand. "I'm so sorry, Lou." Bidge grabbed me by the shoulder and pulled me off. I stood up and looked at him. I was looking at a stranger . . . at a stranger I didn't like. I knew that I had better learn to understand him, and another emotion came flooding over me—fear.

"How could you do this? Lou didn't mean anything. He wanted to say something nice."

"This isn't going to work out. I don't want to be with three men who are lusting after my wife. Is that so hard for you to understand? Or are you lusting after them also? Go up to our room, I will see you there later."

I walked slowly back and up the stairs to our pie-shaped room. I looked out of the windows over the roofs of Rome. How I love you, Rome. I heard some of the churches striking the hour.

What had seemed like a playful fun situation of four men and a girl had turned into a nightmare. Like taking the lid off a box and finding it full of snakes and strange animals.

It's just natural jealousy, I reassured myself. Maybe I should feel flattered. But natural jealousy shouldn't end up with a bloody nose and a broken friendship. It was the dark anger in his eyes that had frightened me—like a gate swinging open to an unknown territory. I wished I were back home where things were simple and easy to understand.

When Bidge came upstairs, he had a satisfied look on his face.

"We are leaving," he said. "In a few hours. We are going to Sardinia." He pulled out of his jacket pocket guides and maps of Sardinia. "Look these over and acquaint yourself with some of the sights that we will see so that you won't be completely ignorant and so that I can have someone to talk to intelligently." I felt that now that he no longer had the boys to hear and witness, he was going to drop his manners of politeness. His whole appearance seemed to have changed. He seemed rougher all over.

"Where are the boys?"

"Oh, they are going to North Africa, they said to say good-bye. I think they thought that travelling with a woman slowed them up."

Maybe, maybe, I thought, but I don't believe they said that.

From then on I began to watch him, to observe. I had taken him before as a normal young guy, with an unusually good mind and a bit of arrogance. But, I thought, there is something else here. His gestures were jerky, his reactions surprising and unexpected. His relationship with Tony, Dale, and Lou fluctuated between "you're a good fellow" and a kind of hidden contempt. They, on their side, seemed to admire him, admired his scholarship, his style in talking and dressing. He always seemed to be ahead of the game, attracted attention wherever he went. He had been voted "the most likely to succeed." Sometimes he stood in the doorway or silhouetted against a window and he always looked striking. His sentences always put an end to an argument. He had a way of putting a cap on everything and leaving everyone with the feeling that there was no more to be said on the subject.

I was left torn between feeling pleased that I was married to a man of seemingly superior ability and resentment at his arrogance. Was I imagining that he had a sinister element?

I never saw the boys again, and I missed them. They seemed to take the hard edges off my relationship to Bidge. Whenever Bidge said something rough and I looked at their kind faces, I felt comforted and reassured. Their presence gave a color of good fellowship. Now I would be all alone with He-him. There would be no relief. Things looked pretty bleak.

In my mind I began to go over the past few weeks. There were many things I did not understand.

"I don't want any pictures of your family around," he had said once and he took a picture of my sisters off the dresser and put it in the wastebasket. I wasn't angry: I was hurt. I got it out of the wastebasket and put it face down on the bed. He gave it a brief look and turned away.

Once he grabbed me by the shoulders and looked and said, "How can you like this big ugly face?"

"I don't think it is big and ugly."

And he swung away and picked up a book.

He gradually slipped into deeper dark moods—nothing pleased him.

He would sit by the window, and when I spoke to him, he would not answer. When I touched his arm trying to make contact, he would shrink back.

The silences between us increased until there was more silence than anything else.

Once he burst out, "Are you going to leave me? If you do I will kill myself."

In my heart, I believed him. I was looking forward to the day when our trip would end, when we would be in the U.S.A. I felt I was losing my sanity. There was no one nearby who could advise me.

When Bidge no longer wanted to leave the room, I began going out for walks alone. When I would come back, I used to be afraid to open the door. Would he still be there? And in what condition? I took to knocking on the door so that I would not startle him.

On the way home, we stopped over in Paris. I had made up my mind to tell him that it was no use. I wanted out of the marriage. I looked at him across the table as we sat in the little French cafe.

It looked wrong for the announcement I was going to make. I was going to say, "I don't think that you and I, we, are going to make it. I'm not right for you. When we get home, let's call it off." But instead I said—I had to say: "I'm pregnant, I'm going to have a baby." He looked startled, his eyebrows drew together in that long threatening line.

Would the baby look like him, I thought? God forbid. It's bad enough to have a husband like that, but to duplicate him? That's pretty terrible, that's unforgivable. What am I talking about?

"How long have you known?" And he took his silver pencil with its sharp point and started calculating. "It will be born in January."

I could feel the cold of New York and the crying baby. Would I be nursing it? Would he treat the baby well? Would he love the baby?

Suddenly he didn't seem so important anymore. He faded into the background. The baby took center stage. He began to look better to me—maybe having a baby would change him. I couldn't leave now. Babies should have fathers. I felt myself reaching out to him.

"Let's have some wine to celebrate; people always celebrate when they are going to have a baby." I waved my hand at the waiter. Following my impulse, I said in French, "We want wine, we are going to have a baby."

With Gaelic gallantry he responded. "Felicitation. Oh, que belles nouvelles!" and he clasped his hands together. I felt I was being carried away by the situation.

What was I being so happy about? Didn't I still want out? How did the baby change anything? I felt I was two people: the one who knows that the relationship is no good and won't get better and the other who wants to make it good by having a baby.

"I'll be a mother," I cried happily.

A dim smile lit my husband's face, and he covered my hands with his. "And I'll be a father."

"We'll be different people."

He leaned forward across the table, his face close to mine.

The two me's reacted—one pulling back, the other pushing forward and pressing my lips against his.

On the boat crossing, I began to feel sick in the early morning. I hung over the basin. He began looking at me in disgust.

"Is this how you're going to be for the whole nine months?"

I felt apologetic, as though, as usual, I wasn't doing things properly. I tried to stand up but threw up over the basin, making matters worse.

Then I said, "It's only supposed to last three months."

"Well, I hope so. I'm going to the dining room for breakfast. If you feel better come down."

"Go and eat your breakfast," I wanted to yell at him, "and I hope you choke on it."

Wet and messy, I changed my clothes and rang for the steward. He came neat and clean in his white jacket.

"Yes, Miss."

"I'm not Miss," I wanted to say. "I'm Mrs. now, Mrs. who's morning sick and going to have a baby."

"Please bring me some tea and dry toast."

I felt alone in the world—a baby in my stomach and just me.

I stayed in the cabin all day, and late that afternoon I went to the bar and ordered a drink—a nice long drink—"Planter's Punch." The man next to me at the bar was a handsome blond man with gold-rimmed glasses. I felt myself longing to be single and free!

I believe that inside every woman, at least during her sex awareness years, there lives a little creature with a pointed nose, big eyes, and ears who when she meets a male gives out verdicts.

Possible, impossible. I may, I will, I won't. He is very close to what I want, not at all, forget it. The music at the bar was slow and sentimental and the man leaned towards me.

"That's a real woman's drink, Planter's Punch," and he smiled, a warm, loving smile spreading over his face.

"I guess so. What are you having?"

"Scotch on the rocks."

"A real man's drink," I said, and we moved a little closer to each other.

"Do you like this ship?" I asked him.

"I do now. Do you?"

"I do now, too." Everything seemed transformed. I felt good, I was swimming in his approval.

My husband's voice interrupted.

"Are you going to introduce me to your new

friend?"

"Oh yes, this is my husband—I don't know your name—"

But my new friend had already. turned away.

10

We returned to New York in the summer of 1928. I was pregnant with Denis. We had moved into a ten-room penthouse on East 86th Street for which my father had provided the money. When you looked out bedroom window, you could see a little park on the East River surrounding the Gracie Mansion, where the mayor lived.

The apartment was on two floors. The first floor contained an office and four bedrooms. A staircase led to the large living room on the second floor. Beyond it was the dining room and then the kitchen. Outside, a patio surrounded the penthouse on three sides.

Bidge decorated the apartment in a striking fashion: The carpets were black, the walls a deep blue with white trim, and we had the art deco furniture by Ruhlmann that we had bought in Paris on our honeymoon. We acquired some works of art during this period: a painting by Odilon Redon and several lithographs by Matisse.

Bidge was a creative and brilliant designer with exquisite taste. He was working for Ely Kahn one of New York's eminent architects for $75 a week—a pittance, but the fact he had a job on the eve of the

Great Depression was impressive.

My mother and my sister Juliette were in Europe, and my father was living alone in his big white marble palazzo on Riverside Drive. These were very sad days for him, and he seemed so lonely. He would send his car once or twice a week to pick me up, and we would go for a ride, usually into Westchester to see our country house.

His hair seemed so thin, and the lines in his face were much deeper. He'd puff on his cigar, which seemed to be one of his remaining small comforts, and say in his badly broken English, "Here I am, a very rich man, and yet I am all alone. Everyone has deserted me. I live in that big house with strangers who order the food and cook the meals."

I felt sorry for him; in his way he had been a very good, kind, and generous father, but he could not accept American customs and ways. He had a wife and three daughters that he wanted to literally keep under lock and key. Surrounded by the free American society, there were constant screaming battles between him and my mother. My mother and Juliette had escaped to Paris. Victoria and I escaped into a marriages that proved to be a deeper trap than the one we had experienced living at home.

It was up to me now to comfort him and this I did by accompanying him on these rides to the country.

When I told him about the baby, and his face lit up.

"My first grandchild," he said. "I am so glad. I hope it is a boy, but boy or girl, I want you to let it stay with me, here at the house, every weekend. We will have a second set of clothes and toys for him, and I will buy nursery furniture. Where would you like him to be?"

"Upstairs, on the third floor," I said, "in my old room. It is nice and sunny there."

Dear father, I thought, if only my husband were as happy about this as you are.

Everything about my father was special and made to order. The car we rode in was especially made to be bigger: the roof of it higher so if he wanted to stand up in it, he could.

The marble that had been used to build the house was imported from Italy, and all the furniture specially designed and made to order to fit the house. For someone who had been born in a small dusty town in Turkey, had run barefoot in the streets until he was fifteen, had gone on a cattle boat to Alexandria, Egypt, had literally no schooling, my father was endowed with exquisite taste. When I came back from Paris, and brought with me art deco furniture designed by Ruhlmann, which was considered very strange and avant garde when most people were furnishing their apartments with copies of Louis XIV and XV's, my father had carefully looked it over and given it his approval. He smiled and patted me on the back and said, "You're all right, Tunchy."

My father died in 1929, right before Denis was born. It was a very sad day because I knew how much he had been looking forward to having a grandchild.

My father had a painful two weeks before his death. He had angina and suffered much.

He had gone on a trip prior to his illness, travelling with a couple, Dr. and Mrs. Gardner, and they told me that he was very unhappy because my mother had left him.

They had gone to an old hotel in Lenox, Massachusetts, and after dinner one night when the three-piece orchestra was playing music, he had gone out on the dance floor alone and danced much as Zorba the Greek must have danced, trying to recapture his youth, trying to find some joy forever lost. Of course, they felt embarrassed for him, and the hotel guests laughed at him, but before it was over, he collapsed on the floor. He was taken home and carried to his room, to his big bed on the second floor.

Mrs. Gardner called me up and said, "You had better come and live in the house and be with your father. He is a very sick man."

Bidge grudgingly agreed to go and live in the house. I spent most of my time in the sitting room next to my father's bedroom.

Mrs. Gardner had given him a small black pomeranian who spent his time on my father's bed, and my father seemed to like him and would play with him. There were day and night nurses, and my father had times when he was in great pain.

The doctor came and brought more doctors, one of whom was old and deaf and another who saw badly and was almost blind—but famous doctors.

My father said, "Why do you bring me these old sick doctors who can't help me?"

I sat on his bed and held his hand. I asked him, "Do you want me to call mother and tell her to come home?" She and my sister Juliette were still in Europe. He said no very bitterly: "I don't want to see her anymore."

That night he slipped into a coma, and two days later, he died. I was glad I had been with him to give him a little comfort. I wished I had some.

In his will, my father had left a lot of money to hospitals, including one to be built in his hometown of Manissa, Turkey. That hospital still stands today, and it's called The Morris Schinasi International Hospital.

My husband seemed more and more removed from me as time went on. I sometimes thought that to him I was just a woman with a big stomach, and I felt when walking with him he would walk ahead as though he didn't want people to think we were together.

Once at the theatre during intermission we were standing in the lobby, and he said to me, "You look like a sack of potatoes, can't you do something to look better?" All the women standing around me seemed to be unusually glamorous and beautiful, only I was out of shape and deformed. I walked away and back to my seat. That was one of the last times I would go out with him at night.

One day over lunch, my sister Victoria looked at me pityingly. "You'll lose your figure, you know, you'll never get it back. You'll be all baggy and

loose. Too bad, because you're such a young girl."
My sister was four years older than I was.

"Don't you ever want to have a baby?" I asked
her.

She flicked the ash off her cigarette and put the
cigarette back into her red lipsticked mouth. "God,
no," she said. "Whatever for? I like men and sex,
babies are a rude interruption. I'm happy the way I
am."

She took a deep breath and her breasts peeked
through her sweater. She was smooth and svelte
all the way down to her crotch.

The months went by. It was getting harder and
harder to move. Soon, I couldn't lean over any
more to put on my shoes, and I began to wear
loose shoes that I could slip into. It's a good thing
I'm an artist, I thought. I'm wearing a smock for
two reasons, to keep the paint off me and to hide
my pregnancy.

I began to read books—*My Baby's First Year,
Natural Childbirth.* I knew it was going to hurt. I
would probably die in childbirth—"And I am only
twenty," I whispered to myself piteously. "How did I
ever get into this mess? And there is no way out.
This is the first thing I've ever done that if it turns
out to be a mistake I can't get out of. No ticket to
Europe, no other adventure."

I began to count the days. I got a big calendar
and put it up in the studio and put a cross on
every day that passed.

"What's that?" Bidge asked me as he rubbed his
finger on the dates.

"Nothing, nothing."

My husband had been his usual up and down self. For two or three days he would go without stopping, inviting people to the house, playing the record player loud and wild, inventing games to play, insisting on food and drink at all hours. We had a cook, butler, and chambermaid, and he would think nothing of waking them up at one o'clock when we had come home from a theatre party and demanding that they cook a meal for us and friends he'd brought home with him.

After these periods of frenetic activity, he would sometimes lie in bed for two or three days, hardly moving and uninterested in everything.

During Bidge's periods of depression, I would call his boss and report that he had the flu so he was able to keep his job in spite of his absences.

The world around me seemed to be getting worse. The Depression deepened. Men in Brooks Brothers suits were on the sidewalks, selling apples. At least my husband had a job, and we had the money my father had left me.

Stories began to come from Europe. Hitler was rising in Germany. Stories of Jew hatred and Jew killing were in the newspapers. Were the stories true or false?

Was this all there was going to be to life? An uncertain and fearful world? Living with this uncertain man, never knowing if he was going to wake up manic or depressive?

The hospital was across the street, not far to go. I could always walk there if worse came to the worst. What was I thinking of? The worst was that

He-him would not be there to take me. He was drinking heavily and getting home later and later at night; more and more often I was eating dinner alone.

But the doorman was a nice man. I knew he would walk me across the street and carry my suitcase. I was counting on him for that—even if he didn't know it. I gave him large tips every month. He was kind, and he usually patted me on the back when I came out.

"We're getting along now, aren't we?" he would say. "It won't be too long now."

Was I the only woman in New York who was depending on a doorman to take her to the hospital instead of a husband?

But it didn't happen that way. My mother was there when the first pains came, and she sat beside me and held my hand.

"Mother, shouldn't we pack my suitcase? It's in the closet. I already put some things in it."

"You won't need much. They give you everything at the hospital."

"Let's call the doctor."

Dr. Hellman was short, stubby, and cheerful. He was a great hand patter and squeezer.

He answered the phone. "Count the minutes between pains and when it gets to be two to three minutes call me, go to the hospital, and I will meet you there."

The pains were coming every six to seven minutes. They weren't sharp but more like severe menstrual pains.

"Mother, you won't leave me now, will you?"

"Of course not. I am here for you. Where is Buddy?" She always called my husband Buddy.

"I don't know," I admitted, feeling ashamed.

This wasn't what it should be. There should be an adoring husband leaning over, suffering each pain with me, anxiously awaiting the arrival of this baby he had created.

Things didn't turn out like they did in movies and books. Schopenhauer was right when he said women shouldn't read novels—it just gave them the wrong ideas.

We were conscientious. When the pains came every two to three minutes, we called the doctor, closed the suitcase, and went downstairs. The doorman blew his whistle and got a cab.

"No point in walking," my mother said. "The taxi man will help us get out."

The desk at the hospital expected us. I was put in a wheelchair. By now I was squirming and moaning with pain.

I kept asking everyone, "Will it get worse? For how long?"

"Wait until you see the baby," they'd say. "You'll forget all this pain."

Up in the bed, they put my feet in stirrups. The intern came. "Push," they all said, "push. That will make the baby come sooner."

"But if I push I'll come apart, I'm afraid—I'm afraid to push."

Dr. Hellman arrived, chubby, motherly.

"We'll give you a little rest now," he said, and he put an injection in what felt like my spine. For a while there was peace, and then it started up again, more hideously painful than before. I heard myself crying and screaming. He-him appeared in the door, but his presence didn't matter to me one way or the other. I didn't feel it was his baby. It was just mine.

Then they were lifting me onto a stretcher and I was in a room with glaring lights and doctors and nurses in white with masks. A mask was put over my face, and then everything became like a whirlpool of pain and cries and the cries and the pain were mine and then a cry that was not mine and the voice of the doctor. "We have a fine boy here." And then I lost consciousness, and when I woke up I was back in my room, my mother sitting quietly in a chair. "Thank you mother," I wanted to say. "Thank you for not leaving me."

When they brought me my baby, I could see that he was beautiful. He had a big round head; his features seemed to be perfect. His head was crowned with dark hair, and he had thick long eyelashes. He looked quite peaceful and happy. He opened his mouth and yawned. "Are you bored already," I thought, "and tired of it all—and you haven't been here very long."

Denis was everything he promised to be; healthy, beautiful, and happy.

I remember giving him his first bath and being afraid my hand would slip and he would drown. I always seemed to be afraid I would do the wrong thing. Once when he was at the crawling stage and it was summer time, the window was open and we lived on the twelfth floor. I went out of the room for a minute, and when I came back, he was outside

the window on the ledge. My heart stopped
beating. I went towards him ever so slowly, and he
crawled back into my arms.

The next day we had people putting up bars on
all the windows. How could I have been so stupid!

It was fun taking him out in his carriage with all
the mothers in Central Park. Of course he was the
best looking, best dressed baby of all.

But even having Denis was not enough to make
me feel better towards Bidge. Whenever the
thought crossed my mind, I'd say to myself, "I'd
like to leave He-him. What would it feel like to
contemplate a day without his presence?' But I
didn't want to deny Denis a father. It didn't seem
right, and Bidge did love him, and Denis did love
his father.

I can't say he was a bad father. After the birth,
he would bring his friends to the hospital so that
they could see me nursing the baby. We were the
first in our group to have a child.

My mother decided to move back to France,
where she felt happier and more at home. Since my
father had died and left us all a lot of money, she
had enough so that she could help her sister and
her sister's family to take a nice apartment in Paris
where they could all live. Paris was, and still is, I
suppose, one of the most wonderful cities in the
world to live in. You never had to wonder how to
spend the day in Paris. Once out in the streets, you
were surrounded by beautiful buildings and sites.
If you came out on the Champs Elysee with its
great avenue leading to Napoleon's Etoile, you

could walk towards this sculpture-covered archway that lead out of Paris, strolling leisurely and without stress; or you could stop at one of the many cafes, buy a newspaper and sit at a small round table, sip coffee, and observe the people walking by. Or if you came out and found yourself in the old part, on the Ile de la Cité, in front of Notre Dame, you could sit in the Cathedral and in the mist and under the great arches of the nave and enjoy the beauty of its stained glass windows.

If you wanted to see the modern parts of Paris, there were the shops with their exquisite wares for sale. There was something for everyone. The Bois de Boulogne for children, and Punch and Judy shows, and on Sundays the horses on the bridle paths, ridden by stylish men and women.

You could be purposeless in Paris and the city gave you purpose. It was not like other cities where to go out you had to have something specific that you needed to accomplish. If you loved books, you could wander by the Seine and thumb through the old books, stacked up on the sides. There was music in the parks. Paintings in the museums. Civilized life was there.

Bidge was doing well as a young architect. He had a good job with a prominent architect, the man who had built the Squibb Building. It was the era in New York when the monumental skyscrapers were going up: The Daily News Building, the Chrysler Building, the Empire State. It was the time for the appreciation and glorification of architects. The newspapers ran articles about them and their characteristics as they do now about movie actors: Architects were the stars of the twenties and thirties. But the biggest star, Frank Lloyd Wright, was not represented by any structure in the city. This was probably due to his difficult and controversial personality. I once heard an architect say, "If only he were dead, then we could lay wreaths and flowers on his grave."

Bidge didn't make much money, but he was given a lot of respect. He resented the fact that I had so much more money than he did. I sometimes wondered if there was anything about me that he approved. Later when I was married to my second husband, Eric, I told someone, "It feels so great. Eric thinks I am wonderful. What a change!"

Bidge had had some prominent clients. One of them was Lilly Dache, a famous New York hat designer. She had an extraordinary facility for making hats: If you went into her salon, she would take a piece of material—it would be just the right color—and she'd twist it into a shape for you to wear. Then she'd turn it over to her hat maker, and the next time you came in, it would be the perfect hat for you. She didn't have much taste in anything else.

Her business was booming, and she intended to build a new building off Fifth Avenue to house it, and, of course, Bidge hoped to be the architect.

He had designed and furnished Miss Dache's apartment for her, and she gave a party. When we arrived, she had put big teddy bears and dolls all over. When Bidge saw these dolls on his carefully designed furniture, in a fury he raced around, picked up the dolls and bears, walked into the kitchen, and put them in the trash can.

Lilly Dache was not happy, and when it came time to do her new building, she did not give him the assignment.

He-him never took into account anyone's feeling but his own.

Denis got to be one and then two years. He was always happy and bouncy. Bidge and I decided that summer to take a trip to the Black Forest in Germany, a place we had never been.

The inn we'd selected was quaint and beautiful. The manager showed us, all smiles and bows, into a lovely room with a view of the forest.

But Denis did not feel well and spent most of the night crying. At seven o'clock, the manager arrived, knocking loudly at our door. When we let him in, he said, "You will have to leave. I give you two hours to pack and be downstairs. Everyone has been complaining about your child crying." He spit out his word crying as though it were the worst sin against humanity.

It was my first experience with the German character that goes from maudlin sweetness to black brutality.

"Start packing," he said and left, banging the door behind him.

We felt like criminals, and we packed and went downstairs. We boarded the taxi waiting at the door and left. We spent a few weeks with my mother in her apartment in Paris, and then headed for home.

On the boat, we met a couple from Hagerstown, Maryland. The husband was sleek and blonde and good looking, and he and I we had an immediate attraction. His name was Lynn, and he seemed silky smooth compared to Bidge. I remember the trip mostly as grabbing occasions to kiss in dark stairways until we reached New York.

Bidge and I promised to go to visit them in Hagerstown at Thanksgiving.

In the fall, Lynn used to come to New York to see me, and he'd wait outside my dance class, where I was dancing with Doris Humphreys. Our feelings for each other were heating up.

I never mentioned Lynn's visits to Bidge.

On our visit to their home at Thanksgiving, Lynn wanted me to tell him that I would leave Bidge and marry him. I knew that I might some day leave Bidge, but I also knew I would never marry Lynn. He was attractive and sweet, but he lacked the intellectuality that I always needed in a man. I told him this, and he took it very hard.

He went into the bathroom and took carbolic acid. We called the doctor, who had to pump out his stomach. It was a nightmare, and Bidge knew I was responsible. Going home on the train, he sat at a distance from me—my judge and executioner. Once home, he left and went to his masculine hideaway, the Yale Club. In those days Yale men always went to the Yale Club when they had domestic troubles. No woman was allowed to enter their sacred portals.

If I had had any brains I would have let him

stay there, but being so filled with guilt, I begged him to come back.

Once back, he began drumming at me to have another child.

I wanted expiation . . .

In 1931, Terry was born. He was long and slender with dark soulful eyes. When I brought him back from the hospital and undressed him, I saw that his body was covered with a rash. When the doctor arrived, he said it came from the bathing of the babies in unclean basins so that a germ was passed from one body to another.

"Sue them," everyone said. "This is an outrage that at a hospital your baby should get an infection." They were right, but I didn't want to be involved in a lawsuit. This was a definite flaw in my character. I hadn't learned to be willing to fight to rectify injury done to me and mine. I shook my shoulders and said, "It just boils down to collecting money, which I don't need and don't want," ignoring the obvious fact that it was much more, that it could protect future babies from being harmed, forcing the hospital to be more careful.

I had to keep Terry home for two months until he was cured, and then I took him out with his brother Denis in a big carriage to Central Park.

My great achievement—two beautiful boys.

But my husband was his usual up and down self. One moment the house would be swarming with people, and then just as suddenly, everybody would be gone, the house would be empty, and he would be still, lying immobilized in his bed. Finally,

Denis & Terry Sanders

I became frightened and called the doctor. He came, he took his pulse, blood pressure.

"Your husband," he said, "is a 'manic depressive'. That's his pattern—hyperactive and hyper-passive."

"Well," I thought, "now we have a label for it—a recognizable illness. Is that supposed to make it better? Easier to have around?"

I asked the doctor, "So what do I do?"

"Do? Nothing to do. There are some new drugs now on the market. Maybe we could try some." And he left.

11

At the end of the year after Terry's birth, I felt I was entitled to go back to working at my art. It had been three years; and it was all piling up inside of me. Denis at three was old enough to stay with the cook. I began looking for a nurse for Terry, and I found an old German nurse who clearly loved babies, and with whom I felt it was safe to leave him during the day.

Her name was Miss Schlabitz. She was pretty ugly, a big nose and beady eyes, but her hands were big and purposeful. Terry seemed to like her, and she adored him.

I rented a small studio on Madison Avenue where I could walk to work. It was just a square white box of a place, nothing like René's studio that was surrounded by all the beauty of Paris. Mine was surrounded by small commercial stores evoking nothing romantic or exciting.

Still it was a space, a place to work, quiet and apart from the routines of the house.

I bought an easel, a drafting board, paints, brushes, crayons, pastels—I didn't know what I wanted to do or make. I bought a book called *The Natural Way to Draw* by a famous teacher at the

Art Students League. It was a series of exercises on the many ways to approach drawing and painting and nature and to express the different aspects of whatever you were looking at. One exercise helped me learn to understand the sensitive line that surrounds natural objects. I would hold up my hand and let my eye and pencil slowly follow the outline of each finger. Thus I gained an awareness and sensitivity that I didn't have before. Another exercise was on the heaviness or weight of each object, from a leaf to an animal, and this I did with a pen scratching, so the heavier it was, the darker the ink.

The white walls began to get on my nerves, and so I approached them and found myself drawing and then painting the skyscrapers and buildings of New York. In a few weeks the walls were crowded and jostling with these images of strong buildings, and when I used to come in the morning, I was filled with a sense of joy and accomplishment.

The walls divided themselves into three aspects—early morning, when the light on the buildings made them seem ethereal and lacy, the colors gentle and pastel-like. Noon, when they were strong, and bright blue skies outlined their shapes, and the streets below were crowded with people, black bugs on the pavement. Then night, when in darkness the light illuminated the buildings and formed dim chasms between them.

I used to go up into some of the tall buildings at twilight to observe the day changing into night and the buildings responding to the changes of light. Then I would go back to the studio and try to render all that I had seen. I didn't forget that plastered up against the big edifices were the small brownstones, houses of another era.

I didn't ask anyone to come to the studio to see what I was doing. It was an intimate experience just for me.

But one day I received a call from a man who said he was a friend of René's from Paris. His name was Alexi Brodevitch. He was a White Russian. At this time New York was full of White Russians, the nobility who had fled the Revolution. They manned taxi cabs, were doormen, waiters, washed dishes, and among the more enterprising, opened nightclubs, where sad and melancholy music was played, or lent their names to fancy perfumes, while the women crocheted or made exquisite silk scarfs based on Russian imperial designs which they sold in the expensive boutiques of the city.

They had an enclave outside of New York where they met on Saturday nights. It was on a strip of land given to them by Americans enamored of Royalty and Titles.

They lit it with candles and oil burning lanterns so that it had an eerie and romantic feeling—and they furnished it with tables and chairs and an upright piano. It was a long shed-like room that had once been the meeting place for Girl Scouts who had abandoned it for better quarters. At the end of the shed was a tall dark chair decorated with Russian symbols painted in gold on which the grand duchess sat. She was the head of the clan. She wore a dark red dress with a lace shawl. She always held her head high, but her face looked drawn and tired, a result probably of her hours of working as a salesgirl at Saks Fifth Avenue.

When they would arrive they would first go to pay their respects to her, and then retreat backwards as would be the royal custom. I never approached her as I was afraid that since I was not used to walking backwards I might fall over and I could imagine the laughter after my fall.

There was a Russian prince by the name of Orbeliani who was a wonderful pianist and gave music lessons to support himself and whose primary food was alcohol. He would play Russian songs and dances at the little upright piano.

After the greetings had finished, the fun would begin and vodka and the corks of champagne bottles would pop—and the singing and dancing would start.

If you shut your eyes and pushed it a little you could imagine, listening to the voices and the stomping of boots, that you were in some faraway kingdom on the other side of the world.

There was something moving and touching and brave in this invented recreation of a lost world—and a nobility—to these people in their garments of paupers.

Impulsively, perhaps because I missed René and this was a way of seeing him, I asked Brodevitch to come to my studio.

When he arrived, I looked at him carefully. He was of medium size, pale, and blue eyes like precious stones seemed to shine in his face.

He told me that he belonged to the intellectual

class in Russia, his father having been a scientist and his mother an artist. He, himself, was a graphic artist, and the articles I read later about him said that he brought a touch of magic to everything he did.

He said he had a position in Philadelphia in the fall at the University of Pennsylvania to head the art department and teach graphic art; but that he had the summer free to travel and discover America. He had been in Paris for ten years and had come to seek his future in America.

I told him of our plans to take a cottage in Westport and suggested he might like to take a cottage there too. It was on the water and a good place to make trips from. He agreed to look there for a place.

As with a few rare people, I felt after an hour of conversation that we were close friends. I trusted him and felt I could tell him things that I would never ever tell to anyone. We parted, and I knew we would be friends. He came several times after that and our feelings and understanding grew.

He told me that he had a wife. Her name was Nina, and a twelve-year-old son, Petri. When I first saw his son Petri, in Westport where they had taken a cottage close to ours, I noted that he was unusual in appearance. His head seemed too large for his body and his eyes large and pale stared out of his countenance. No children came to play with him, and he was always with his mother Nina.

His mother looked like a stereotype of what a healthy, sturdy Russian peasant would look like. She had a pleasant smile and large competent hands. Good smells of cooking came from their house.

After they moved in, I went over to welcome them as neighbors. They greeted me warmly and gave me coffee and a piece of wonderful cake that Nina had made. Alexi sat somewhat apart. The closeness we had first felt at our first meeting had disappeared. His wife and son separated us like two blocks of stone.

When I got home I told Bidge about my visit there.

"I don't want you going over there," he said. "If you want to see them they can come over here. They don't have a good reputation here—they are known as foreigners."

"But," I put in, "he is supposed to be a good artist."

"I know, if he weren't he wouldn't have been invited by the University of Pennsylvania to head up their Art Department. Still I don't want to get mixed up with them."

"Oh shit," I thought, "will I always have to be living by his rules?" I was doing my best to keep my marriage going—because of my two children; and having them made up for a lot of things, but not for everything—no.

One afternoon I heard screams from the house next door, and I looked out of the window and saw Petri in the garden, squeezing a cat, and the cat was letting out fierce squeals. I saw Nina come rushing out, separating him from the cat and dragging him into the house, his legs kicking and flaying.

Cruelty to animals was high on my list of sins, and seeds of doubt and fear were sown in me.

I knew I was dealing with people out of the ordinary.

One morning as I was leaving to go out sketching Nina waved to me to stop my car.

"I want to ask you something," she said in pleasantly Russian-accented English. "I see you are an artist. My husband Alexi is an artist, and he would like to go out into the countryside sketching. He does not drive. Could he go with you?"

I hesitated, not really wanting to relinquish my solitude and independence.

"He will not bother you," Nina said. "In France he is a famous artist."

"All right," I said, and that "all right" sealed my fate.

"Wait please now. I will tell him." And she went back into the house.

Alexi came back alone, his sketch material under his arm, and he climbed into the car. After a few minutes I broke the silence. "I thought," I said, "of going to a small village nearby that has a white church sitting on a square of green lawn, the houses of the village surround it. It is all white and green and very New England and austere."

"That sounds very nice," he said. We drove in silence.

I turned and looked at him. He was very handsome in a quiet way—his face ivory pale, his eyes alive like two blue-gray birds, and his hair falling over his forehead, gold in color.

Unexpectedly, I felt as I looked at him, a longing to know him better. He was, I could tell, so different from He-him. His hands as he held his sketchbook almost seemed to tremble.

I knew he would be no good at small talk, but we were not yet in deep enough to talk the big talk.

I was suddenly filled with hope. It seemed

possible that things could change, that my dreary life with Bidge could be transformed, that getting up in the morning with no promise of a fulfilling day would no longer have to be.

I felt an urge to tell him all about myself and find out all about him at the same time.

The landscape changed and we were now on the outskirts of the New England village—the white church gleamed in the sun and the green lawn in front of it was more exquisitely green than even I had remembered.

"Here," Alexi said, "let's stop here." He seemed very excited by the scene.

He took out his white paper.

"What kind of paper is that?" I asked.

"It isn't really paper; it has layers that I can scrape away to give it a third dimension."

"Do you mind if I watch you?"

I followed him out, bringing my fold-up stool with me. I sat near him.

The whiteness of the paper gradually disappeared and he scratched the outline of the church and embedded in it colored stained glass windows and soft gray shadows. The blue of the sky penetrated parts of the church and entered into the green grass in front. It all had a jewel-like quality but still kept its religious austerity. I was witnessing the transformation of a scene after it has passed through a poetic imagination onto a piece of—albeit special—white paper.

All I could say and I meant it, was, "That's wonderful." He smiled back at me, and I felt that we had joined together again, and I knew that he felt it too. It was as it had been in the New York studio.

That night when I got home, I heard myself singing as I prepared the dinner for all of us. I ran to the car and went to the station to pick up Bidge.

He was looking sweaty and tired on the station platform. "What are you so happy about?" he asked, and he gave me a scowl.

"Just glad to see you," I lied, but I didn't mind lying—nothing seemed to matter any more, nothing but the fact that the next day I would be going out with Alexi, into the magical world of his vision.

"What is your husband like?" Alexi asked me the next day.

"Well, he's an architect, he's very bright, but he doesn't really understand anything—and he doesn't like anything."

"His children . . . ?"

"I think he likes his children, but he's always correcting them, so he makes them cry a lot. And Nina?"

"She's a good woman. She does her best to make me happy."

"And does she?"

"No, not really, but I am not easy to be made happy."

He leaned towards me, and I leaned in turn towards him, our faces close. I wanted to say, "I love you, I love you—you have changed my world. You have made me feel that life could be wonderful, could be full of unexpected beauty and joy, that I could get away from the dreariness of living with He-him. I want to live with you, close to you. Please say that you love me too."

I gradually began to absorb Alexi's way of

looking and seeing, and my work took on a wholly different quality—as did my life.

The days were light and full of bloom and only Alexi stood out three-dimensional and in full color—all the other people were like unimportant shadows in the background.

Then one afternoon when we had finished sketching, we walked down towards a brook. The grass was green and dry, and I sat down and let my hands glide in the water of the brook. It all felt so peaceful and happy. I wished it could go on like this forever. Alexi leaned towards me and I towards him, and we kissed, but his kiss was not like the kiss a man gives a woman. It was not what I expected. I felt as though I had been walking and then stopped dead in my tracks. I knew from the kiss that there was some sort of impediment in his manhood. I knew I was a normal woman who needed sexual love and that he didn't have it to give me. I knew he wanted to, but he couldn't. This would eventually change my feeling for him, but now at this moment in spite of this realization, my feelings for him were very strong.

And words came out of love. "I love you. I am so happy being near you."

"How can you stay with that man?" he asked me.

"How can you stay with Nina?"

"That's different."

We went back unresolved.

The summer was over and we faced separation. He had taken an apartment in Philadelphia. He was going to teach at the University.

Back in New York, I felt as though I'd returned to living with a beast and a tyrant. With Bidge, I withered and became impotent. He was so harsh in his criticism of everything that I did, that I ceased doing anything at all, lying in bed for hours, waiting for the time to go by. One day I realized I just didn't want to get up ever again. That evening after coming home from a meal where all evening I had observed Bidge with distaste, I knew I was at some sort of crossroad of decision. I sat on the edge of the bed and looked up at him. A voice that I hardly recognized as my own came out of me. "I want a divorce. I don't want to go on with this marriage."

Bidge looked at me, startled, surprised. "You mean you want me to leave?"

I nodded my head, hardly believing the scene.

He walked over to the closet and took out an empty suitcase and started packing. He went into the bathroom. "Is it all right if I take the toothpaste?"

I nodded yes.

"I'll be at the Yale Club. When you come to your senses you can call me up there."

Then I heard the front door bang closed, and he was gone.

I went to the phone and called up Alexi.

"I am leaving my husband," I said. "You were right. I cannot stay with him anymore."

I remember there was a stunned silence.

"Oh no," he said. "You can't do that."

"Isn't that what you wanted me to do? I thought you loved me."

"I do, I do. But you don't understand." I did understand, but I was filled with anger, the childish side of me was saying I thought it would all end, that I would be with Alexi and live in his wonderful world of imagination happily ever after. But with the deeper side of me, I knew that Alexi was impotent or else that afternoon we had kissed on the grass, something would have happened and nothing did; and I sensed that much of his desperate melancholia came from his anger with his impotence.

But my disappointment was great. Getting out of my marriage I wanted something wonderful to happen, to recompense me for those difficult and dreary years.

"I never want to see you again," I yelled into the telephone, and banged it closed.

I went to the phone and called my girlfriend Adele's husband who was a lawyer.

"I want a divorce," I said over the phone. "What should I do?"

His name was Mac Brandwen. "Meet me tomorrow afternoon at the Biltmore under the clock at five-thirty."

Under the clock at the Biltmore seemed to be a meeting place for people with important decisions. Beginning an affair, ending an affair, or making future commitments.

I was there at 5:30, watching the clock with anxious eyes. At 5:45 Mac appeared. He was, I noted even in my preoccupation with my own problems, tall, dark, and handsome. Flashing through my mind came the thought, "Gosh, I wish I had a guy like that—responsible. A problem solver, a lawyer.

"I want a divorce," I said.

Mac leaned over and took my hands.

"I'll help you," he said, and then surprisingly enough he added, "You know I've always loved you, since the first time I saw you at your father's house when you were only eighteen and I came with my wife after we had just married."

I took a deep swallow. It didn't seem to be the right time to deal with this piece of information.

"Oh," I said. "Oh."

"Well," he said, "let's talk about you and your problems. I never did like that guy you were married to."

After two or three days, Bidge must have thought he'd made a mistake to leave so hurriedly. He tried to come back, but my lawyer was already preparing the divorce. Bidge was very angry when he found out. He told people that I was out of my mind; they told me he had a gun and he was twirling it around his finger. That scared me. I called Mac and told him what was happening with Bidge. "I'd like to take my children and go to France to see my mother."

"Good idea," Mac said. "I'll arrange for your passage, and when you get back we'll see about dealing with a divorce."

But the next day, I found myself, unbelievably, sitting in a train opposite Nina, going to Philadelphia, watching her face set in hard lines. She had come early in the morning to the apartment, unannounced, into my room. I stood looking at her.

Without waiting for a greeting she had said, "You must come with me now—to see Alexi—he is desperate since you called him—and I am afraid that he might hurt himself."

"Why? How?"

"You don't understand Alexi—he is not like other men, but he loves you. He has formed a deep attachment to you and you cannot just break it off like this. You cannot destroy him. Alexi and Petri are all I have in the world, all I care about." I looked deeply into her face, and I knew she was sincere; I also felt, though, that it was strange for a wife to want to bring another woman to her husband. But I knew, once again, that I was not dealing with ordinary people.

Alexi met us at the door, his face very pale against his dark blue sweater and there were bandages around his left wrist. Nina went off to the kitchen and left me alone with Alexi. Petri came in and sat with us.

"What are those bandages?"

"I'll tell you later."

We sat in silence. "Petri, go in and help your mother." Petri got up, fixing his pale eyes on me and not wanting to go. Nina's voice came from the kitchen: "Petri," and a phrase in Russian, ending in "Petri." He left.

"I'm going to Europe tomorrow," I said. "I want to see my mother. My husband has left. It does not affect what there was between us. I just don't want to be with him anymore."

Alexi nodded. "We can talk after dinner. What did Nina tell you?"

"That you were very upset because I was angry with you and that she was afraid that you might hurt yourself."

"She was right. Nina understands how I feel about you. Nina is my mother, my sister and my wife. You are my love. When I am with you, I am glad. I am happy. I do not know if I can go on without you."

I was silent. What was there to say? "Did you

really cut your wrists?"

"Yes, in a moment of Russian despair."

"But now, you feel better?"

"Well, yes, at least you cared enough to come and see me." He leaned forward and took my hands. The old wave of love I had felt for him came over me, but I pulled back—I didn't want to feel for him anymore, I wanted to leave, I felt I was in a tangled web that Nina and Alexi had made and I didn't belong here.

We ate dinner silently, hardly looking at each other. Borscht and black bread, heavy red wine, followed by baklava. "Nina," I said, "you are a good cook."

"Eat in times of stress," said Nina, "to keep up your strength. Alexi and I have lived through bad times and learned how to live from day to day. The future will take care of itself."

We got through dinner, and then Nina got up and made into a bed the small couch that was against the wall.

"Get undressed," she told me, "and knock on the wall when you are ready. Alexi will come to you." And they both stood up and went up the stairs.

I was alone. Fear swept over me. I felt I was in the power of Alexi and Nina. I did not want to see Alexi or be with him when Nina was upstairs. It was a plot, a plan. What did they want of me? There were two, I was one, alone. I am in danger. What kind of danger? I don't know, but I want to flee from here. They seem so sure of themselves. Am I to be part of their family plan, of keeping Alexi happy? It was too strange and foreign. Nina cooperating. It was too different from my conventional kind of thinking, way of doing things.

Nina had no resentment of me or my relationship with Alexi. She even liked me. She wanted to control me. Alexi seemed very weak. Nina was the strong one. I would just be part of her plan to keep her family afloat.

I went to the phone and speaking as softly as I could I called a taxi. I was cold and trembling. I went out on the stoop and waited.

When the taxi arrived, I told him to take me to the railroad station. There was a train leaving at midnight for New York. Though the weather was not cold, I was cold and trembling. I got on the train, and in three hours I was back in New York. Back in my apartment—safe—safe. I don't know what I was so afraid of, but Alexi had changed for me into a mysterious and threatening person that I did not know or understand. I started packing and the activity quieted me down. Tomorrow I would be on an ocean liner with my children and their old nurse, and soon after that I would be in France and I would see my mother.

I knew Alexi was desperate, but I thought not for me, but for his manhood. I knew now that Alexi had been the key for opening up life for me, for giving me the courage to leave my marriage. I was grateful to him for that.

I am not a psychologist, but I wonder if his sexual impotence did not channel his sexual drive into his art and turn it into the burning, flaming images that he was able to project on the pages of his drawings and paintings. Alexi Brodevitch did become a famous designer in New York City and was, I think, the arts editor of *Vanity Fair.*

12

I suppose I would describe the night in 1933 when I set foot on the gangplank of the steamship "Europa," fleeing with my two babies to Europe to be out of the control of my husband, as the time in my life when I felt most fragile and terrified and on a precarious road. Mac advised me that I should get out of the country as quietly and as speedily as possible to avoid having my husband serve me with an interdiction against taking my two children out of the United States into a foreign jurisdiction. Mac got us tickets on the Europa—a German ship. Hitler was already in power, and I recognized with a deep throb, I was sailing on a Nazi ship.

"I told the Captain," Mac said, "of your situation, that he was not to allow your husband on the ship, and he said that if he came, he would put him in irons and fling him into the hold." Mac said this with a gleam of conquest in his eye—and my spirits fell even lower. It was as though my life and my decision were all being taken out of my hands and in a violent, frightening way. I walked up the plank carrying Terry and the nurse followed behind leading Denis. On a leash I had a very small Chihuahua dog.

All night long that first night, I kept looking at the porthole and being afraid that I would jump out of it into the ocean, thinking, hoping that it was too small a window to allow me to slip through it. I got through the night—with the aid of my two children who needed a lot of attention since they were uneasy and afraid and missing their beds and their room at home. I still had my dog with me, and she also was whimpering. Next day, as was the custom, they took the dog and put it in a kennel upstairs.

In the morning, there was a knock on the door, and the head steward arrived with a letter in his hand. He bowed deeply and in correct, but heavily accented English, he said, "The Captain invites you to sit at his table, and dinner will be at eight o'clock this evening."

"Thank you," I said.

He bowed and asked, "What shall I say to him?"

"Of course, I would be delighted." I felt as though Hitler had invited me to dinner.

Our old German nurse was happy; her eyes gleamed through her glasses—what an honor! And on this big ship. And I was praying that if and when I went, I might not vomit.

The invitation hung over me like a pall—like a sentence of death. I dressed carefully; I felt so cold. I did everything carefully. I watched the clock. At five minutes to eight, I was at the head of the staircase going down to the dining room. Here I am a Jewish woman going to sit at a place of honor on a Nazi ship. I was placed to the left of the captain. The place at the right was reserved for Toscanini. I was seated facing an American couple. The woman had a sweet tired face, her husband stiff and unsmiling: an important official in the telephone company. The captain arrived late—a rosy, smiling benign-looking man, not what I expected from what he had said about putting my husband in irons. He patted my hand gently and asked me if I had decided what I wanted to eat. "I can recommend," he said, and his fat finger pointed to the roast beef with mushrooms and stuffed cabbage. "I think we could afford to get a little more flesh on these bones. You are beautiful, but with a little more weight, you would be even more beautiful." What are you doing to the Jewish women in Germany? I wanted to scream. You are stripping the flesh off their bones, aren't you?

I, instead, gave a slight smile and thanked him.

I had a way of endearing myself to people and eliciting from them a protective manner and mantle that they draped over me. The lady across from me decided I was in deep trouble and wanted to help me. She came down to my cabin and told me of hard times she had in her life. I began to like her a little until she began talking about the "Jewish question"—wherever I looked there it was staring back at me: the "Jewish question." Fortunately, being regarded as someone in deep trouble, I was able to avoid political discussions. You seem like such a nice lady, I thought, why do you want to hurt and kill people who would wish you no harm, who just want to be left alone?

I don't know what I was afraid of. Realistically as an American citizen, no one could come and drag me and my children off the ship. I was safe, but I didn't feel safe. I was living in this atmosphere of the Germanic superman. The superiority—I felt it in all the stewards, in all the service. They seemed to carry themselves with such arrogance, such pride. Anti-Semitism was not a new phenomena for me; I had been aware of it from the first day that I went to school. My parents in wanting what they thought was the best for their children had sent me to a New England boarding school, a white Protestant school that took in a token Jewish girl, a token Japanese, and a token Catholic. The Blacks had not yet reached even the token stage. They were simply taboo.

I had over the years become rather skilled at concealing my identity—I never denied it, nor did I concede what I was. It was a game of avoidance. I succeeded in being voted the most popular girl in my class, I was nominated for President of the "Christian Association," though I thought this was a bit much and said I preferred not to run. I confided to my roommate that I was Jewish and that my father was foreign born. "That's all right," she answered. "I won't tell my father." Many years later during the German occupation of Paris, I read that the Germans had asked all the Jews to come down and register. Henry Bergson, a noted Jewish scientist and philosopher had been among the first to come to register himself as a Jew. I thought at the time, "I don't admire him; I think he is a fool." Why should anyone feel obliged to tell the truth to a thug? That is a false pride. It is like a man whose head is on the block of the guillotine who moves his head over to accommodate the blade that will descend on him.

Sitting at the Captain's table, I felt ashamed that I was flying under false colors, receiving all this warmth and hospitality. What if I were to say, "Look, I am Jewish." I could hear the frozen silence. Then what? The Captain would clear his throat, and he would maybe try to coat it over: "We are not saying all Jews are bad; there is a lot of false propaganda going around."

No—to announce that I was Jewish would be a gesture, I thought, that would look good on the screen, but I am not on the screen. I am trying to find a solution to my present difficult situation. I am really not concerned with these people sitting around this table. On the day that we land in France, I can be through with them forever. Why take everything so seriously?

The next day, the steward arrived at my cabin with some long-stemmed red roses. He laid them on my bed. "The captain wishes you to have these." He bowed and left.

After I put them in water, I thought, What shall I do? I must go up to his cabin and thank him. I stopped at the purser's office and told him I would like to go to the Captain's quarters to thank him. He picked up the phone and then said, "The Captain would be pleased to receive you."

I climbed up to the upper deck and stood in front of the door. I heard voices inside, and I knocked. The door opened and the Captain asked me to come in. Toscanini was seated inside. "I don't want to interrupt you. I just wanted to thank you for the flowers."

"Please come in; I was telling Mr. Toscanini about your situation."

I felt pleased that I was important enough to be brought to the attention of this great man. Here he was talking to the Captain of a Nazi ship, and there didn't seem to be anything wrong with that. They were probably two nice men caught in a political situation that they chose to ignore and just talk like two human beings.

Toscanini took my hand, and I found myself sitting next to him. He had such a fine, sensitive face and fire in his eyes. He asked me about my children and said when I got to Europe I should go to Italy, where the climate was mild in the winter. I don't remember much of the conversation, but just the feeling of being pleased to be there.

The next day we arrived in Cherbourg, France. My uncle David had come all the way from Paris to meet us at the boat. He was a very shy and tender man, and he loved children and flowers. His face broke into smiles when he saw Denis and Terry. He was especially attracted to the baby, and stretched out his arms for him. He held Terry in his arms for the whole six hours that it took to get to Paris.

Toscanini and another man shared our compartment. It was comfortable enough. I sat near the window and looked out. We had the dog in a cage, and in spite of the cage, he was glad to be with us again. Toscanini watched the children, and I watched Toscanini.

At times, Denis and I sat on the trunks played cards with a deck I had brought along so we could pass the time. When we stopped at a station, I would get out and buy sandwiches and fruit to give the nurse and Denis and Uncle David. I was beginning to feel quite happy as though I were on a holiday. It felt good to be away from the German atmosphere, and I wanted to throw my arms around all the French, kiss them on both cheeks, and say, "Thank you for being French."

My uncle and my aunt had settled in Paris after leaving the U.S. My aunt loved Paris. Until the apartment my mother had bought was altered, Uncle David and my aunt were living in a very modest apartment. All the money they used to have in Greece had been confiscated, and they lived on the income from their savings. My uncle went every day to the Bourse stock exchange to do a little trading. He told me about my aunt and my mother and about the nice new apartment in which they would all live once the changes had been made.

Like everything in France, the train moved at a snail's pace. I fell asleep during the ride. I felt very tired—tired by the strain of the trip on the Europa and the strain from the fact that my life was uprooted.

At the Paris station, my Italian brother-in-law, Victoria's husband, had come to meet Toscanini. He was a tremendous snot and had always felt that I was below him, but now when Toscanini turned towards us on the platform to say good-bye and wish me well and kiss my hand, I could feel my brother-in-law's surprise. It caused him to greet me warmly.

The first thing I said to my mother when I saw her was, "If you tell me to go back, I will kill myself."

"I have no intention of telling you that," she said. "I know you, and I know you did your best. All I want for you is to be happy."

She worried, though, because I jumped at unexpected noises, and she thought I was very pale, thin, and run down.

"I think you should go to Switzerland, to the clinic where Marcel is recuperating," she said. Auntie Rachel's twenty-three-year-old son had contracted multiple sclerosis two years before; he'd lost the use of his limbs, and he was just learning to walk again.

I felt ashamed to think how cowardly I must seem to my mother. Marcel was still semi-paralyzed and would have to face a future in a wheelchair, and yet he was still pleasant and agreeable instead of angry and depressed and beating his hands against a fate that had so condemned him. He and Auntie Rachel had been facing such severe physical and psychological problems; she'd lost her youngest son, twelve-year-old Raymond, to death right after I'd married, and now she had to look at another in such a poor condition. I tried to put my feelings into words for my mother. There was no answer she could give me. She patted my hand gently.

The next day, I found myself in a Swiss clinic, so clean and well-ordered that you knew it had been scrubbed at least twice each day.

I was given a small room next to Marcel. I kept remembering him as the small dark beautiful little boy with black wavy hair that I had first met.

He was beginning to walk a little with the aid of crutches or canes. He told me about a young Swiss girl that he had made friends with and whom he was hoping would consent to marry him.

I sent up a silent prayer that this could happen and that he could have some normal joys. My prayer was answered. They married two years later.

Breathing the clean Swiss air and taking long walks made me feel a good deal better.

I was under no stress here, and every time I thought of problems ahead, I developed the ability to pull down a white shade in my brain and block them out.

Lying on my bed and reading, I began to feel as I used to feel when things were going smoothly.

The Swiss doctor would come and check me every day although physically I had nothing wrong. We would engage in a little quiet conversation. He wanted to know about the U.S.A., in what ways it differed from Switzerland.

The first difference I thought of was speed. Everything moved so fast in the U.S. while in Switzerland it was a slow, measured pace. There seemed to be time for everything.

In the U.S., you knew you were in a powerful country, throbbing with vitality. Children left home at eighteen to make their way. In Switzerland, they remained with their parents until they married.

We had many conversations along these lines.

René Bensussan, Self-portrait

The time passed and I was ready to go back to Paris.

We all settled in at my mother's hotel in Paris. I told my mother about the trip over, about the growing anti-Semitism. Of course she knew about it. Anti-Semitism is one of the threads in my life that seems to reappear; and now it was looming large and ominous in the person of Adolf Hitler. In the early days it was just a question of social discrimination—now it was to become a question of life and death.

My mother's uncle Isaac Ben Rubi, a philosopher who worked with Bergson, formed the habit of coming every day to see the children. He had never married. His work and studies were his whole life, but he seemed to miss having children and took great pleasure in playing with Denis. He always wore a formal suit—striped trousers and a long gray topcoat with tails. I think it was the only suit he had, and he had chosen that style for when he would be invited for an occasion.

My mother was very fond of him. He reminded her of her father, and she always prepared special lunches for him. I think she thought he was poor and did not eat properly. He always seemed very peaceful and happy and never complained about anything. I made many drawings of him.

I began going to see René at his studio, but our relationship since my marriage had changed. It had lost its pure quality of my being a young virgin.

We used to go to sketch every day at an open class with no instructor; it was called "La Grande

Chaumiere." The models were unusual, sometimes
very ethnic, Jewish, German, Russian—they all
had a lot of character. I still have some drawings
from that time that René made, and they are
among my treasured possessions. He drew in
pencil, and they all had a three-dimensional
spirituality that made my drawings seem flat and
superficial.

The people in the class were all shaggy and
interesting. There was not much communication
between us. I noticed when I spoke to anyone,
René would reproach me as though I were doing
something I ought not to be doing. I realized that
he was very jealous.

He told me once of the story of his mother, who
was one of the beauties of her time. His father was
much older and quite ugly. His mother, Dulcita,
met a Turk in the marketplace in Salonica, Greece.
He was handsome and prominent and was to go to
America as ambassador for Turkey. They fell
deeply in love, and she would meet him daily,
disguised as a Turkish woman with a veil.

When the time came for him to leave for
America, he asked her to come with him. She
agreed, and that night at midnight when everyone
was asleep she slipped out of her room, went down
the stairs, and then remembered she had forgotten
her jewels. She went back upstairs, but her
husband had awakened. He seized her and for a
year she was locked in her room and not allowed to
go out.

René was not allowed to see her, and though he
loved her very much, his father had drilled into

him that she was a bad and faithless woman. His
father died during the next year, and so she was
allowed to come out of her room and to care for her
children. But René had developed a deep mistrust
of women. He said that he would never marry and
be made a fool of. So that was, I suppose, at the
root of his exaggerated jealousy.

When we would go to a restaurant, he would
falsely accuse me of flirting with someone there. If I
had even considered of marrying him, I now
dismissed the idea.

I knew that I would have to be going back soon.
The strain of being away was showing on Denis.
When I took him to a "Punch and Judy" show, he
wanted to know why people all talked so funny. I
took him to a children's party. He said to a little
boy, "If you don't stop talking so funny, I'm going
to hit you."

My lawyer, Mac Brandwen, who had helped me
flee Bidge, had called me several times. At one time
he said to me, "You know, I have always loved you,
since the first time I saw you in your father's
house, when you were eighteen and I had just
married."

There wasn't much to reply, but I began to have
fantasies about him. I knew I didn't want to be
single. I wanted somebody on whom I could
depend, and he was that kind of a man. Still I had
a relationship with his wife, Adele. She had been a
good friend to me, so helpful and kind.

An hour before we arrived back in New York, I
sat on a deck chair next to a man I had made
friends with on the boat. We invented a game to

pass the time as the passengers walked past us on the deck, some of whom we knew and some of whom we didn't know. We labeled each one with what we thought to be their salient quality—the quality that they lived by. A pretty woman with extreme makeup—eyeshadow, eyeliner, long lashes, dyed hair—we labeled "Vanity." A middle-aged stocky man who walked with sure rapid steps, who always got the front seat, the best table, had the loudest voice, we labeled "Aggression". The captain as he walked by: "Responsibility."

My companion turned to me. "What label would you give me?"

"Kindness," I answered.

"And to you," he replied, "I would give the label Courage."

I was startled and pleased. I remember that as a fifteen-year-old girl I had read a novel by Hugh Walpole, and its theme was, "It isn't life that counts, it's the courage you bring to it." My companion was right. Courage was the quality I admired most and I tried to live by. Courage to me meant doing something you were deadly afraid to do, fearing, but doing it anyhow. Courage was what enabled me to leave my marriage and face the world with my two children that I would make fatherless. And I had to thank Alexi for that even if that courage had come to me in the strange and twisted relationship I had had with him.

Leaning against the railing of the ship, I wondered what awaited me. What would happen now? Mac's words on the phone came back to me: "I have always loved you." He was the kind of man I would like to have as a—no, not as a lover—as a husband, but there was that little hitch. He was married. It didn't seem right to be messing around with Adele's husband. But then the image of Mac came before me. He was so handsome. He was very masculine. I could imagine that he was very passionate. I imagined he had a big penis. What was their sex life like? She always seemed to me to be too neat and self-contained to have a good sex life—as though she would hesitate to get her hair messed up. She approached every act with scientific deliberation. Her body, her health, her looks must in no way be damaged. Shut up, I said to my thoughts: forget it.

I leaned against the rail of the ship. The engines had stopped and the tugs were pushing on the sides of our big steamer, guiding us into the harbor. The Statue of Liberty with her arm held high and the New York skyline always aroused in me patriotic feelings. I was glad to be American, glad to be a New Yorker, but not sure I was glad to be home.

Altina

13

I looked down into the sea of faces on the dock—the welcoming committee for the travelers returning. But no one there for me. I felt a loud bang of self pity. Poor little me, so good, so sweet, and no one to welcome me home.

But, hey, stop—in that sea of faces I saw Mac. And then and there, I made a decision: if he still wanted me—and his being there must mean that he did—I would proceed. We could start as lovers and progress towards husband and wife, yours hopefully yours—

I looked down at my son Denis; he too was scanning the faces hopefully. I knew he was looking for his father.

"My poor little darling," I thought. "I'm robbing you of your father. I will try to make it up to you." I put my arm around him and gave him a big squeezy hug. He lifted his face and smiled. I think he understood what I was feeling. He was always good at understanding me, at reading my feelings in my face. Some people have that gift and others "ain't got it."

There was Mac. Tall, dark, and handsome, and rich and a lawyer. What more could a woman want? With his brains and knowledge he could take care of me, solve all my problems or at least some of them.

At the bottom of the gangplank, Mac came towards me and gave me a brotherly kiss on the cheek and a reassuring pat on the back. He also patted the children.

He talked us through the customs, and pretty soon we were in a taxi.

New York streets.

I was glad to be home if for no other reason than to see our cook Christina with her shiny warm face. She kissed us all warmly. "It is good that you are home again. Your husband has been calling every day."

"Don't tell me, Christina. I don't want to see him anymore."

"But what about the children?"

"I will always care for them. They will be happy. In time they will forget him."

Denis was in his room, looking at his favorite things. He stroked them gently and a grin lit up his face.

"We'll have dinner soon," I said. "Are you hungry?"

"Where's Daddy?" he asked.

"He won't be living here anymore, " I said and turned away so as not to see the disappointment in his face.

The telephone rang. It was Adele, Mac's wife.

Her voice was warm. "Your 'boyfriend' wants us to go out dancing tonight if you feel up to it."

Why did she call him my "boyfriend"? It hit a jarring note, but I answered, "Yes. I'll finish having dinner with the children."

"We'll come and pick you up in about an hour."

I was downstairs waiting for them. I didn't want the children to know I was going out. What if they should tell their father when he called?

Once in the cab, I turned to Adele. "What's been happening here?"

"Well, the panic has died down. Roosevelt really took over. He has these fireside talks and everyone feels he is talking directly to them. They keep repeating what he said - 'All you have to fear is fear itself.' And that seems to ring a bell."

Roosevelt's face flashed before me, his jutting chin, his cigarette cocked at an angle, and his friendly grin. He was looking directly at me, or so it seemed. I felt as though I had been there to hear his words.

"We're lucky to have such a leader," I said.

Adele continued: "When he closed the banks and put in a barter system, everyone seemed to enjoy it."

"Well, I wouldn't say enjoy," Mac interrupted. "That's going a little far—"

"Well, I mean, exchanging a pillow for some groceries did seem funny and playful."

"Is that what you did, really?" I leaned forward, laughing. "That is funny."

"I don't know."

Mac said, "We had cash, and Adele had plenty

of cash."

"You're lucky," I said.

The brakes on the cab screeched. "Here we are," Adele said. "The Mocambo Club. I hope there are some attractive men here. You can have Mac."

I felt myself blushing. It must be great to have a husband who always has cash.

We got out of the cab into the dark, dimly lit interior. The music was dance music, soft, sexy, appealing. It was like walking into a warm cocoon, separate and safe from the cold outside.

The maître d' took us to our reserved table at the edge of the dance floor. The tables were all close together. Two attractive men, apparently single, were seated next to us.

"Oh boy," Adele said to Mac. "Maybe we're in luck. Go ahead and dance, I'll order your drinks. What do you want, Tina?"

"A Tom Collins. That will be good." At first, I could not help watching Adele. I was not quite clear about the plan. But then once I started dancing with Mac and felt the warmth and movement of his body, I forgot everything else. I knew that at least our physical relationship could only end one way.

We danced two sessions of music. Many dancers went back to their tables but we continued to dance. "This must be dirty dancing," I thought, but we didn't talk at all.

When we got back, Adele was leaning over to the other table, her hand on one man's arm. The other man had left the table. He was talking to the maître d', and was now coming back. The maître d' came over and whispered into Mac's ear.

Mac nodded and looked angry. "This gentleman," he said to Adele, and he emphasized the word "gentleman" in a sarcastic way, "this gentleman says you are embarrassing him." He waved his arm and asked for the check. We got up and left.

In the cab, Adele was crying. I didn't know what to say. We drove in awkward silence. I got out. "Please don't see me to the door," I said to Mac and went upstairs.

I was beginning to understand. I was to be Mac's girlfriend and Adele would be looking for a boyfriend. But, somehow, this offended me. What I wanted with Mac should be serious business. This other arrangement seemed so flippant, so frivolous. It wasn't what I wanted.

I didn't want a just "pass the time" relationship. I wanted a "HUSBAND"!

The next night the doorbell rang, and Mac was standing there. If I had been able to read the future, I would have slammed the door shut and said, "Please go away—You are a thief for me; you will steal from me eight years of my life, put me in a turmoil, on the edge of deep depression and breakdown, of inner conflict and war with myself. The sex part will be great, but it won't warrant the pain."

But did I? No, I opened wide the door and said, "Come in Disaster, I can hardly wait."

We went upstairs.

"Do you like martinis?"

He smiled. "Yes, I do, I do."

Martinis are great. In no time your head is spinning, your eyes are shining, the room is floating around you and lightheaded happiness is floating there, too.

Mac put his hand over mine, and I felt it was a position I would like to hold forever.

There should be some system where you could hold the great moments for at least five times their normal time—and skim over the bad times in five times less than their normal. It would have been a nice arrangement.

"Hurry, hurry," I said inside of me, though. "After dinner we will go to the couch by the window, look out over the city. He will do more than hold my hand—I know it."

So it happened—the beginning of disaster. Christina served us a bang up dinner; she seemed happy there was a man in the house. We drank many martinis and rose higher and higher into the sky of unreality. Everything seemed wonderful, and I never wanted to come back to earth.

After dinner we went to the little couch in the living room. I sat down and looked out over the city: Beautiful city, I love you. Mac followed and the world exploded into sex and love and that was all that mattered. The wonderful sex explosion, two people both hungry for sex love, love sex that made everything else seem unimportant, that stood over both of us big, overpowering, in command.

He was a very powerful lover, and our embraces had an animal-like ferocity.

He was everything I wanted. The road ahead

was definitely going to be intertwined for me with Mac.

But a small question came.

"How are you with her?"

"I'm not. We don't have sex anymore. She understands."

So did I, for awhile.

He would snatch time for us between leaving his office and going home for dinner. It was wonderful having sex with someone you loved and admired, so different from sex with just a body and no soul.

After that I seemed to live only for our next encounter. When you start a love affair, the only thing that matters is sex and love. You never think of food, or headaches, or shopping. Your head and body are all immersed in love: when, where, how. People around are like shadows—bodies without substance, in the way: Hello—hello; good-bye—good-bye; you're in my way; please leave; oh, where's the bed?; where's the couch?; don't talk dirty; surely it's more than that; why should it be more?; okay settle down now.

He was everything I wanted. The road ahead was definitely going to be intertwined for me with Mac.

At first Adele was very friendly and would refer to Mac as my "boyfriend." I didn't like that; it was a false front: I wanted her to know that I was serious about wanting her husband. It would be easier if she would deal with me as an enemy and not a false friend.

Mac told her how he felt about me.

"You'll soon get tired of her," she said. "Your

little plaything. She won't last."

A plaything? Me? We'll see, my fine lady, if I am a plaything, something not to be taken seriously. We'll see, my fine lady, once I get my divorce. You'll soon know that I am not something to be brushed aside lightly—

In New York divorce was only possible if one or the other committed an infidelity.

"We'll have to get someone to tag him," said Mac.

"A detective?"

"Yes, a detective."

This seemed so patently unfair. Here I was being unfaithful, but I would be posing as the injured party if they caught him.

"You have to do things like that to get what you want," said Mac. "I didn't invent the law nor did you; but we have to go with it."

Mac did put a detective onto Bidge. It was all not very nice, and I decided to go to Mexico to get a divorce. A Mexican divorce wasn't worth very much, but it was still a divorce.

I booked passage for me, my children, my mother, and my dog, and we all sailed for Mexico. From the port, we took the train to Mexico City. It was quite a trip in those days.

Bidge had sent word to the consul in Mexico City, asking him to find me and to stop me from getting a divorce, but the consul was very nice to me. He said, "As far as I'm concerned, it's your business. I won't stop you."

However, in the meantime, the detective had photographed Bidge with a woman, and Mac got word to me that we had the evidence we needed and could proceed with the divorce in the New York courts. So we set sail for home.

After I returned from Mexico, I missed my period.

I began receiving calls from He-Him. "Let's call it off. I don't want a divorce. I want my children back. If we do get a divorce, I want to have Denis. You can keep the baby, but I want Denis."

"No, no, I'm sorry but I wouldn't want to separate the children."

His voice got rough then, and rude.

"We'll see when we get to court which of us is the better parent."

My period—one, two, three weeks.

I would have to tell Mac.

Please let him want the baby. I never wanted to have a baby with He-Him, but I really do want a baby with Mac—to have a baby with someone I really loved—

Bidge continued calling: "I don't want a divorce. It's silly, and if we do get a divorce I want to have Denis. You can keep the baby."

I'd hang up and rush into the kids' room and grab them both and hold them tight. I loved Mac. But I would not ever want to lose my children. Anything but that.

I was filled with happiness at the thought of having Mac's baby. I began to dream. He—it would be a he—he would be dark and beautiful, and the baby would help him to leave Adele. He would have to.

I didn't know how I would tell him.

I would watch his face. I would look for joy and acceptance.

Please, God, let him want it.

The time came.

"I think I'm pregnant," I said. He made a quick turn and looked straight at me. "Are you sure?"

His face didn't reveal anything.

"What are you going to do?" he asked.

My hopes were sinking fast.

"I don't know. What should I do?"

"This is not a good time to have a baby."

"I know that. Bidge wants Denis, and this would be his excuse to take him. That I'm an unfit mother."

We were skirting his side of it.

Was I the only one that wanted this baby? And I wanted it so much.

I had to balance losing Denis to have this baby I didn't know yet.

"What do you want to do?"

There was what I wanted and what I could hope for. "I want the baby and I want to keep Denis."

It ended up that I found myself in Dr. Hellman's office, the doctor who had delivered both my children.

He shook his head sadly. "I'm sorry to hear that. You're asking me to do an abortion—"

"Yes."

"You know it's against the law. If it is discovered I would lose my license. I might even be put in jail."

"I know it is asking a lot, maybe too much."

Dr. Hellman stood up. "I will call you. I will let you know."

I went slinking out of his office, my head down. I felt ashamed. In my heart I was hoping he would say no and I would be forced to have the baby. The decision would have been taken out of my hands.

I knew I wouldn't go to some shady doctor in a back alley who might be clumsy and dangerous. That night, in my prayers, I prayed that he would say no. And then in the morning I looked at Denis and prayed that he would say yes.

It all seemed now to be a choice between a new baby and Denis. Mac, I would have to deal with later.

It turned out that he said yes. "I can do it for you in your apartment, and I will bring a nurse with me."

"No, not in my apartment on account of the children, but we can do it in my mother's apartment. I will ask her."

My mother agreed, and it was on a Saturday afternoon in her kitchen on a kitchen table that we arranged to have it done.

Saturday: Mac was there, my mother was there; the doorbell rang, and the doctor and nurse arrived.

I had taken one of my nightgowns and slit it down the back and sewed it so it was like a hospital gown.

I felt apprehensive, nervous, and angry.

I laid down on the wooden table. I looked at the table next to me holding shining instruments. Oh, God. Why did life have to be like this? I began to think, to worry, and one thought came on top of another. I would die, the baby would die, and it would be discovered why. The police would come and ask questions. They would find out I had had an abortion and that Dr. Hellman had done it, and they would search him out and find him and arrest him. And they would take away his license, and he would never deliver another baby, and they would cart him off to jail, and his nurse would have to go too because she had helped him. And then they would talk to Mac, and he would lie and say he was only there because he was doing legal work for my mother, but they would find out that he had been coming to see me every night, and so they would arrest him, too, for being an accessory, and the Bar Association would kick him out and his firm would take his name off the letterhead on the stationary. It wouldn't read Szold and Brandwen, but only Szold. He'd lose his license to practice, too, and he'd have to move to another state, and his wife would be glad because she'd been right that I was bad news and could only bring him trouble; and she'd be angry and furious because she had to suffer also for his wrongdoing. And the people who ran the apartment house on Park Avenue where my mother lived would come to see my mother to tell her that she had hurt the reputation of the apartment house and perhaps she should leave, but they'd gradually forget about it since she was such a good tenant. They'd let her stay. They felt she had suffered enough with the death of her daughter. And He-Him got the two children and the trust fund and he was appointed guardian and he spent all the money in his manic moods until there was very little left and they all had to move to a small, small apartment and the children kept asking, "Where is Mama, where is mama?"

All these thoughts piled in as they clapped the gas mask over my face and I slipped away. I felt sharp pain and heard myself cry out, and then they must have given me more anesthesia, and then I woke up. And there was Dr. Hellman, smiling and patting my hand, and Mac and mother standing behind. They all looked happy and relieved.

"Everything went very well."

How could they say that? There was all this blood coming out of me and my baby was gone and I turned my face to the wall, and I cried and cried.

After that I never loved Mac as much. I couldn't forgive him and my feeling for him went down. Why did I stay with him?

He was under six feet, but he seemed bigger. He had a very big penis, and that was fulfilling. Everything about him seemed passionate. He gave me an awareness of my body that I had never had before. I used to lie on my bed and feel my body alive and beloved. I had feeling of pride and pleasure in it. My below-the-surface life would ebb and flow like a stormy wave of the sea, and above it my mind might be occupied with trivia. "Where shall I go tomorrow? What shall I do?" Everything sat on the satisfying surge of passion that filled my being.

Words steamed out of his mouth, sometimes vindictive, sometimes full of praise, and you could feel yourself ascending on his rhetoric so you would want to yell and clap: Yes, that's the way it is.

I always felt protected when I was with him. My other men friends seemed inadequate and frail by comparison. Although there were among them ones who were brave and laid down their lives for the causes of liberation of people in other countries.

Mac always had an opinion on every subject and his reasons were well organized and convincing. When I was in doubt about something, I always asked him what he thought. If there was a case of injustice, he would do everything in his power to rectify it. He would write letters, give speeches, give money. Like the case of the Rosenbergs who were executed as spies.

I think Mac had a Mafia philosophy. He was super tender and kind with the ones who belonged to him, and ruthless with the ones who did not.

Sometimes he could be very cruel to people he considered stupid or inferior.

Once in a taxi the driver took a wrong turn and Mac let him have it.

The driver turned and said, "Look mister, if I had a big brain, I wouldn't be driving a cab."

This set Mac back, and he laughed.

He considered the world a jungle. "It's a jungle out there," he would say. "You have to fight your way through."

He had been born on the wrong side of the tracks in Pittsburgh. He used to deliver newspapers to the homes of wealthy people. His fingers would freeze as he delivered papers at four o'clock in the morning.

Because of his high grades he got a scholarship to Harvard and graduated from law school summa cum laude and became a partner in an eminent Jewish law firm.

I admired him.

He had rich clients for the money part, but he worked free for the labor unions. He was the lawyer for the Amalgamated Clothing Workers and labor leader Sidney Hillman's right-hand man. So when we started to arm for World War II, Hillman was called to Washington to coordinate the efforts of labor and Mac went with him.

I always felt when I was with Mac that he knew where he wanted to go, where he wanted to be. He was always purposeful. And he was very rigid in some ways. Once I said to him, "Let's go see a movie, down the block. I hear it's good."

He looked at me as though he thought I were crazy: "At eleven o'clock in the morning on a weekday?"

Our best times outside of the bed times, were when we went to the theatre. He was very receptive to good theatre, good acting, good writing, and idealistic themes. And in the darkness of the theatre he would be carried away.

It was always his dream to write a good play, but as well as he spoke, so poorly did he write. It was ponderous and heavy-handed.

In small details and little things like matters of good taste in dressing he was sometimes very insecure. He had to attend a Cabinet meeting once, and he made me go to a store with him to select a tie that I thought would be appropriate.

There was always the struggle between us. It was like a live animal lying there. We would meet and the struggle would come.

Sometimes quiescent if we were sharing an enjoyable time; at other times it would spring out into a fervid life, and we would part angry—and then wait for the phone to ring and make it all up again, the fear of loss surmounting the anger. And there would be peace again for a while.

Mac never bored me, as did other people. Perhaps because he was always dynamic and intense.

The day the judge was to rule on my divorce finally came. I went to court with my mother. I was amazed that the courtroom was filled with mutual friends from our married days. I went up to one of them and asked him, "Why are you here?"

"Just curiosity," he said. "And maybe to help out."

I didn't pursue it but took my seat at the front of the courtroom.

When I called to the stand, Bidge's attorney, who was a woman, began an attack, trying to say that I was a rich woman who only cared to enjoy herself, who had gone to Europe to have a good time. Because of this, she said, her client would like to have custody of the two boys.

When she was through, my attorney, an assistant in Mac's office, began questioning me as to why I had gone to Europe.

"Part of the time," I said, "I was in a clinic to rest as I was run down and nervous."

The judge seemed to like me and said, "Sit back and relax. No one is going to hurt you."

I felt reassured after that and answered the questions as well as I could.

The judge ruled that he had no intention of giving the children to Bidge and taking them away from their mother. He also stated that although we had not asked for anything, that Bidge should pay $100 a month for the children's support until they reached the age of twenty-one.

The day was over. I was free, and I had my two kids.

I settled down with Mac into a routine of "seeing each other." He had a special phone with a special number installed in my room so I knew when it rang it could only be he. He came by twice a week for dinner and sex. And he'd stop in every afternoon at six and stay until eight. Then he'd go home for dinner with Adele.

"Will she ever let you go?" I'd ask.

"No, I don't think so."

"Is this the way it will always be? These interludes between your real life—and I am the interlude."

"But it's such a beautiful interlude," he would answer. "Can't we enjoy it and not worry it with all these questions? I can't punish her; she hasn't done anything to deserve punishment."

"Nor have I—"

We had this conversation over and over. Each time we made love it happened.

Then the blow came. One evening he told me

very definitely that he had promised Adele he would never leave her. That was hard for me: before that, I'd been able to sustain myself with promises, promises: *just be patient; just wait.* I finally realized that our relationship would never materialize into a marriage, but I would always remain his sex life, a recipient of extravagant gifts and indulgences. It wasn't what I wanted. I always felt guilty and a doer of wrong. I didn't want to fool anybody or lie or be sneaky, and I felt badly about his wife.

So then I began to look around me.

This is not the world I want to live in. I must change it.

Inside me was a very strong voice saying, You've got to make something of yourself; get moving; don't sit around expecting wonderful things to happen; it's up to you to make them happen.

I took a job with Peter Copeland, designing windows for 5th Avenue stores. I loved the excitement of installing them at midnight and then sometimes as late as three o'clock in the morning going out to view them with my fellow workers. Afterwords, we'd go to an all-night automat, exhilarated and hungry, exchanging silly cracks and jokes, enjoying the satisfaction at work well done.

Salvador Dali arrived at our workshop one day followed by his wife, Gala, to whom he was utterly devoted. Bonwit Teller had commissioned him to design two windows, and they were to be built in our shop. I recall that one of the windows had a large female figure draped in white with her face obscured entirely by red roses. The ground was of desert sand, and a melted watch was folded over a wall. It was striking and beautiful.

Dali, himself, was a small man and exquisitely made. We got used to working with him, but it wasn't easy. He would arrive in an ankle-length fur coat, step out of the back elevator into the workroom, come over to where we were working, and explode angrily that nothing we were doing was right. He would wave his hands dramatically and speak in Spanish except for a few words in English. Then he would stride over to the elevator, but not ring the bell, just stand there. When none of us moved to stop him, he would turn around and come back. And then he would tell us precisely and calmly what he wanted.

So his window got built, and the time came to install it. Installing windows on Fifth Avenue was generally done in the early hours of the morning when there was no traffic. Dali and his wife arrived in a taxi. They got out, and when they reached the sidewalk in front of the store, he pretended to try to take off her clothes to make love to her. A policeman came by and was ready to arrest him for indecent behavior when he was told it was Dali's wife. The policeman went off, shaking his head.

Dali liked to do what the French called "epatee le bourgeois," or "confound the staid, middle-class person," and he was very good at it.

When Ed Murrow interviewed him, Dali had an electric light in his tie that would turn on when he wanted to speak. Murrow was disgusted with him. If they had been animals instead of people, it would have been like seeing a porcupine having a conversation with a lobster. Both would be sincere, but they lived in such different worlds and had had such different experiences that communication was impossible.

Looking back, I wonder why I was so anxious to get a job to earn some money? Maybe it was to prove I had some worth. I hated the idea of being a rich man's daughter, idly passing her time amusing herself. Did I or did I not have talent? Taking a job was one way to find out. True, the boss was my friend and more or less in love with me, so I did not feel I was getting the job on my own merits. I learned quite a bit, though. I did learn what it was to work from nine to five, but actually that wasn't so different from being at school. I did learn something about window displays. I did learn how the customers treated the workers. And I met interesting people, among them Dali. It was exciting working down on 23rd Street—although I'd have my chauffeur drop me a few blocks away and then I'd walk to work.

Mac treated what I was doing as a strange but allowable entertainment that would pass when I had had enough of it.

I had long admired a German artist named George Grosz. He had fled from Germany and was put on Hitler's blacklist of enemies to be found and executed. He had done a drawing of Christ on the cross with a gas mask and dedicated it to the Nazis with the title, "Here is your Christ!"

Grosz could say more with a line than any artist living. I poured over his drawings and books. If only I could draw as he did; if only I could see as he did! Seeing: that was the first prerequisite. I had nothing to say yet of any importance. I didn't like the way things were—in my life or anyone else's.

When I heard that he was setting up a school with the painter Maurice Sterne, I went and registered for his class. Grosz had been on faculty at the Art Students League, but they'd come to think his trip to Russia on his flight from Germany indicated he was a communist and had asked him to leave. The League's loss was my gain.

On a Monday morning, he appeared. I was surprised by his appearance. He was a handsome blond good looking man of forty-five who seemed to be in the best of health and happy—until you looked at his eyes; they told another story—

I don't know why I expected him to be dark, gaunt, highly nervous, and maybe Jewish— probably because of his drawings. When I first got the book *Interregnum*, which contained most of the drawings he'd done in Germany between the two wars and the rise of Hitler, I found it so terrifying that I never looked at it unless there was someone with me.

The class consisted of about twelve men and women, a mixture of the unemployed and of affluent women with liberal ideas. A strange mix, but a good one.

George Grosz was not an articulate teacher. He

would come around and say, "Altina, I think you are increasing," and to illustrate what he meant, he would make wonderful little drawings in the margins of my paper. Of course, I treasured these.

The class monitor was a man called Marshall Glazier. He was rough and rude in manner, but tender and gentle of heart. His drawings were an imitation of Grosz's—as all of our drawings were to become. It was impossible to see a drawing of Grosz's without wanting to go along that path.

Even if Grosz wasn't a great teacher, we all knew we were in the presence of a great man. He talked to us of Europe and the tense and terrible situation there. He'd invite us to his house sometimes on a Sunday, and he would feed us and regale us with stories of his youth. His warm, fatherly personality was in strong contrast to his bitter student drawings, but we only saw the warm side of him.

Once at lunchtime, three of us went out with Grosz. He was smoking a pipe. A woman darted out of the noonday crowd, opened her dress and exposed her breasts. She pointed to Grosz and screamed, "That man burned my breasts with his pipe." The crowd gathered, including a policeman and stared at her unblemished breasts. The policeman said, "Okay, come down to the station."

The woman yelled, "No, last time I ended up at Bellevue Hospital."

The policeman was disgusted and said, "You're all nuts," and walked off.

Grosz, who felt very precarious in his situation as an immigrant, shook his head.

"Of all the people she had to pick on, it had to be me."

Because the depression was at its height and because most the students were living on the $22.50 a week that the government allotted to those who were unemployed, they were very often hungry and so my house became a sort of watering hole for destitute artists.

It was a time rich in conversation; ideas were bandied about. We had Christina, whom everyone loved, cook us great meals. The children were part of the group.

I made some good friends from that group. There was Lorraine Brevannes, a secretary who was married to a painter with a short temper. It was told that he had a show and not liking the expression of one of the viewers went up to him and said, "You don't like my painting?" and without waiting for an answer, knocked him to the ground.

Another friend was Lester Polakov a small young nineteen-year-old kid with a lot of talent. Glazier called him Palooka, and he stayed with that name until he was thirty and had become a respected scene designer. Grosz once said to him, "Why do you draw so small?"

So Palooka started drawing figures five feet high. And then Grosz said to him, "Why do you draw so big?" And so he went back to drawing as he used to.

My closest friend was Ben Edwards. He was nineteen, and he came from Union Springs,

Alabama. He was handsome in a classical Greek way, and he fit the description of being a gentleman. He was studying to be a stage designer; in those days he was unknown and miserably poor, but now he is quite famous and is head of the scene designers union.

Ben taught my young son Terry how to tie his first shoelaces. He, also, did some beautiful drawings of Terry, who had such a sensitive face and sad brown eyes. Lester painted a big mural of Pinocchio in Denis' room.

Salvador Dali used to come to the class to use the model. He made exquisite detailed drawings of a foot, a hand, an ear, and we would watch him with fascination. In the class, he was very quiet and intense about his drawing, but he didn't seem to mind our watching him.

Grosz drew and painted plants and female nudes, disappointing many of his admirers. People wondered why he didn't make the sharp cruel drawings of the bad things in the U.S. as he had done in Germany.

"Why? Because the U.S. has been good to me. This is my last port of call."

14

New York in those days was a pleasant city to live in. I could wander around the streets at night with a companion and feel no fear of being robbed or mugged.

I lived in an area named Yorkville, which was on the Upper East Side and went down to the East River. The neighborhood held an assortment of small stores and bars, and some evenings we would go into a bar and stand around a person playing the piano and we would all sing. It had a homey informal atmosphere.

One such evening, I went with a friend to a local movie theatre—fifty cents a ticket. Coming out, we decided to explore one of the side streets. We passed an optician's window. In it stood a large oil painting of a young blond woman: on her face had been placed a pair of rimless eyeglasses with gold ear pieces. She looked like a nurse in a hospital, antiseptic and utterly unromantic, and I remembered Dorothy Parker's line, "Men never make passes at girls who wear glasses."

As we walked on, my head was on fire, thoughts were flying through my brain. "Surely, there must be some way to design eyeglasses that could be attractive! What looks good on a face? What adds to a face? What could a woman wear on her face that would be romantic?"

An image of a masked ball and people wearing small black masks came to me. "Yes," I thought. "Masks are beautiful—black and seductive looking. They have mystery and whimsy. I could design eyeglasses in the shape of a mask—and black! They must be in black."

I hurried home, said good-bye to my companion, and went to the studio.

I got out different issues of *Life* magazine and cut out large pictures of women's faces. Then I began drawing on them different possible shapes of masks.

Not bad.

I didn't sleep much that night. Bright and early the next morning, I went to the nearest toy store and bought three black masks. Back at my studio, I started cutting them into shapes like eyeglasses. I sat in front of a mirror and put them on. They slanted up at the corner, and the black lines framed my eyes. They looked startling. They looked good. People would surely like them, I thought.

I got more and more excited; I could feel in my bones that I had stumbled on a new and exciting idea. I knew, though, that a lot of work had to be done to bridge the space between these paper eyeglasses and the final marketable product.

The first thing to do was to get a model made in plastic, and that meant finding a model maker who could do it.

In those days, if you wanted to do or to find

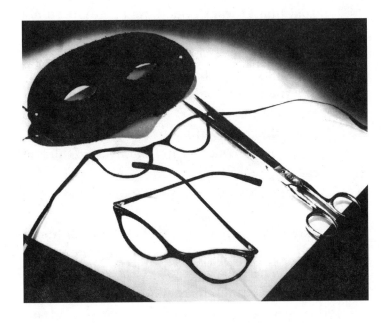

Harlequin Worksheet

something unusual, you went to Greenwich Village, where the free souls lived away from Park Avenue's stodgy, respectability and odd people pursued odd occupations. There I found an old man who had a dusty studio full of models for inventions that had never been born. He looked at my sketches and my paper model and seemed to understand the problem.

I told him, "I want something I can put on my face and wear. It must have a fitted nose piece and an upward tilt to the shape around the eyes."

"I'll do my best," he said. He was a pleasant-looking man, and his hands seemed strong and hopefully effective.

"And, oh, yes. I want it to be in black plastic, and while you are making it, I want you to think of a mask."

I came back in three days as he had told me to do.

The frames were on the table in front of him. I picked them up, put them on, and went to a mirror. I knew they were too small to be optically correct. But I thought they were attractive and perhaps good enough to have a picture made so that I would have something to take around to help sell my idea.

I decided I wanted a photograph not just of a woman wearing the new eyeglasses, but of a romantic scene that she was involved in. So I called my friend Ben Edwards who was the handsomest man I knew, and I called my friend Virginia Bolan who was exquisitely beautiful and very photogenic. Virginia had run away from home

Virginia & Ben Modeling for Harlequin Eyeglasses

when she was fifteen, and she made her living as a model, but since she was so small, she didn't model clothes: she modeled hats, shoes, stockings, and such.

They both agreed to pose. I bought a triangular black hat for Virginia and rented a harlequin costume for Ben. And the name for the eyeglasses sprung up on its own: Harlequin eyeglasses.

Another friend, a photographer named Marcus Bleckman, took photographs, and they were very beautiful and romantic. Armed with these photographs I decided to go around to the manufacturers of frames. But I needed one thing more: a male companion. In those days, women were not respected as promoters, and were always or almost always brushed aside and not given a fair hearing.

I thought of André Boutemy, a friend of mine who was in the jewelry business. André dressed well, was a pleasant companion, had a good sense of humor, and was French, which was a decided bonus because French men had a reputation for style. I asked him if for twenty-five percent of the profits (if there were any) he would help me in my effort to get my business established. He agreed. He was happily married so we could have a strictly platonic relationship.

We went to all the major manufacturers— American Optical, Bausch and Lomb, Ray Ban, etc.—and in every case we were shown the door. We then called on Meyerowitz Opticals on Fifth Avenue, where Mr. Meyerowitz said, "When I get a call from a lunatic asylum, I'll let you know."

We went to the big retailers. At one, a big fat disagreeable-looking manager agreed to see us. He handled the frame as though it were something that had fallen out of the ash can.

"You don't know anything about the optical business, do you?"

I had to agree that I didn't.

"Women," he said, "want to look dignified. They wouldn't wear anything like this."

I wanted to say, "You don't know much about women," but I didn't.

Interestingly, I was not put off by the accumulation of rejections. I knew that sooner or later Harlequins would be accepted.

We decided that the place to go would be a small retail store that catered to stylish women.

There was such a shop on Madison Avenue called Lugene's. We went there, and the head clerk shook his head: "No, no." But "Fate" or "Chance" intervened in the form of Mr. Lugene walking in the front door. He passed us, looked at the photograph, and said "Follow me."

In his private office, he took the photograph and studied it carefully. "I like it," he said. "I will work with you if you'll give me an exclusive for six months."

I pretended to hesitate, and then I agreed.

We showed him the plastic model.

"I would have to make these optically correct and wearable," he said.

He was our Santa Claus.

Within a week, he'd had a frame made that was optically correct. I made arrangements with a small manufacturer to make them, and I offered to design his front window.

We spent a few days decorating his front window, blowing up the photo of Ben and Virginia to life size. People on the street stopped and looked.

Within a week, Mr. Lugene had sold the first pair to Clare Booth Luce, then to the actress Katharine Cornell, and after that to many social and theatrical stars, all stylish women, all well-known.

It was beginning to be fun.

I applied for a patent. I couldn't get a mechanical patent but I did get a design patent.

I had a friend in the advertising business, and he said, "You need a public relations person," and he recommended Constance Hope, who did P.R. for Metropolitan Opera stars.

We met. She was plump and beaming and the nice person my friend had said she was. She wanted $75 a week on a contract of six months. That seemed reasonable.

In those days, New York had many newspapers—*The Times, The Tribune, The Daily News,* and an afternoon papers, *The World Telegram.* The first thing she arranged was for *The World Telegram* to send both a man for an interview and a photographer to take a picture of me wearing Harlequin glasses. Story and photo appeared on the first page of the second section. The next day, I got calls from American Optical, Bausch and Lomb, Ray Ban, and the other major companies; they all wanted to come in on the deal. I told them that Lugene had an exclusive for six months, but after that I was free.

I made an arrangement with all who were interested that they could manufacture the frames and pay me a ten-cent royalty on each pair that they sold. On paper it looked fine. In practice, there was no way to know the amount they sold. Their books were too easy to disguise.

I had enough money from a trust fund from my father to live comfortably, but not enough to start a factory and be the sole manufacturer.

I decided to open an office and get a small manufacturer to supply me and then distribute them myself.

So I did. I took a small office on Fifth Avenue and 43rd Street. My staff consisted of a bookkeeper, a manager, a shipping clerk, and three cigar-smoking salesmen—one for the East, one Midwest, and one for the Coast. I took ads out in *Mademoiselle* and *Vogue*. And thanks to Constance Hope, we got a lot of free publicity in many magazines and newspapers. This was one: "With all the yodeling that it is sad to need glasses, many of our fond perusers will be delighted with this news. Glasses with glamma, with zip, with silliness—you know—to make you look as if you don't mind wearing them. They're called 'Harlequin', being patterned after the becoming mask this Droll One usually wears. We understand that they own complete optical efficiency, and we do know that they give the eyes an amused, tilted look, and the face a kind of whatthehell expression—"so I wear glasses, so what." But you'd have to try them on yourself to see what we mean. Lugene, 600 Madison Avenue. $8 for the frames." And a cartoon appeared in *Barron's*, the financial newspaper. Two men see a woman wearing

Harlequin glasses, and one says to the other, "Oh, Boy—she has specs appeal."

Within a year we were doing well.

My day consisted of going to the office from ten to four, and then going home to be with my kids.

I received a good deal of free publicity. It was the first time in all these years that eyeglasses entered the style area instead of the medical correction field.

The war in Europe was heating up. Hitler had invaded France. England declared war on Germany. And Churchill proclaimed: "Give us the tools and we will win the war." Roosevelt called the heads of Industry and Labor to come to Washington, and Mac went with Hillman.

I began trekking to Washington during the week to be with Mac, and he would come to New York weekends.

It was a nervous time for the whole world. It was a nervous time for me.

One day going down in an elevator on Wall Street with two prosperous men, one said to the other, "What Hitler is doing to the Jews is nothing as to what we will do to them." I looked up into his face. It was an ordinary face. Is this what these killers look like—just ordinary people?

When I got home that night, I sat in a warm tub. "Not me," I thought, "They won't get me. If that knock should come on my door, I'll kill myself. I'll kill my children. I will not let them starve, beat, humiliate us. Death will be sweet. How are you going to do it? I don't know, but I'll find a way. New York has so many tall buildings—we'll just step out of one of them into the air.

Having decided that, I felt more at peace.

15

In 1939, the war in Europe was going on full swing. The stories of Jew killing seemed to get worse. I didn't know what I could do to help relieve the suffering in Germany and Austria until one day my beautiful Viennese friend Camilla Spear leaned over the table, her blue eyes filled with tears, her lips trembling. "It's so bad now in Vienna, since Hitler came. My friends are all in hiding. Would you sign an affidavit for me? It is for a very dear friend. He is a physician. I think we can get him out. He is being helped by gentile friends who are hiding him, and once out if he has an affidavit to come here, he will be safe. He can make a new life. His name is Eric Barasch, and he is thirty-four years of age."

I hardly waited for her to finish her sentence. "Of course I will sign it."

Camille was very warm and sentimental, and she got up and put her arms around me.

Five months later the phone rang. It was mid-winter, and I was in bed with the flu.

A nice voice with a strong foreign accent came over the line. "Madame," it said, "I am arrived." I knew he was nice as soon as he came into the

Eric Barrett

room. He moved with such lightness and grace—and he moved into my life.

I learned that he was not only a physician but that he also had a law degree. He'd always wanted to be a physician; but his father thought it was too hard a life, and so he persuaded him to study law. In obedience to his father, whom he loved and respected, he did, and when he had completed his studies, he told his father that he still wanted to be a physician. So he went to medical school and got his degree. He was also a gifted pianist and sometimes gave recitals.

Eric had been working on the staff of a hospital when Hitler came and took over Austria. The second or third day after the takeover, Nazi authorities arrived at the hospital. They lined up all the staff and said, "All members of the Jewish faith, step forward."

Although Eric had converted to Catholicism, he was classified as a Jew—as were about a third of the staff.

Said the Nazis: "Your services here are no longer required. Pack up your things and leave." Although Eric had been expecting this, when it happened it was still a shock.

Active persecution of the Jews had not yet started, but everyone knew it was just a matter of time. Jews were still allowed to leave Austria, but they could only take their clothing with them. Eric bought himself twenty suits and a black coat lined with mink, hoping to sell it if he should be able to come to this country. He went to live with a close friend of his, a professor at the university, who was a member of the Nazi party. At the end of the war when the Allies had won and they were rounding up the Nazis and putting them to work cleaning the streets, etc., Eric wrote the American authorities that this man had helped him and sheltered him and not done him any harm. We later learned that the professor had been allowed to go back to the university.

While Eric was living with this friend in Austria, waiting for an exit visa, the attacks against the Jews began. The windows of their shops and houses and synagogues were broken. It became known as the "Night of the Broken Glass."

Eric's visa came, and his friend, at risk to himself, drove him to the airport and put him on a plane for Paris. In Paris, Eric got my affidavit and boarded a plane for the U.S.

Eric got a small room on the upper part of Riverside Drive. He picked up English very quickly—probably for two reasons: he was such a great student, but more than that he'd developed such a dislike for the Nazis and the Germans that he wouldn't talk German to anybody if he could possibly avoid it.

In spite of the hard times he had gone through, his excitement about living hadn't been diminished. Eric was filled with a curiosity and determination to make a new life.

One day he asked me if we could go to a concert. We went to Carnegie Hall, that center of music on 57th Street, to hear the Philharmonic. As he sat and listened, I could feel that he was completely taken over by the music, and when he turned to me during intermission, his face was suffused with joy. I felt in that moment great affection for him, for his feelings. When we got home, we sat on the edge of the bed. He put his arms around me and said, "I am so glad to be here, so glad to know someone like you."

"I feel the same." I returned his embrace, and we made love. Later, lying in bed with him, I noticed that he coughed a lot.

"Do you have a cold?"

"No, I think it is from smoking." I didn't think much about it, but later, later when I used to hear him cough, my heart would sink in fear.

My growing feelings for Eric began to eat away at my relationship with Mac. I'd long realized it wasn't going to lead to marriage. Adele had told him, "Frankly, if you leave me, you'll never practice law again." And it was true she could have made a lot of trouble for him with the Bar Association. So he was at times afraid of her, and at times he felt it would not be moral to leave her.

My growing attachment to Eric, countered some of the pain. We were very happy most of the time. I enjoyed seeing New York through his eyes. We would go down to Wall Street late at night and walk; it was deserted at that hour and the tall buildings cut into the sky and the city belonged to us. Then the 1939 World's Fair arrived, and we would go there every night. We went to exotic restaurants in the different pavilions, tasted exotic foods and listened to the music of all the different countries. The Fair was crowded every night and every night there were fireworks. The world and all its troubles were far away, but—

We worried a lot of the time. England was being bombed. It looked as though Hitler might win, so over our happiness was a constant veil of fear. We would turn on the radio at night and between ads for underwear we would listen to "Kaltenborn," the famous analyst who always sounded like an undertaker, describing the bombings in England. Then: Winston Churchill telling of the bravery of the English people and describing how they would fight block by block but never surrender. Our hearts were with them: "Give us the tools and we will do the job." Our factories revved up and began sending goods overseas.

"I want to talk to you, seriously," Eric said. I sat down by his side, and he took my hands gently into his. "In this world, so full of hate and with a devil like Hitler killing and conquering, you cannot afford to stay Jewish."

"But," I protested, "the United States is not Germany or Austria. It cannot happen here." But then I thought of the two men in the elevator talking about what they would do to the Jews here if Hitler won.

"So, what are you thinking?" I asked.

"You must become Catholic, you and the children. You must be registered as a Catholic—so you are on a list. You will be protected."

"Until they find that Jewish grandmother."

"They may not have the same laws here that they had in Germany and Austria. It may be enough that you belong to a church. Let me bring a priest here to talk to you."

Unlike Henry Bergson, I didn't mind lying to a thug who wants to kill me, but I didn't feel I could lie to a priest who came to my home in good faith.

"Well," Eric said, "just do this for me: just see and speak to the priest that I will bring."

When the priest came, he asked me, "Why do you want to become a Catholic?"

"I'm afraid if Hitler comes, they will follow his lead and kill all the Jews."

"I sympathize with what you're saying," he said. "But that's not a good reason. It would have to be more than that. I brought you some books to read—about religion, about faith. Read them and then call me."

I took the books and they lay on my night table for two weeks. I never read them. Even if the Catholics wanted me, I knew I could not go through with it. The words would stick in my throat. Maybe the Jewish God would strike me dead.

I called up the priest. "I would like to return your books. Thank you for your time, but I guess the answer is no."

Eric began giving my son Terry piano lessons. Terry hated his former piano teacher and used to get on the floor and bite her ankles. She finally gave up and left. Terry seemed to like Eric, though.

When Eric played the piano his touch was exquisitely precise and light. I was in love with his playing. There seemed to be no end to his talents.

When I would take him out to dinner to meet my friends, he was always the smartest and the brightest. We fell more and more in love. We continued to go to the Fair. It was breathtaking—every nation with its pavilion. We went everywhere, explored everything, it was a feast every night. Fireworks exploding in the sky.

My Harlequin glasses were selling to all the smart women. If only Hitler would have disappeared, what a wonderful world it would be. I had love, I had work, I had health, I had money—I had two beautiful children.

Eric had to serve one years' internship in a hospital before taking his medical exam to get a license. He began sending letters all over the country, and a Catholic hospital in Colorado Springs accepted him, and he was to start in July. I was happy and sad, happy because it was a step in the right direction, sad because it would mean separation. But we decided that once Denis was off to his father's for summer vacation, Terry and I would follow. We planned to be married when I arrived.

I wanted to tell Mac now about Eric and me. I knew he already knew, but I hadn't stated it. Saying it would make it true. I looked at him as though he were a stranger. He looked different to me. Where once I had thought his eyes were dark and appealing, now he looked more like a sly fox. Slippery. Whatever he would say to me would be oiled with the grease of his legal mind. I felt I had become for him a convenience like a gas station.

"Fill 'er up."

But then he surprised me. "You don't seem to realize that I love you deeply," he said.

There was so much I could have said, but I didn't. We could have had this conversation, but we didn't. I would have said, "How can I believe you really love me when you have let me suffer all these years? You knew how I was struggling with the idea of being your mistress and how I hated it."

He would answer, "But you wanted me to leave Adele, to mortally wound her. I couldn't have lived with myself if I had done that. I would have grown to hate you for making me do that."

And I'd say, "That psychiatrist was right when he said that you were having a love affair with your wife and a sex affair with me.' When I go to your office, I feel ashamed. When you were in the hospital and I was sitting by the bed holding your hand, your friend came in to see you and you withdrew your hand. You didn't introduce me to him. It was as though I had disappeared and no one was sitting in that chair. Your friend seemed embarrassed. I sort of expected him to acknowledge me, to say, 'So this is your girlfriend.' He didn't. Instead he said, 'How's Adele? Give her my love.' I wanted to throw something at him. Did he think I had no feelings at all or that my feelings couldn't possibly matter? That only people with legal relationships would have feelings to be respected? You turned that funny color red that you turn when you're feeling guilty.

"Remember that day we were having lunch at your favorite restaurant, the St. Regis, and Adele and her friend walked in and came over to you and you stood up. Nobody looked at me. I was a "non-person," and your face and neck were fiery red. As for me, I felt I was pale white. I don't remember any words, only feelings that were flashing across the table. And then they went to a table across the room, and we canceled our order and left. I felt like a rat leaving a sinking ship. That was the way it always was with your friends. My friends accepted and liked you. They didn't know Adele, so their only loyalty was to me. If I liked you, you were an okay guy."

I didn't say any of that, but I did say, "Eric got a letter from a Catholic Hospital in Colorado, and he's going there for his internship."

"The Catholics help each other out," said Mac. "Eric's a nice fellow. I wish him all the best."

"I may go out there in August, for a vacation—"

There was a silence. Mac leaned over and patted my hand. "I'm sorry about everything. You deserve any happiness that you can find."

How civilized, I thought. But my feelings were stronger than this civilized response. We stood up, and I raised my hand and slapped him full in the face, a strong hard slap. I looked at my hand. Did you do that? Did I order you to do that?

Mac stood silent, then turned and walked away.

The day came for Eric to leave, and we went down to Grand Central station to see him off. It was filled with kids going to camp, and we ran to the gate to Eric's train. Eric always ran, he never walked, and years later after he had died, I saw a bird, a road runner, and I thought, "You must be a reincarnation of Eric, and you've come to be near me and help me in my loneliness."

At first Eric's letters were buoyed up. The sisters were good to him, and he liked his patients. But he was disillusioned with the doctors. They divided the patients into two classes. The "good patients" were the ones with money, the "bad patients" the ones without money.

He called a doctor once at midnight: there had been an accident, and the patient needed surgery.

"Is it a 'good' patient or a 'bad' one?" the doctor asked. "I will only come for a good patient."

"I don't know," Eric answered. "It's a patient."

This answer put him on the doctor's blacklist, and after that he always made things hard for Eric.

Schatsie was his Austrian nickname for me, and he'd write, "Come soon, Schatsie. The people here are so dull."

And then one day came the shattering news:

I am lying in bed, my darling. I had a physical exam, and I was diagnosed positive for T.B.

The patients pass by my bed and their faces are concerned and their eyes are sad as they take my hand and say, 'I am so sorry Doctor.'

I will be in this bed surely for at least a year.

I could not stop trembling for hours after I read the letter. In those days they had nothing to cure T.B. except bed rest.

I told my mother. She was very firm about her opinion. "You cannot go out there nor take Terry. T.B. is very contagious. You do not have the right to endanger yourself or your child. Ask anyone and they will tell you the same thing."

I went to a doctor friend. "Forget him," he said. "You are young, desirable. Do not tie your life to a seriously sick man."

Practically speaking, all of them were right. But emotionally, they were all wrong.

16

The years after Eric had left and before he returned were nervous, anxious years. Mac had gone out to California to be with his wife. I hadn't cared before, but after Eric left, I wished he were in New York.

For a month after I heard he had T.B., I couldn't seem to be able to go out. If someone called to invite me for dinner, I refused and then tried to explain that I was ill, too ill to go out.

I went to the theater once with a friend, and I had to leave. The place seemed like a nightmare. The people all seemed threatening and ugly. I was afraid I might scream.

I decided to go to a psychiatrist, but I didn't realize that a neurologist was not a psychiatrist, and I ended up in a waiting room with patients who had trouble walking and other sorts of physical problems.

I knew I didn't belong there, but it was too late to leave. The door opened, and the nurse called my name.

I went in and the doctor was seated. His glasses were so thick I didn't know how he could see anything.

I told him of my fear of public places and how I was afraid I might scream.

"Did you?" he asked.

"No."

"Then you are all right. Don't worry so much."

"What an idiot," I thought. I got up and left.

After a few months of being a recluse, I began to go out again. I began going to my office two or three hours a day. Harlequins were doing well. Mac was back, but when we went out, I felt very low and very sad. I let him think that it was because he had gone to California to see his wife, but I suspect he knew I was mourning for Eric.

The boys asked about Eric and I had to tell them he was ill and I didn't know when or if he would be back.

They were both curious about him, especially Terry, who said, "If he can't teach me the piano, I don't want another teacher." I didn't tell them that Eric had T.B. and I don't suppose they would have known what T.B. was, but I wanted to protect Eric and I didn't want to spread the story. Perhaps not admitting and telling it made it seem less true.

We started writing each other long weekly letters.

He said the sisters were very kind to him and he was being treated for free. I began sending them money and thanking them for their kindness. He said they would come over to his bed and say, "You have a very good friend who likes you very much."

I went to Florida with my aunt Rachel for a rest

in the sun. I brought Terry, but not Denis, who was away at school. Julian, our chauffeur, came along, too. We had a little house on the beach, and every day we would take long walks and runs on the beach. We "adopted" an Indian boy, who very cute. He used to run along the beach with us.

We spent a lot of time at Marine Land, a famous tourist attraction where bus loads of people came every day. It had a restaurant, where we ate every night.

My sister Victoria and her husband Henry Broadwater came to visit. He was the only decent husband she ever had. After his untimely death, I often asked why he had to die. But there's no point in asking why.

While I was in Florida, Eric sent me a telegram, signing off with "oceans of love." The delivery man was laughing as he gave it to me.

We had fun in Florida, and I did gain back quite a bit of health.

Then one day, Mac called to say I'd won the 1939 Lord and Taylor Annual American Design Award for Harlequin glasses and that I should come home.

I found myself in an elevator at the Waldorf Astoria going up to the hall where the awards were to be given. The elevator was crowded with all the most famous designers of New York. I knew one of them and greeted her, but she only gave me the slightest of smiles. I clued in: I was not important enough to get anything more. I went up on the platform, where Walter Hoving was in charge of giving awards. He took my hands and greeted me warmly and said, "Now you must design something for me to wear. We want to be beautiful, too." I sat next to a famous industrial designer who was receiving an award for a new type of refrigerator. All the designs were for serious industrial products. When they called my name, I walked up to Mr. Hoving, and he gave me a check for a thousand dollars for "distinguished designing in the field of eyeglass fashion." I thought that was pretty good. There were speeches about the value of designers, applause, and the whole event was very impressive to me. Going down in the elevator after the awards, all the people beamed at me and offered me congratulations. I felt pretty good. I felt I had made it!

Harlequin eyeglasses were talked up in *Vogue*, *Life*, and different magazines. I had "revolutionized" the eye-wear industry, and orders poured in. I was pleased, but the novelty of being in business soon wore off.

In my mixed up insides I would say to myself, "I'll show my father; he always thought I would starve to death if left to my own resources. I'll show my father." But then I'd say, "Your father is dead, you fool."

I had countless friends who admired me because I had made it on my own, with my talents and designs; but I felt I was worthless. I had no husband. That was a cardinal lack. I looked down on single women above thirty, and I was now thirty-two. My lover was very generous and gave me anything I asked for, but all I wanted was a husband with whom I could do ordinary things like going to a drugstore and buying toothpaste or aspirin. I was absorbed and tied to the bourgeois ideal; I looked enviously at the women who waddled by with their husbands, their arms securely locked in his, as they walked down the street, as he opened the taxi door and helped them in.

Marriage was my principle occupation. My talents and creative abilities were secondary and to be set aside if there was any conflict between them and marriage. A submissive wife was the character I cast for myself. I carried inside me the ideal of the woman who would die for her man. I listened in a hushed audience to Fannie Brice singing, "There never was a man just like my man, never was a man loved like he can. He beats me too . . . I always come back."

I was unable to appreciate all the good things I had; I longed for the things I didn't have. As I look back, I wonder why I didn't enjoy all the good things: two beautiful children, plenty of friends, plenty of money, plenty of success.

So what was ruling me? These twisted up ideas of what a woman should be, of what a woman should have. Number 1 in big letters: "A Man." No! More than that: "A Husband."

I continued my relationship with Mac, though with fewer and fewer hopes that he'd leave Adele to marry me. One day Bidge called me to say he'd been in Washington, D.C., and saw Mac kissing a woman in a taxi.

The political situation was getting worse, and it was clear that Roosevelt wanted to enter the war against Hitler. But there were too many people in the country who were isolationists, among them Charles Lindbergh, who was an idol of the people. Lindbergh had visited Germany and had been very well received there. They had shown him their armaments, and he was convinced that if we entered the war against them, we would be defeated.

He either didn't seem to know or to care about the atrocities that the Germans were committing. Many people believed, as perhaps he did, that the stories were all lies and propaganda to turn public opinion against the Germans. Because of this, Roosevelt could not risk pushing us into war and sending our men overseas.

But then Japan struck at Pearl Harbor, destroying half our fleet. I remember it was a Sunday afternoon, December 7th, and I was at a cocktail party at the home of an artist friend. We heard the strong voice of Roosevelt over the radio: "This is a day that will live in infamy." It sent a shudder through all of us.

We declared war on the Japanese, and as the Japanese and Germans were allies, the Germans declared war on us. Thus fate played into Roosevelt's hands, and he did turn on the Germans.

All the men I knew now had an active part to

play. Ben ended up in the Air Force. Lester started training as a bombardier. And, of course, Mac was in Washington working for Hillman. The whole country was swept by a wave of patriotism.

The work time for Mac to be away from New York was Monday through Friday and home for weekends. He asked me if I would go to Washington one day a week—Tuesday or Wednesday—to see him. I agreed. And this went on for a year. But my nervousness returned. The panic grew in me. Coming home on the plane once, I felt a desire to scream. More than a desire—a conviction that I would scream.

I felt myself trembling and rang for the stewardess.

"Could I have a glass of water," I asked. She brought me some. I drank the water slowly, sip by sip and the panic passed. But I decided no more trips to Washington. It was too risky; I feared loss of control.

There was a fear that the Germans would bomb New York. I became an air raid warden. The man who recruited me had a hard steely face. "You know what would happen to you if there were an air raid? You would be blown to shreds." I wondered what pleasure he was getting in telling me this.

My beat was patrolling three or four blocks in the neighborhood of my apartment. I went to a class twice a week to be instructed on what to do in the event of an air raid. I think sometimes that they gave us the wrong class and that it was more a class in first aid. There was a section on how to treat snake bites. This made a lot of us laugh, including the instructor who was a young policeman.

Out on the sidewalk, I used to think, "God help New York if they are depending on me."

One memorable evening, I and another warden received a shower of water that I could see was coming from my apartment on the fourteenth floor. I said, "I'll go and do something about those horrible kids." I did not admit they were mine. When I got to my apartment, I found that the superintendent was already there. He said to me, "If you don't spank these kids, I will."

Denis, with his usual flair for taking charge, went into the bathroom and came out with a brush. "Sit down, Ma. You can start spanking me."

At least they didn't do it again.

Yorkville where I lived, was a section of New York City that was primarily inhabited by Germans and Jews. It had bars where there was all-night singing of German folk songs. A single piano, around it were groups of people with beer mugs and bellies.

The Jewish merchants had small family stores where you could buy the things you had forgotten to buy on your weekly shopping trips. As the time progressed and the news from Germany and Hitler became more threatening, the Jewish stores began boarding up their windows at night, and when you passed the bars the Germans were singing "Deutschland Uber Alles." It was struggle in miniature that reflected the picture of the world that came over the radio and in the newspaper.

People in the streets had a worried and tense look, and while I lived two or more blocks away from the center of Yorkville, the security in and around my building was also tightened. And although the boys were growing up, I didn't feel it was safe to have them walk to school, so I would drive them every day in the car.

Summertime came, and we rented a little house in the country on the beach. One morning I went to the window and heard our house guests talking and laughing below. I yelled down, "What's all the excitement?" They waved a newspaper and said yelling, "Hitler has attacked Russia!"

I can still feel the song of thanksgiving that rose within me. "Now, we will have a chance. We will win the war! What a fool Hitler is, after all!" Hadn't he read history well enough not to make the same mistake that Napoleon had made that ended in his defeat? All those men freezing to death on the snow-covered steppes? Russia was not a country to be conquered; it was just too big.

It has never been clear to me why Hitler made this decision to attack Russia. However, one explanation became clear when Hess, one of Hitler's close advisors, flew to England to ask them to join with Hitler to fight Russian communism. England refused and Hitler was forced to battle alone. Hess, in fact, was taken prisoner by the British, and was later imprisoned for life.

I believe that on the outer crust of our

psychological being we reflect and respond to the news and radio. We hear of the happenings in the world around us in some deep center of our beings. Every time we hear of a monstrous cruel act, a throb goes through us and our balance and sanity are stressed.

My own personal life and balance was not good. To me, the foundation seemed rotten because of my affair with Mac.

My mother was a good but unsophisticated woman who had never approved of the affair, and I came to dread going to see her because her theme song to me was: "Break it off, break it off."

My aunt, who lived with her, was much more sophisticated. "Many women in Europe," she would say, "live happily as a mistress to a good man. It is possible. Just try to enjoy your life. Don't worry so much."

She was right. But right doesn't mean possible. So I continued to nag at myself. I thought my only satisfactory relationship with Mac would be if we were married.

At one point in our relationship, he left Adele and went to live in a hotel. In those few days, his treatment of me began to change. Instead of my being perfect, he began to make sounds like, "The coffee is no good. Is it fresh? My sheets aren't pressed as they should be." He began to sound like a husband instead of a lover, and I began to clue in to how being married might change the idyllic tone of the relationship. But still I was not happy. I felt degraded being a mistress, a sexual object, and I felt full of guilt and anger at myself for participating in behavior that was causing so much pain to his wife, whom I basically admired and considered a good person who did not deserve this kind of humiliation.

I think Mac felt that he was doing the right thing, satisfying his sexual needs but not abandoning Adele. He told me sad stories of how she was suffering and how she had offered for him to have an affair with her cousin, an attractive, sexy-looking blonde who would satisfy his needs and not betray Adele.

So I went around and around in what to me seemed to be an unsolvable mess.

Bodies respond: I had hideous headaches. I would come home from the office, lie down on the bed, and wonder what I could do to stop the banging in my head. I came across a book called *Release from Nervous Tension* that taught how to relax oneself muscle by muscle, beginning at your head and gradually working down to your feet.

It helped, it helped. It taught me to *concentrate* on each small portion of my body, and I suppose it diverted me from the problems of my relationship with Mac.

I didn't seem to have the strength to break away since I was dependent on Mac to help me make all the decisions in living: for the children, for my business, for my future plans.

Fortunately I had friends—and my circle of people was varied and interesting. Ben Edwards was my best friend. At that time, he was a homosexual—although later in his life he became bisexual and married and had two children—so there was no question of sexual involvement between us. We were both artists and on the same beam, we were completely empathic. Except for the time I spent with Mac and my children, I was with Ben.

He also loved people as I did and so we invited a constant stream of different people to the house.

My other close friend, next after Ben, was Iris Whitney. She would classify as a high-grade call girl. Her male friends were all upper crust and it was nothing for them to leave a thousand dollar bill in an envelope for her.

She was very beautiful and had a lighthearted gaiety about her that changed the color of the world around her.

She lived in an apartment with high ceilings off Washington Square.

Once Ben and I dropped in to see her without calling first, and there were four good looking young men seated around her looking as though they were waiting for something to happen.

One of them pointed to me, and Iris put her hands up to her face, shaking her head, laughing, and saying, "No, no, no."

We took the hint and left.

New York was wonderful in those days: the theater and Broadway were jammed with shows, and the tickets all priced at five and six dollars. Once or twice a week we would go downtown and pick out a show and walk in.

Sometimes we would get on a ferry boat and go to Staten Island and look in wonder at the skyline of New York slipping behind us.

I had a friend who was the chief of the Prison Island on the east side. We used to go to lunch there, and his Trustee prisoners would cook and serve it to us.

Sometimes I would ask, "What is he in for?" The chief would say of a solid, nice-looking man, "Oh, he killed his wife." I didn't want to look at him then; I'd feel squeamish.

When we'd walked past the cells, sometimes the catcalls were frightening. But my friend the chief would yell out, "Shut up," and complete silence would follow.

I admired him for his fearless authority.

I continued to work in my office and make Harlequin glasses. A cartoon appeared, though, in *The New Yorker*—a woman throwing away her glasses because the tilted eyes looked too Japanese. There was also a shortage of materials for making anything that did not contribute to the war effort. So production slowed down, and my time at the office decreased. I was losing interest anyway. It had been fun for awhile, but it became boring and repetitious.

My life with Mac was also becoming boring and repetitious.

But letters from Eric were more cheerful. He had tested negative and was resuming his work as an intern. It looked as though if he remained negative he could return.

One evening coming home from the office, I opened the front door and heard the piano being played. I thought unrealistically, "Oh, if that were only Eric!"

I walked up the staircase slowly, and there was a young man seated and playing. He stopped when he saw me, and he had a very sweet, hesitant smile. His gesture had a naturalness and spontaneity about it, and his face, unusual in an adult, a kind of innocence that I used to note in the faces of Renaissance angels, a face that had always aroused in me a feeling of tenderness. I noticed now he wore a hearing aid—a "Renaissance angel with a hearing aid," I thought. "Poor guy—to be a musician and deaf. Almost like being a sculptor and blind."

"I hope I didn't startle you," he said, " but Nell dropped me off here. She had some errands to do, and she wanted me to meet you."

Nell was a good friend, an actress whose actor husband, Erford Gage, was in the Army, stationed in the Pacific.

"Nell talks so much about you," he said, and as he spoke he leaned forward and cupped his hand around his ear. "I'm deaf," he said, "and you may have to talk a little louder, although I am pretty good at reading lips."

I had felt an immediate and strong draw towards him. He was very good looking in a "help me I'm in trouble" sort of way. And when he raised his face up in a hopeful gesture of trying to hear what I was saying, I was won over to his side. "I'll help you, I'll help you," I said inside of myself. And to him I said, "I am so glad you came. It's been a long time since anyone played this piano."

"Oh, would you like it if I played some more?"

"Yes, I would."

I sat on the bench beside him and watched his hands as they travelled with lightness and precision over the keys. I felt I was listening to an extraordinary musician.

My body close to his, I followed as he played, and inside of me, I followed and moved with the sounds. We were knit together by the warmth of our bodies and the sound of the music as though a magic net had been slipped over us to hold us together.

It had always been so for me with music. It wasn't that I was a musical expert in any way. I couldn't even distinguish Strauss from Mozart, Haydn from Handel, Beethoven from Bach. In my own field of art and art graphics, I could identify with hardly a glance a Pissaro from a Bonnard, Roualt, van Gogh; a da Vinci drawing from a Dali, Jasper Jones, Warhol. It was as easy as telling asparagus from an artichoke.

But when it came to music it was as though I had walked over a bridge into a dark pool of emotion that left words and intellectual reasoning behind and that made me feel complete, overwhelmed, and surrounded.

If at that moment I could have chosen a time to be frozen in eternity, I would have chosen that moment. It seemed part of the same moment when later that evening he put his arms around me and we lay side by side on the couch and expressed our feelings.

He played popular music from musical comedies and then he played some of his own music that he had composed. It was very romantic music, and he began singing the lyrics in a low but not unattractive way.

"Who writes your lyrics?" I asked.

"A friend of mine called Alex. We're hoping to get them into a Broadway show. We play for different producers. Alex is homosexual—do you mind that?"

"No, not at all. If he writes good lyrics that's all that matters."

I soon learned to talk to him, not loudly but by pronouncing every word clearly and moving my lips so that it helped him read them even when he couldn't hear.

"Would you like a drink?" I asked.

"That would be nice."

I went to the kitchen. Christina had been standing listening to the piano. She seemed happy that something nice was happening in the house.

"Would you make us some martinis and some good little things to eat?"

"Of course," she said, and her kind face shone.

Pretty soon we were drinking martinis, and I noticed that he drank them in a hurry and was always ready for more. It crossed my mind that he might be a boozer.

The doorbell rang, and Nell came skipping up the stairs. She was beautiful and her straight blond hair covered half her face, outlining her delicate profile. I had done a few portraits of her. She greeted me warmly and said, "So you know Billie now."

I realized that I didn't know his name, although

I felt I knew him.

Billie Provost.

"Let's all have dinner," I said.

I found Billie very attractive physically, and after meeting him, I went through many restless days. I knew I wanted to make love with him, and finally after a week, he called. I invited him over.

We talked about his music, he played the piano and sang, we drank martinis, and we found ourselves in bed.

And so my friendship with Billie started. And a love affair (or let us say a sex affair) went with it.

Lying alone in my bed that night, under the cool sheets, I slipped into the darkness, filled with glorious hopes and promises for the future.

The speed with which our "rapport" was established may have been, in part, due to the tedium of my long affair with a married man, emasculated as I was by the affair's limitations, the constricted boundaries of the relationship. I'd find myself wishing to do something simple, domestic, sometimes even prosaic like going to the drugstore and buying talcum powder, a toothbrush, an evening paper instead of long-stemmed red roses, opera tickets, sex, and caviar, and then out into the night and back to his wife.

I had made a habit of compartmentalizing my life. There was my work at Harlequin.

That was one compartment. Then there was my social life with good pals: weekends tramping in the country and swing dancing in Harlem.

In the third compartment went my long-standing affair with Mac, which was becoming less and less satisfactory.

Now I had a chance to get involved with someone who needed me, to keep and care for someone who elicited my sympathy, admiration, appreciation.

Perhaps it was this that laid the ground for my surge of feeling for Billie so that a few hours of music, sex, and booze and a feeling of sadness, pity, and identity with the black hearing aid attached to the back of his ear had laid the strong terrain for at least the limited time that I knew I would spend with him.

Billie picked me up the next day at the Design Center where I worked and said we were to meet Alex at my apartment: "Alex, you know, who writes my lyrics. We're working on a musical play, almost completed."

I anticipated the meeting with Alex, expecting I'd like him and wanting him to like me. I wanted to be part of everything that touched Billie.

The setting sun glistened on the sidewalk, and I felt such a rush of happiness. Why, I wondered, should the sight of sun glistening on a sidewalk arouse in me such joy? But it had always been so—joy coming at unexpected and unheralded moments, usually connected with the sun: like climbing out of the pool after swimming and looking behind me at the water below as I slipped my foot out and watched the drops fall from it. "A glistening fish in the sun." Where had I read that phrase? Always these phrases darting through my mind. Bad ones too: read or invented. In bad situations, I would sometimes think, "I am a lamb being led to the slaughter" or "I am a turkey on a platter, being offered up to be eaten."

When I met Alex, I got my first premonition that perhaps the future was not going follow my expectations.

Alex sat in my winged chair, his hands folded carefully, one over the other. He had the sharp pointed nose and black piercing eyes of a hunting dog. He saw his prey and was sniffing his way towards it. He rose imperiously and held out his hand for me to take. It was cold and strong and bony—as though it had a capacity to be precise and hurtful when necessary. He peered down at me, making me feel—as he always would do—that I was standing several steps below him. I knew he was judging me, and I felt I could read his thoughts: "Nice-looking girl—not a beauty, but attractive—and self-supporting, a reputation as a very talented designer. Her apartment is supposed to be outstanding—a good place for us to entertain in: that should be a help. Better than the other girls that Billie brings around—pretty, helpless, like wet kittens, coming in out of the rain."

"Billie has a new friend," he said, and I felt he was seeing right through me. "I hope I have, too."

"I'm sure we'll be friends," I answered and pulled my hand away, saying to myself, "Liar, liar."

He was witty and hard, sharp and piercing, and untrustworthy, I felt, but talented and good for Billie, and that was all that counted.

"I think you can be of great help to Billie," he

said. "You look sensible and reliable. He needs someone like you."

Billie went into the kitchen to make drinks.

"How long have you known him?"

"Part of a week," I answered.

"Not long enough, I guess, to know that he has a drinking problem . . . . "

We were silent for a moment before he continued. "Do you think you can at least help to replace booze in his life?"

"I don't know," I said.

"None of the other girls did," he said.

All my happiness disappeared.

The three of us were always together. Did we like each other? Love each other? Just want to use each other? All those things? We all wanted to be famous, and we lived in that great, overwhelming metropolis called New York City, so most of the time we were just groping our way, acting as though we knew what it was all about, what it would all add up to. We looked around, and everyone else seemed to know what they were up to. Everyone else seemed to move with an assured air. Maybe they were all just faking it, too.

And that's how we got by—faking it—at least part of the time. But a part of the time, we all felt as though we were in small dark dungeons all alone and scared. That was the time when one of us would reach for the booze, grab the telephone, say: "come on over" or "listen to this tune I just wrote" or "hey, I've got the lyric to go with it"—

Many nights found us at 10:30 p.m., finding our

way to one of the smaller nightclubs around 52nd
Street. They were usually two or three steps down
from the street, a basement to be exact, where
fellow musicians were beating it out, and in those
settings Billie was a big star. We'd walk in, and the
players would stop and greet us and lead Billie
over to the piano. I'd trail behind, feeling proud
and somewhat possessive—he was my guy.

People would cluster around Billie, and Alex
would sing his lyrics, and the drummer would
make the place vibrate with the sound of his
drums, and the silky smooth black singer named
Julie would drape herself around Billie's neck.
Later he would say, "She's a romantic bitch," and I
would be left with a feeling of jealousy and a
question: "Has he ever been with her? Is he still?"

And then the place was thundering with music
and rhythm and passion and excitement, and I'd
be seated at a small table near the piano with a
drink in front of me.

At dawn we'd find ourselves out on the cool blue
sidewalks, going back home to his or my
apartment, finishing the night wrapped around
each other.

Getting up and going to work the next morning
was like walking through a wet fog.

There were the nights when I needed help to get
him home and one of the guys would come with me
and help to lay him on the bed, wave a friendly
hand, and exit.

"You're looking beat, Tina," I began to hear at
the office.

"I'm feeling beat," I'd say, meaning it.

He was a kid, twenty-three-years old and nine years younger than I. I entered into his world ignorant but learned fast of agents, auditions, night-playing musicians, girl singers in nightclubs, people all looking for the "big break."

My own occupation seemed much more solid, much less ethereal, something you could see, touch, and feel—far from the atmosphere of the rooms filled with sounds of music and excitement where I seemed to be carried away on the winds of feeling and sound.

Coming out into the early hours of the morning, I would feel transported, overwhelmed by the way Billie was looked upon by his fellow musicians—the great composer of ballads—the way he was applauded and idolized by the audience.

We had a lot of fun together.

One afternoon sticks out in my memory. Billie and I had driven to the country to get away from the concrete and lack of trees or green in New York. We left the car on the side of a dirt road and started walking. It was spring and the smell of the grass and the flowers beginning to bloom was intoxicating to us after the grayness of the city. Suddenly the sky grew dark and there was a rumble of thunder and the rain poured down on us hard and straight. We were ready to run, but we were pretty far away from the car, and we thought hopefully that there might be a house that could give us shelter. We started running and could see in the distance a long low building. As we approached, we could make out a cross on the roof. I turned to Billie: "It looks like some kind of convent."

"Well, maybe we struck it lucky and as good Christians they'll give us shelter." We were soaking wet, but it seemed like a lot of fun.

We approached the building and knocked on the big wooden door. A few seconds later it was opened, and a sister in her long black dress, her face framed in her nun's headdress said, "Come in, my children."

We didn't want to get everything wet, and we went to a portal near the house to wipe off some of the rain. Then we came back and went through the open door. We found ourselves in a long room with a stained glass window at the end that filtered in a soft yellow and blue light. There was a piano in the middle of the room, and Billie walked towards it as though drawn by a magnet. He sat down and started to play. I looked at the sister, and her face was smiling. Pretty soon other sisters came in and crowded around the piano.

The first sister said, "Look what the Lord has sent us—someone to make us beautiful music."

This scene was among the beautiful scenes I witnessed with Billie.

But there were the bad times, too. I was an older woman, and he admired beautiful young girls. In restaurants when they walked by, he would say, "Boy, there's a romantic bitch," which meant he wanted to have sex with her. I wasn't crazy about this, but I was lonely. No Eric. Mac was in Washington most of the time. Ben and Lester were in the army. "Beggars can't be choosers," I said to myself. But my friends didn't like him. "He doesn't appreciate you," Iris would say. "He's too immature. Get rid of him!"

Trying to hang on to everything. Holding on to Mac. Holding on to Billie. Having two men at the same time. Double dealing. Double loving. Oh, no. It won't do. If I see another penis, I'll puke. It's got to stop. Do they both trust me? Yes. No. Of course not.

Getting Billie out of the house on Friday nights when Mac comes from Washington.

"What is this?" Billie would say. "Does he come here on Friday nights to fuck you?"

"Of course not," I'd answer, very prim and proper. "How can you think such a thing?"

But Friday nights became a terror.

"Call me, kid, when I can come back."

I dunno. I don't like this. And Saturday afternoon at the theatre, during intermission. "Sorry, Mac, I have to make a call." Out to a pay phone. Call Billie.

"Hi, honey. I'll be home later. After dinner." Back to Mac. Neither man is dumb. No one is asking questions.

When they meet finally, there is a dull, dumb silence, a silly giggle on my part.

What do I want? Neither one or both. This is awful. This can't go on—

I tell my mother. She tells me to clean up my act. "You're not made for this sort of thing."

"No," I cry, "all I want is a nice, simple life, a nice, simple husband, my two kids, everything happy and simple."

These late hours, nightclubs, going to work strung out.

Where is my self-respect? Gone down the drain.

They don't love me. I don't love them.

Cross and double cross. I'd like to go to sleep and forget the whole bloody thing.

I soon found out that Billie's favorite companion in his loneliness and fear was Booze. His deafness cast him into a lonely world, and he had a great fear of losing his hearing completely and not being able to hear his own or anyone else's music. He'd feel most alone at parties when the chatter of people surrounded him like a wave of unknown sound. Then he was never without a glass in his hand, and by the end of the evening, he would be lying on the floor or on the couch snoring loudly. People would leave and cast pitying glances at him.

The days went into weeks and more and more of them seemed to end up with Billie passing out and with me rolling him over and covering him with a blanket. The lighthearted fun times seemed to be draining away and being replaced by the lost days of haze and alcohol and sullen anger.

I knew music poured out of Billie—as long as it was not too mixed up with booze—so I began hiding all the bottles in my apartment. But he would arrive with his own bottle. Still he would work three to four hours a day; the musical was almost finished, and he and Alex were waiting for that call.

Alex insisted that once success came, Billie would sober up, that his drinking was just his depression at the long struggle. I knew what I had known from the beginning—alcohol would be a companion of Billie's, meaningful and maybe inseparable, an overshadowing companion that would tinge and color everything else. He had chosen. His world was deafness, music, and booze.

I was assigned my role: right under booze— or maybe money. Music, booze, money and me—in that order. Music (deafness booze) money and me to mitigate the loneliness of being deaf, the reality that he was getting progressively deafer, the fear that one day he would no longer hear at all—not even his own music. Money: just enough to get by, playing in sleazy night clubs sustained by people holding glasses in their hands and giving him admiration and affection, albeit temporary.

I wanted to be his solace, his companion, his helper, but he had already spoken for Booze to be all those things.

I started feeling a missionary zeal in trying to keep him from drinking, to save a great talent from destruction. I started substituting hard drinks with beer, which seemed less damaging; agreeing with him that tomorrow he would "go on the wagon." And I began trying to cover for him when he missed appointments.

I had a message service on my telephone, and Billie had asked if he could give out my number so people could call and leave him messages. I'd agreed. How many times was I greeted by Alex's angry messages saying something like: "Where the hell have you been? I stayed in Schultz's office waiting for you until he threw me out." I began dreading getting the messages when I came home at night.

When I'd relay Alex's messages, Billie would carelessly wave his hand and say, "He'll get over it. Poor Alex, he needs me more than I need him."

I began to realize that Billie never had had any real feeling for me, never had been interested in my work. "I's okay," he would say. "Doing fine."

It was the hours of music, sex, and magic that held me.

Somehow word was getting around that this deaf kid could write some cool music.

And then the long awaited call came—*the* Desmond Jones had heard about Billie Provost and wanted to hear his music.

Desmond Jones—a famous producer of Broadway plays—invited Billie up to his apartment for an audition. It was a sign in the music community that something great could happen.

Maybe this would be the day; maybe Alex was right: maybe success would make Billie turn away from Booze.

I applied my makeup carefully. I wanted to look as attractive as I could--not that the way I looked would affect the result of the audition. Still, it could add a little to the ambience of the hour.

I arrived a few minutes late and followed Billie and Alex up in the elevator of the plush Park Avenue building. We found ourselves on the twelfth floor and being greeted at the door by Mrs. Desmond Jones. She was graceful and tall and exquisitely dressed in a Fortuny gown of a thousand small pleats that clung to her figure.

"I like to encourage young composers," she said as she met us at the door. She led us in. "Desmond will be down in a minute."

Everything in the room appeared to be luminous gray—even the design on the curtains and couches slipped from satin smooth to shiny to resembling slabs of wood that had been tempered gray by the sea. The room was an evocation of sea and sand and nature at its most delicate and exquisite. I feared that even the smallest finger placed on a cushion might leave a mark and destroy its surface. It was clear that in such a room, it would be necessary to walk with care, respect, and even reverence for its exquisite delicacy.

I had been praying that Billie was sober. Earlier Alex had been saying to me, "If that bastard isn't sober, I'm going to kill him. This is our big chance if we can make it." But I knew as soon as I'd seen Billie that it wasn't going to be good. His eyes and head moved in a slow, uncontrolled way. "Alex," I wanted to scream, "let's call it off." But Alex with a firm step was following Mrs. Jones and then gracefully sliding onto the couch beside her. Billie stood with his hand to his earphone, leaning slightly forward trying to catch their words. Mrs. Jones looked towards him, as though with pity and understanding for his deafness. She reached out and patted his hand reassuringly.

Billie and Alex went to the piano. I sat close to Mrs. Jones. Alex announced the title of the musical. "Our first," he said, and there was a mincing smirk about him that came on when he wanted to make a good impression. God, I wish he wouldn't do that, I thought, it makes him seem so subservient and so obviously homosexual.

Desmond Jones slipped in almost unnoticed. He, too, was dressed in tones of gray and wore a large satin cravat with a pearl stickpin in its folds. He was dark and delicately handsome and clearly of the same third sex as Alex, so, I thought, perhaps he won't mind. He crossed his fashionably clothed pearl gray trouser legs and leaned back in his chair.

When Billie sat down to play, I found myself

looking at his back and loving it, and as his hands touched the keys, the memory of our first meeting came flooding back. So much promise.

I looked at the straight figure of Alex, his hands folded in front of him as he prepared to sing out as best he could his treasured lyrics. His eyes were on Billie as he struck the first note.

At first it seemed to be all right, but then Billie's fingers began sliding and abruptly he came crashing down on the keys. I knew it would only be a matter of seconds and he would lose control and it would be all over. Their long waited for chance would have slipped away. Please God, I thought, don't let him vomit; if I'm never granted another prayer as long as I live let this be granted. But Billie started throwing up on the pearl gray carpet. I felt a trembling go all through me. Desmond Jones sprang to his feet. Mrs. Jones sat rigid in her chair. Alex's mouth stayed open, biting on the lyrics he had written; then the pointed end of his nose turned red with anger. I moved fast towards Billie and tried to hold him straight up while Alex half led, half carried him to the door. Ooze dripped slowly out of Billie's mouth and onto his suit and touched Alex's suit in places.

I turned and saw Mrs. Jones was looking at me. "I'm sorry, so sorry," I said. "He's been under a terrible strain. Please forgive us, and thank you for your time."

Mrs. Jones came forward and took my hand between both of hers. "A word of advice I would like to give you: there are some situations to which there is only one solution. If you want to survive, just walk away, and don't look back. He is too troubled a young man."

I stood silently until the elevator came up, and when the door opened, Alex pushed Billie in.

Alex was the first out downstairs. A taxi pulled up and he dumped Billie in, then stepped back. "Get in," he said to me. "He's all yours now." He turned and walked down the avenue. I could feel him washing his hands of the whole mess.

When we got to my apartment, the doorman helped me get Billie out of the taxi, into the elevator, and upstairs. We took him into the study and laid him on the couch where he dropped into the deep slumber of alcohol. I stood looking at him and felt as though I were staring at the corpse of our relationship.

I knew I never wanted to touch him again.

The fallen angel.

I went to my room, and soon I was asleep in my bed. The next morning I got up and looked at my image in the mirror. It looked pale, drawn with lines of anxiety etched on.

You're going to have to decide soon, I said to my reflection. Okay, so Billie is a talented man, a wonderful musician, sexy as hell, beautiful to look at, fun to be with—but he has a drinking problem. You can't go on living with a drunk and survive—no matter how talented he is, no matter how much you may love and care for him. Ultimately, you have yourself, you have your own talent to think about, your own desire to live and prosper.

There was only one thing to do now: What Mrs. Desmond Jones had said. "Walk away and don't look back." I offered him a ticket to Hollywood, and he accepted and went. He called me once or twice, but I never saw him again.

17

Finally in 1942, the moment I'd been waiting for arrived. I got a letter from Eric: "I am testing negative. Shall I come back?"

My answer was "YES, YES, YES."

When he got back, he looked the same, though a little older and a little more tired and worn. But other than that he hadn't changed, and the intervening years disappeared. It was as though he had never left. I wasn't the only one delighted with his return. Denis and Terry—Terry especially—were glad to see Eric again.

Springtime is a good time in New York. We used to go and sit on the benches in Central Park and have a pleasant time watching the city go by. Summer is not so nice, and Eric had saved up enough money from his salary to rent a house for the season. He wanted to find a place on a lake so we could rent a boat and go sailing. He loved to sail, and it had been so many years since his early carefree days in Austria when he'd been able to do it. Eric promised to teach me how, and I was looking forward to living again.

We wrote and found a house in New Hampshire. Our plan was to have the kids go to camp and when it was over to come to New Hampshire and spend the rest of the summer with us.

We had our tickets for the train and a picnic basket filled with sandwiches and cold drinks to eat on the way up. Sitting next to him, I watched his face, so kind and gentle, and his beautiful hands as he held the basket on his lap. My love for him had never disappeared, and I vowed to love and keep him as long as we were both alive.

The lady who rented the house was waiting for us. "Are you brother and sister?" she asked. When I said, "No, we're engaged," I thought her face fell in disappointment. I think she was interested in Eric herself.

We hadn't talked about getting married, but we sort of assumed that we would. "We have to look for a judge," I said. We did, but it was a very small town and there was no judge. But the postmaster, a wispy old man, said that he could marry us. We set a date.

Eric wore a tan linen suit, and I asked him if it was all right if I got married in my shorts. I was always most happy and comfortable wearing shorts. Eric laughed and answered, "I will marry you in any outfit you choose to wear."

We both laughed happily.

We were married in the postmaster's house on the edge of the woods with his daughter as our witness. His wife, almost as old as he, played the wedding march on their battered piano. The postmaster got my name all wrong: He called me Alpina Sinders. At least Eric's was easier for him:

he'd changed it from Barasch to Barrett when he'd become a citizen.

Eric and I had brought a bottle of champagne, and we sat with the postmaster and his family for an hour or so and finished up the whole bottle. They were very sweet people, and I could not imagine having anyone nicer at our wedding.

They were very curious about us, especially about Eric. The war and Hitler seemed very far away in New Hampshire, but they seemed to understand and were sympathetic.

When we left their house, we went down to the lake and found a fifty-five-foot sailboat that was for rent. The lake was very choppy, and despite Eric's skill, we capsized and found ourselves swimming. People in a motorboat came by and pulled us out of the water and put the sailboat back on course. Wet, laughing, and happy we arrived back at the house and spent our first married night.

I wrote to Mac to tell him, and he wrote back, saying he wasn't surprised really and that he would be my friend forever. When I received the letter, I cried; but I think I cried him out of my system, and I never thought much about him after that.

Our little house was on the lake, and we passed our time swimming, sailing, walking, talking, cooking. We felt very domestic, and Eric was teaching me how to cook Viennese dinners. He missed the food from Vienna as he'd missed the sailing. I think he was happiest when he was on the water. It was the first vacation Eric had had in years, and it was great to see him so happy.

Camp ended, and we called for Denis and Terry at the train stop. The first thing Terry asked was "Is my name going to be Barrett now?" I laughed and said, "No. You will always be Sanders."

Denis was ill with a light fever. He coughed all night. "Oh God," I thought. "He has T.B., and everyone will think that he got it from Eric." The long night finally passed, and in the morning I called the local hospital fifty miles away. They sent an ambulance. I went with Denis and left Eric and Terry at the house.

Denis was diagnosed as having viral pneumonia, but after a week he was declared sufficiently well to come home. "Thank you, God," I said over and over again. Of course, I realized that he could not possibly have gotten T.B. from Eric and that it had been a completely unreasonable fear. I still worried about Eric's having T.B., though, and when he would sometimes cough in the night, my heart would sink.

We had a nice two weeks remaining with the boys, and then we packed up and went back to the city.

The first winter that Eric and I were married was a very heavy winter in New York, tremendous snow storms and severe cold. Eric wasn't quite well; he was still pretty delicate. I would think, "If only I could hold out my arms and stop the snow from falling." But the next best thing was to move.

After leaving Colorado Springs, Eric had been to California for a short internship, and there he had a great friend, Anatole Murad, who was an economist and a professor at USC. It was Anatole's brother who, though a member of the Nazi party, had hidden Eric in Austria when he was in danger of being taken by the Nazis and sent to a concentration camp. Anatole's brother had also risked his own life by taking Eric to the airport so he could get to the U.S.

That winter, we received a letter from Anatole, urging us to come to California where the climate was mild with sunshine and blue skies every day.

Eric thought it was a good idea: "California is so beautiful. Why don't we move there?"

It sounded like a good idea to me. I was just a little afraid to tell Bidge because I didn't know if he would object. Still I had the right to take the boys with me, and Eric's health was too fragile to fool with. "Look," I said to the boys. "Don't tell Daddy we are going to California." I hadn't told my sons that we were moving, only that we were going on a trip. They agreed not to tell their father.

Anatole said he'd find us a house so that we wouldn't have to house-hunt from a hotel. He did find one on Bedford Drive in Beverly Hills.

Moving meant that I had to leave my Harlequin business in the hands of my partner, André Boutemy. I went into the office. I felt bad about leaving the people who worked for me, for leaving behind all that I had built up through all the effort and hard work. I looked around me at the signs of my success—my staff, the penthouse office. I felt sad. But Eric was the important person for me now, and whatever price I had to pay to help make him well, I would pay. I decided I could open another office in California.

We went on a train because no one used planes so much in those days. The kids were quite excited and happy. They always loved new adventures. In Chicago, Bidge's sister, Janet, met the train so we could have a little visit. It was March and still very cold and blustery. The sky was gray and snow-filled.

After four days on the train, we reached California, and it was like a miracle. The sky was blue. The sun was shining.

Anatole met us at the station. He was a slender, attractive man, and he seemed so glad to see Eric. "I hope the house I rented for you is okay. They say Greta Garbo used to live in it. Anyhow, I only took it for four months to give you time to find something you want."

It was a beautiful house on a good street in Beverly Hills, but it was large and gloomy, and it didn't have what I wanted most—a swimming pool. It had a little pond out in the garden, but that wasn't enough.

It was a nice house, though, and a big house—sort of grand in an oppressive way. It had large rooms: the master bedroom must have been twenty feet long and the master bathroom was of equal size.

Between the bedroom and the room where Denis and Terry slept, there was a nice sunny room that overlooked the garden: that's where we put Eric. He and I never slept in the same bedroom, in case Eric became reinfected with T.B.

There was a porch off Eric's room, and that's

where we spent a lot of our time.

In Los Angeles, I not only opened an office for Harlequin, I started a little factory, making sunglasses. It was quite a big space—about 3,000 square feet—a big space with quite a lot of workers. There were black workers and white workers, and there were problems between them. The white workers didn't want the black workers to use their restrooms, so I told the blacks they could use mine. That didn't make the whites happy.

For a long time, Anatole was our only friend. He would come every day after his work to sit and talk with us. He was a brilliant, fascinating man who was also a great tennis player. He had a lovely wife and a son, and they lived in a small house in Santa Monica with a big tennis court that had belonged to a tennis champion. We used to visit them every Sunday.

Anatole was trying to get his citizenship, but he was having a very hard time. He was in a real bind because if he couldn't get his citizenship, the university would not keep him. Finally, it was discovered that during one of his interviews at the immigration office, the typist had typed "all we communists" when Anatole had said "all we economists." For a long time, he could not talk them out of their belief that he was a communist, which in those days was equivalent to saying he was a murderer.

Finally after many interviews, he was granted his citizenship.

My friend Nell who'd introduced me to Billie had moved out to California because her husband, Erford Gage, was in the army in the Pacific. In 1945, Roosevelt died, and a few days later we heard that Erford had been killed. We took Nell with us that Sunday out to Santa Monica to Anatole's house on the tennis court. She formed a strong attachment to Eric and wanted to drive him back to our house, but I objected because she was in no condition to drive anybody.

I worried about Eric because he was never really cured. And I was always worried about contagion for the kids and for me. And Eric was worried, too. We had an apparatus to disinfect his sheets, towels, clothes. We were very careful. Luckily, nothing happened.

Eric was never very well. He tired easily and couldn't go out and walk much, so he stayed in the house a lot and played the piano. Because we were so new in California, we didn't know many people at that time. We met up with Nell, and she introduced us to a lot of people. One was Kate Blakely, who later became the mayor of Colorado Springs, strangely enough. She was a big, handsome, blonde girl.

After our lease was up, we decided we wanted to move because we didn't like the house very much. We went looking around for a house to buy or to rent, and we got a house high up in the Hollywood Hills on Davies Way that had a wonderful view of the whole city. And it had a swimming pool, which made me very happy because I love to swim. I've always had an affection for swimming pools. It was a fun house, and we had a good time there. Eric was in good health, and it was easy to enjoy life.

I wasn't happy with the Hollywood public schools, which I thought were terrible. Terry didn't like them either, but he was too young to go away to school. But when Denis said, "How can I study with all those beautiful blondes all around me?" I thought that it was time for him to go to a good school. So I looked for a private school, and it was a question of Thacher or Cate. The funny part is that if the boys had gone to Thacher, Terry would have met his future wife at Thacher. But I chose Cate, a boarding school near Santa Barbara. Denis went to Cate, and Terry stayed home.

In August 1945, the atom bomb was dropped and the war ended.

After my friend Ben Edwards was discharged from the army, he came to visit. He was very sad and very disoriented. He wanted to live with us, but I knew that wasn't possible. It was too hard on Eric. Even though my relationship with Ben had always been platonic, we were very close. At night he'd come into the bedroom; one night he was there at one in the morning. Eric came in and saw us; he turned around quickly and left, but I could see he wasn't happy about it. So I said to Ben, "I think you have to go." That was a big shock to him, but he did go back to New York.

Each day I went to my office in Hollywood where

I promoted my Harlequin glasses. One day, two big thug-looking guys came and said, "Well, Miss, how are you getting along?"

I said, "I think I'm getting along all right."

"Well, we think you need a little protection. Don't you?"

"No. Why do I need that?" I wasn't completely stupid; I knew what they were talking about. They said, "Well, you know, someone could break your windows, or who knows what could happen. We're willing to help you out."

I told them I didn't think I needed their help, but they said, "We'll come back again."

That sort of scared me.

Shortly after that, I found out the sunglasses were made of nitrate—a highly flammable substance—and I thought, Well, I don't really like running a factory. I don't like clocking people in and clocking them out, doing the production, getting the salesmen. The whole thing just didn't appeal to me. To compound it, Eric's health had actually gotten worse, and he wasn't happy about my going to the office every day.

So I decided to close my California factory and to sell Harlequin in New York. Harlequin had been a whole new experience for me, and for awhile, I enjoyed it—and for six years, I made a good bunch of money. But I wanted to move on to other things. I decided it was time to study fine arts and to start painting seriously.

I enrolled in the famous Jepson School of Art in Los Angeles. Many of my classmates were World

War II veterans whom the government had granted free tuition for two years after their service. So they were a very interesting group, much more so than the usual nineteen-year-olds who would go to art school.

Rico Le Brun was the star teacher. He had been a graphic artist in New York and in California, but then he changed to fine art. He made extraordinary drawings pushing the technique way beyond what was usual. And he was always a spellbinding speaker who inspired the students to do their utmost not to disappoint him. He was small, dark, and dynamic.

My teacher, Howard Warshaw, was his student, but was also a teacher at Jepson. Howard was almost le Brun's opposite—tall, heavy and ponderous with piercing blue eyes. He was very hard as a teacher. But he was a wonderful teacher unlike George Grosz, who wasn't a great teacher, but who was a great man. I think that's why I appreciated Grosz so much, but he never actually gave any instruction. He'd draw those wonderful old drawings on your board, but he didn't teach anything.

Warshaw was a very strict teacher—and perhaps a little sadistic, too. I remember working on a painting for two weeks. When he saw it, he took a rag, doused it in turpentine, and scrubbed out the whole painting. "All right," he said. "Now, start all over." And that happened more than once.

It would make me pretty furious, but I would obey. When I first started with him, he had said, "I don't care what you do on your own, but as my student you must do as I tell you. Only that way can you learn what I know." I'd accepted that. It was part of the deal. That was Howard. Grosz would never have done that. He was very tenderhearted.

18

After a year on Davies Way, we decided to buy a home. It took awhile, but we finally found a wonderful house in Coldwater Canyon. It belonged to the great English actor Aubrey Smith, who was eighty-five-years old at the time. His wife was afraid he would die, and she wanted a smaller place.

I fell in love with it. It was a really beautiful house— big and sprawling with a lovely garden. So we bought the house, and we put in a swimming pool.

We stayed in that house for seventeen years.

The house was on three acres. We inherited chickens from Aubrey Smith, and he'd given each of them the name of a famous movie star. They lived out back in cages, as the cement on the ground gave them rheumatism. They supplied us with eggs. Once we ate one of the chickens, and that was a really awful experience. I didn't eat chicken for years after that.

We had a beautiful shepherd dog and a donkey who used to come up on the terrace and look in the window asking to be let in.

We had so many animals there: We had foxes,

coyotes, and once a rattlesnake even came into the house. I called the mountain patrol, and they said, "Is there just one?"

I said "Yes, there's just one."

And they said, "Well if there's one, there'll be more."

That prospect didn't cheer me.

It took them forever to get there, but they finally did get the snake out of the house.

I took a room in the house as my studio and put a sign on the door: "Do not come in unless there's a catastrophe." I wanted to have three hours a day just to myself without interruption, and I really did work very hard. Howard Warshaw came once a week and taught me the techniques of drawing and painting: three packed hours. Sometimes his friend Billy Brice would come. Billy was Fanny Brice's son, and a painter who also taught at Jepson. Gradually I began painting bigger and bigger canvasses. My goal every year was to have a piece selected for the Los Angeles County Museum juried show. I did succeed each year, and there was a satisfaction in that as it was a tough show to get into. But I never particularly felt like competing in the art world; I wasn't working to get famous. It was something I did for myself: I just wanted to be a good painter. I love to paint, but I never thought I was a great painter. I am not and I never will be.

I painted for the joy of it—because it's what I love to do. For me, art is fun. I like to make things. I've always liked to make things. If I couldn't draw it and paint it, then I'd make a pillow or I'd make a quilt or I'd make something. I always had to make something, and I was always looking for ideas for projects. I wanted to use my art to enrich my life.

When I started out, they're weren't that many women painters around. Now it's so easy to be a woman and be a painter: You walk in a gallery, and they don't care if you're a woman or a man. But then the whole attitude was a woman painter should go back to the kitchen. It wasn't quite that bad when I was studying with Howard in the late 40s and the 50s, and he was always very supportive. I was very fond of him.

Howard emphasized techniques of glazing and underpainting. He made you do a tremendous amount of preparation before you would start a painting; he wasn't a spontaneous painter himself, very slow moving. I learned a lot from him about technique, color, drawing; but I think in a way he overtaught me. He sort of took the life out of my approach because he was so hard. It took me a long time to get rid of his influence and to paint my own way and do my own things.

I'm not sure what I feel about teaching art, but I do know I don't think a student should be so much under a master and working so much in his shadow as I was with Howard Warshaw. Sometimes I think the best way to teach art is to have students travel in Europe and see all the great art and make copies of the old masters: That way you learn other ways of painting and learn from the inside out that Rembrandt painted differently from the early Italians.

But I always liked to study; I always liked to

learn something new. I don't think I'm a good teacher, but I am a good student. I like learning. I like to learn something new every day. And studying with Howard was quite inspirational because he was a very, very brilliant man and we used to have wonderful conversations. And then after the lesson, we would go to Eric's room and I would listen to them discussing science, art, and world happenings.

I was truly very happy with Eric. He thought I was wonderful, and I liked being thought of as wonderful. Bidge had always been very critical; he was a very critical man. Whatever I did was wrong, wasn't the right thing to do. And then even though Mac was good to me and loved me, it had been a hard time.

With Eric, all of a sudden everything was peaceful. It was as though I had been rocking around in a boat on a wild sea and then I came into a serene harbor. Everything was calm: it was fun, it was nice, and the kids were fine. The love they developed for Eric because of his wit, intelligence, and concern for them grew stronger each week, each month—as did my love. It was one of the nicest times of my life.

We made a lot of very interesting friends —artists, musicians, and scientists who had worked on the atom bomb—and had an active social life even though Eric was sort of an invalid, though I never thought of him as such. We had quartets, sketch classes, dinner parties, and great discussions and conversations.

We used to play bridge once or twice a week, and a musical friend of mine, a violinist, brought the famous cellist Piatagorsky to play bridge. Piatagorsky loved to play bridge. He was married to the daughter of a Rothschild, but she was very shy and withdrawn and seldom went out while he was a very jovial and friendly man who loved to go out. During our bridge games, he would tell us very funny, ribald jokes and wonderful stories. He also used to comment about Americans and American life. He would say, "They are very musical people. If they want to sell cereal, they make a song about it. They sing about everything."

He was a very tall and handsome man, and he felt very sympathetic towards me because I was married to someone who had T.B. and was trying to make him happy. "A man needs only one angel in life," he would say. He wanted Terry to marry his daughter. I wish he had.

He encouraged me in my painting, and one day I took him down to the gallery where my teacher showed his work. They were very impressed at the gallery by the fact that Piatagorsky had come. The owner drew me aside and said, "You should have told me you were bringing him."

"Why? What would you have done?"

Piatagorsky didn't much like Howard's work. He found it too gray and gloomy.

I always looked forward to the evenings when Piatagorsky would come. He would light up the house.

Another visitor whom we enjoyed was Evelyn

Caldwell. She taught at UCLA. Denis brought her home one night for dinner, and she and Eric became close friends.

She specialized in the study of homosexuals. At that time, it was thought that homosexuality was a physical illness. She did many careful studies of heterosexuals and homosexuals and proved that this was an error. In 1992 a film was made about her and her work, and it received an Academy Award nomination.

She was very beautiful, and she married a Professor Hooker and remained with him until he died.

Denis and Terry seemed quite happy and would bring their friends home so we had many young people around. They had made good friends—Denis had Dick Shapiro and Andre Previn and Terry had Ralph Riskin, the son of a producer. I think Ralph's mother had a crush on Terry because she took him down to Mexico for the weekend and then slept in the same room with him. He said when he came back, "She's really a very bad sleeper!" I guess she didn't try anything but—

After the war, we went into a very bad period with Joe McCarthy, who was persecuting everybody— especially actors. For him, everybody was a communist; I think a lot of those people were communists, but in such a kind of mild way. The government arrested and jailed ten: "The Hollywood Ten." Jack Berry made a film about

Denis & Terry Sanders

them and toured the country with it. That made the government want to arrest him. Jack and his wife were very good friends of ours so we asked them to come and stay with us in the apartment over the garage: We hid him there and snuck him food and supplies. His wife didn't come to stay with him, but she was in touch.

One night Jack disappeared. They'd got away and escaped to France. Before they left, his wife had gone to all the stores in Hollywood and Beverly Hills, and she'd charged a slew of clothes, never expecting to pay. She packed them all up and went to France. That left a bit of mess. I think they stayed in France, but Jack's career was completely ruined.

I had hesitated a bit to shelter Jack, but Eric was absolutely insistent on taking him. He said that we had to help him because this was the kind of thing that happened in Austria. "When these terrible people get into power," he said, "you have to fight them." So he was very much for protecting Berry.

One day, our friend David Gregory called and said, "What is this I hear about your refusing to help Jack Berry?" Although David was both a Hollywood writer and a homosexual, still I thought, "He just might be a spy."

"I don't know what you're talking about," was all I said.

19

Telling about my eleven-year marriage to Eric is like writing about a landscape covered by different clouds, sometimes happy and sometimes sad and sometimes anguished, one scene locking and penetrating into the other. Where was its epicenter?

For many years life was centered in his room in the front of the house, Eric lying in his bed, surrounded by books laying on the floor on both sides of his bed, always one or two people sitting around him, telling him something, asking him something, listening to him speak.

But it hadn't always been like that. In the beginning of our married life together, he was active: the trips on the sailboat, the capsizing, the swimming in to shore—that was all fun.

But the overlay of threatening death was always there so that it lent a blue-grayish cast to everything. There were the constant checks and tests: How was he doing? What was the condition of his health? There were the filled notebooks, the doctors and more doctors.

Life continued. Eric studied, he wrote, he corresponded with distinguished physicians and scientists. He kept himself active intellectually, working out a potassium-based cure for multiple sclerosis that was published in the American Medical Association's journal in January 20, 1951. MS patients from around the world who had success wrote him letters. If Eric had gotten better, he would have gone into practice. That was his plan, his goal.

A new drug had been developed: Streptomycin was touted as a miracle antibiotic that many thought could eradicate T.B. The supply, though, was limited and given out only to a few health clinics and in small amounts that were to be used at the doctors' discretion for patients that they felt would teach them the most about the new drug. I wrote to a lawyer friend of mine in New York who was prominent and influential and good at making things happen. He decided to contact the Mayo Clinic to see if they would allow Eric, who was a physician, to be among those chosen for the experiment of using streptomycin.

After three weeks of waiting, we received an affirmative answer, and our house was filled with hope. The only problem was that Eric's being part of the experiment meant we would have to remain at the Mayo Clinic for six weeks. What to do with Terry?

Denis was at his boarding school in Ojai run by Mr. and Mrs. Cate. Mr. Cate was an old-school aristocratic gentleman, and we had become good friends with him. When we told him of our problem, he offered to let Terry attend the school during the time that we would spend at the Mayo Clinic. Terry didn't like the Hollywood school and was pleased to leave. "No one there cares about studying," he said. "If I study and make good grades, they make jokes about me and call me a long-nosed egghead." So Terry's grades had gone from A's to C's, just barely passing.

I took him up to the Cate's and left him there. It was a big wrench to do this, but I thought, "When we come back, I can always take him out again."

Eric was not feeling too well, and the trip to the Mayo Clinic was a grueling seventeen-hour flight with two changes. We finally arrived at Rochester, a town dominated by the clinic with its tall tower. Hotels to house the patients and their relatives surrounded it. All of them had underground passages to the clinic so that the patients did not have to go outdoors in the long and severe Minnesota winter.

When we arrived, although we had reservations, all the rooms seemed to be taken. We had to spend the first night sleeping on the couches in the lobby, but we were so dead-tired that we could have slept in Grand Central Station. The next day we got a room—pleasant enough and looking out of the window at the Mayo's tall gray tower. The following day at nine a.m., we were in a long room with all the other new patients, waiting to meet the doctor to whom we had been assigned. That was the procedure: You sometimes spent your whole day in the long hall at the convenience of the doctors. At the Mayo, you were charged according to your income. This seemed a fair way to do things.

The people in the hall all looked anxious and subdued. We made acquaintances during mealtime, and the question was always not "What do you do?" but "What have you got?" We heard the history of each person's illness.

Back in the waiting room, we watched the doctors as they came in and wondered which one was ours. A tall, noble-looking man walked into the room. He looked kind. He was identified as the head of the T.B. section. I crossed my fingers. "Eric, I hope we get him!" Someone up there must have heard me: At two o'clock that afternoon, he came out and said, "Dr. Eric Barrett, please follow me."

Dr. Henshaw was as kind as he looked.

"Don't expect miracles," he told Eric, "but this is a very promising drug. Its only weakness is that you might develop a resistance to it after a time. We will start you on small doses." Now they still use streptomycin, but they use it in combination with another drug called ACTH, alternating the two so resistance doesn't develop.

The other person who was getting the drug was a young Catholic priest whose hair was already white. He said he'd been given only a year to live, and this was a great hope for him.

Eric stayed in the hospital that first night, but after that, they let him come to the hotel to sleep. As he told them, I was very nervous about being without him close by.

He spent his days at the clinic, and I searched

the library for books and went to movies, which were all cowboy westerns. I met many relatives of Mayo patients; we used to walk around the town together and search through medical books, looking for information on the different diseases we were concerned with. We also read the lives of the Mayo brothers: it took up an encyclopedia, but the short version was that the father was born in England, had immigrated to the U.S., married, and had two sons. Those sons started the clinic, and their sons continued it. They became probably the best known physicians in the United States.

The weeks gradually passed. Eric showed improvement daily. It was time for us to leave, and we knew that at one stopover in St. Louis we would have to find a doctor to give Eric his injection, which he needed every seven hours. When we arrived in St. Louis, we perused the phone book and found the name and address of a T.B. surgeon. We took a taxi to his office, where we showed the receptionist the letter from the Mayo Clinic explaining the situation. She told us the doctor was out of town. We asked if she could refer us to someone else or if the nurse could sterilize the needle? Time was ticking away. We knew how important it was to keep the medication at specific levels in his body. Finally she agreed to let the nurse sterilize the needle, and Eric administered the shot himself.

We went back to the airport, and in three hours we were home.

Eric was like a different man, full of vitality and

in wonderful health. The next few weeks at home were filled with energy and hope: Eric went out, he started studying to pass the California medical exam, he made plans for practicing medicine.

We went up to Cate School to bring Terry home. Denis wanted to come home too, but that was not possible; he had to finish the school year. Terry said he would like to go to Cate School the following year.

Eric continued to be tested for T.B. After a few months, he began to test positive again. His resistance to streptomycin had started.

It was a great disappointment, but at least we were grateful for the few good months we had had and the hope it had given us for the future.

When Denis graduated from Cate, he went off to Yale. Terry chose Cal Tech. During one of their summer vacations at home, they made a film on drugs with the Los Angeles sheriffs department. It was their first finished film.

Denis transferred to UCLA. Terry developed hepatitis and had to stay in bed for six weeks. Because it was too hard for him to catch up, he too transferred to UCLA.

At that time, the boys' father died. Bidge's sister Rita called from New York, and we were shocked to hear that Bidge had killed himself. She wanted the boys to come back East and get the car their father had left them and his books and personal possessions.

They drove their father's car back to California and decided to take it to Mexico to spend their summer vacation making a film on the Mexican lottery. Lorenzo Tedesco, the painter, went with them. They came back with a good film. Jack Berry saw it and liked it a lot. That experience decided them: they were going into the movie business. They both enrolled in the UCLA film department. In their last year there, they made a film called *A Time Out of War* and won an Academy Award.

Gradually Eric retreated to the inactive life of before, the world of intellectual contemplation. But then the pain got to be too much, and he wanted morphine. The doctors wouldn't give him morphine, but they thought that methadone would be okay. He became very addicted to methadone, though, and when he tried to stop taking it, he would cry.

At times, Eric got very depressed, which I know now can be a side effect of methadone. Both our doctor friend Otto Neurath and Eric's doctor suggested that he might benefit from seeing a psychoanalyst. Eric didn't want to, but he agreed and went to see Dr. Martin Grotjohn who was the head of the psychoanalysis clinic in Beverly Hills.

When Eric came back, he said that Dr. Grotjohn wanted to see me. I went and spent an hour with him. He was an agreeable person. He questioned me about my life with Eric, my painting, my past, my children. At the end of the session, he said, "Tell your husband I will take you, but not him."

"Why?" I asked.

"Because he will resist me. I don't think I can help him."

I went home and told Eric. He said, "Do you want to go?"

I said, "I don't know. I suppose I could learn something if I went. What do you think?"

Eric said, "Well, try if you like; you can always leave."

So I began going once a week. It didn't seem like an analysis. It seemed more like having a pleasant, amusing conversation with a clever man. But I liked him, so I continued to go. It was in many ways a relief from the worries I had about Eric.

After that Eric did go into analysis with Dr. Walter Brill, but he never took to the doctor too much. He was a little too smart to be in analysis. He was smarter than the analyst.

So the cycle began: the pain and the killers of pain. The dependency on the drugs. The desperate fear of being without. The enticement of doctor friends (or were they enemies?) to keep him supplied. The gradual diminishing of his desire to live. The last weeks in and out of hospitals. The hopelessness that permeated the house.

He wasn't really expected to die, but I think at the end he wanted to die. He never played the piano any more; he was tired; he was depressed; he didn't want a life with no prospect of ever getting well. Before he died the only people he wanted to see were Terry and me. He liked the dog's company, too, but he didn't want to see many people.

The two weeks in 1953 before Eric died were unbearable. I knew I was in a struggle against Death—Death, like an enormous black shape standing in the doorway, approaching and unstoppable. I would press my hands against it, and it would be soft and recede; but then my arms would get tired, and I would let go and Death would take its shape again and move forward.

Eric and I slept in separate bedrooms with the door open between them. There was a little chair by my bedside, and during the last days of the last weeks, he would come in and sit in the chair and he would want to talk and I would look at him with love and fear and want to cry out, "Don't bring death in here. I don't want to die. If I go with you now into those journeys that you are making into these dark spaces, I will never come back. I will be lost."

"I know I am very near it now," he'd say. "It is only a matter of weeks or perhaps days. Be patient with me, and then you will be free."

"That's silly," I'd say. "I don't believe you. You are always saying that, but it isn't so. It isn't true."

And he would look at me so sweetly, so wan and so pale, and I knew he was right and my denials were wrong.

I feel guilty now. I shouldn't have cut him off. I should have let him talk. It is little enough to accord someone you love: his right to speak of his fears, to speak of his wondering what would happen to him when he died. But I wasn't big enough or smart enough or understanding enough to allow it. I was too concentrated on my own feelings of dread, my own fear of being left alone. Denial was my only answer.

It was Wednesday. I remember the day but not the date. Exhausted by the pain and tension, I had fallen into a deep sleep Tuesday night, and when I woke, it was ten in the morning, and Eric was calling me from his bed. I went over to him and bent to hear what he had to say: "Get me those pills, on the shelf in the bathroom, quickly." I went and got them and brought them to him with a glass of water, but he seemed too weak to take them. I put the glass and the pills on the table and sat on the bed and took him in my arms. I held him and looked into his eyes. Suddenly the light in them was gone—like a electric bulb that stops shining—and I knew that he was dead.

I couldn't bear to look at him. I laid him down on the pillow, and I ran from the room. I thought of the women who throw themselves on the body of their lovers and husbands, but I didn't. I left. I ran away. I sat in the little entrance to the living room. I was alone in the house, but then I thought, "I must tell someone," so I called Otto, our doctor and friend, and I said, "Otto, please come. I think Eric is dying and maybe . . . maybe . . . " I couldn't get out the word dead.

"I'll be there," Otto said and hung up the phone.

I went back to sit on the little couch in the hall, thinking, "If I don't move, things won't change, things won't get worse.

In minutes, I heard the wail of an ambulance siren coming up the hill. "How stupid," I thought. "What's the use? What's the hurry? Eric's gone, Eric's left, you men in white coats aren't going to do anything, it's all too late now." A man in a white coat came slamming through the door. I pointed to Eric's door, and he went in. Otto arrived. I kept sitting in a corner of the couch. I couldn't move. It was as though I were paralyzed.

There was a small service for Eric, but I didn't go. I didn't want to go. I just couldn't stand it. My sons were there, and Howard, and all the friends, but I couldn't. I was distraught, beside myself with grief. Eric was the first man that I really adored. He was a wonderful man, so brilliant, so gentle and tender. Just a perfect, lovely person with a warm sense of humor.

When Eric died, my world fell apart.

Two weeks after his death, I was lying on my bed, deciding whether to live or to die. It was mid-August, and I could hear the heavy buzz in the garden outside. I got up and went out. I brushed my hands over the late-blooming flowers, feeling the softness of their petals against my skin. Then I felt a sting on my forehead, between my eyebrows. It hurt, so I went in. In the bathroom, I looked in the mirror and saw a small red spot. Then I probably did the worst possible thing: I soaked a washcloth in very hot water and pressed it to the spot. I went back to lying on my bed and fell asleep. About an hour later, I woke up and my body seemed to be paralyzed. I felt frightened. I had been living the last weeks in a kind of purgatory, not wanting to live or die. But now, feeling such a strong sensation of death surrounding me, the urge to live swept over me like a passion. I was alone in the house but for my niece Jackie who lived in a wing beyond the kitchen. I had to get to her.

I couldn't walk, but I could still move, so I

lowered myself over the side of the bed and began to crawl across the floor with only one thought in mind: I must reach Jackie. My crawl seemed to be at the rate of two inches an hour; I tried to stay on the wood floors and avoid the rugs, as the wood was smooth and propelled me forward. In the living room, I went around the edges of thick carpet I had designed and sent to China to have made. But the artist there had sung her own creative song, and it had come back transformed, not even remotely resembling my design. Even as I crawled, I thought of this, and I found myself smiling. I made my way through the hall and dining room and into the kitchen. The linoleum floor felt cool.

I felt like an animal in a cocoon, dragging my cocoon with me, but I was determined to reach my niece's room: I wanted to survive. "This," I thought, "is my crawl for survival." I reached her door and like an animal, scratched on it, thinking, "Oh, Jackie, please hear me." The door opened, and Jackie let out a cry, her face twisting in fear. She picked me up and put me in her bed and covered me with a blanket. I felt I had been saved. I heard her voice on the phone, calling our friend Sam, who was a doctor, and then I fell asleep. Next thing I knew, Sam was sitting on the bed, holding my hand. "I'm going to give you a shot," he said, "and when you wake up you will feel better."

He turned me over on my stomach and slapped my buttock as he put the needle in. That was his original way of giving a shot. The slap distracted the patient from feeling the needle.

When I woke up I felt sad and tears kept coming down my cheeks, but one thing I knew for sure: I wanted to live, I wanted to survive.

20

When Denis got the news that Eric had died, he cut short his mini-bike trip in Europe and hurried from Italy to his grandmother's in Switzerland. He told her that he was going home to be with me to comfort me in my despair. Terry did just the opposite. He left me after two weeks to go to New York to be with his girlfriend.

When I saw Denis, I experienced great comfort and joy. We had always been very close, and he was almost the only person I had to whom I could talk freely. He had the gift of listening and not responding with either praise or condemnation. He was simply a pitcher waiting to be filled with whatever I had at the time—joy or sorrow—and I think I provided him with the same receptivity.

The weeks went by, and my tears seemed to stop. When I did not go out with Denis, I went out with Howard, my teacher, and he gave me intellectual solace. I was very lucky in that way to love and be loved by two unique individuals.

I decided to go with Denis for a few days to San Francisco. Dr. Hinshaw from the Mayo Clinic was there, and that gave me a feeling of security. Denis and I stayed at the St. Francis Hotel up on the hill, and we went to a fine restaurant that night. I had only a spinach salad, but I probably overate. When I came back to the hotel, I felt uneasy and, after going to bed, experienced panic. I called Denis' room, and he came over and called Dr. Hinshaw, who sent over a colleague who gave me a sedative. Denis lay beside me on the bed, and finally I fell asleep.

I was depressed with the thought that I didn't dare travel alone. What if I should get an attack and be alone in some foreign country? So the first year after Eric's death, I stayed in California. But then I decided to go to France to see my mother, and she paid for a cruise to Greece with my nephew Richard. After that, I came back to California, but I soon left again for Guatemala. I just had to get away from the sad surroundings: to experience new scenes, new people, and to try to begin to live again with a situation that had no Eric in it.

So it was that I found myself on the steps of the church in the marketplace in Chichicastenango, up in the highlands of Guatemala. The rough white church might have been hand-built by one lonely missionary with the help of his converted flock. A black figure of a priest stood swinging an incense lamp, and clouds of incense floated over the square and hung suspended in the air. A musky rich odor came with it.

It was afternoon, and I was seated on a stone bench surrounded by the village children. In my lap was a small black sketch book. I had discovered long ago that a sketch book and a pencil were a sort of international passport that introduced me to at least all the children all over the world and to those who had time enough left over to be curious. Guatemala was no different, and the children pressed closely around me.

I looked towards the end of the marketplace beyond the small figures of the Indians who stood in knotted groups in their colors of deep blue and red, looking like wonderful antique encrusted stones against the gray-white of the square. I looked beyond, to the figure of a man, lithe and curved like a figure S. He could have been of any nationality: American, English, German, Czech, or perhaps a native Guatemalan. There were some that looked that way—descendants of the Spanish conquerors—blonde, blue-eyed, big. He surveyed the marketplace as though it were his. He dominated the figures around him, not only because of his height, but because of the relationship that the people seemed to have to him. They moved around him and laid affectionate hands on him: the boys playing marbles raised their heads and called out to him, and his answers must have been warm and encouraging for smiles would flash across their faces; a man carrying a heavy table on his head stopped to talk to him even though I felt he surely must be in a hurry to put his burden down. It was like a pantomime of human exchange and gesture running through the workaday theme—or a ballet of a sun in the sky with small bodies turning about it. The words "a kind cock of the roost" flashed through my mind as I watched this man.

I opened my book, and on the white page, I idly drew the proud silhouette of a cock. I made its beak shoot out of its head and each feather stand out on its body with a pride all its own. And then I saw that the man was looking towards me. I lowered my eyes and then half raised them again. I saw that he was moving towards me. He walked slowly and gracefully and surely, and his feet with their cowboy boots and high heels looked like small upturned snakes on the stones. His clothes were faded and worn, but tight to his body, and the muscles of his thighs curved through them.

The children made way for him, and he laid his hand affectionately on the head of the child at my left as I got up to make room for him.

"What are you doing?" he asked in the carefully spaced English that he must have learned for tourists.

I felt a strong desire to communicate with him. I decided to try to avoid the trap that is so easy for a tourist to fall into, that of talking over-simple English to a native, and by thus talking, of falling into the confusion of thinking that his intelligence was only equal to the oversimplified, fumbling words.

"I am drawing you," I answered.

"That," and he laid his finger on the cock and smiled, "Is that how I looked to you?" And now he laughed.

I looked up at him and saw that his face was brown and his eyes intensely blue, and I was reminded of the ceremonial dance masks of pale brown balsa wood with brilliant blue glass eyes that I had seen the Indians making that morning up in the mountains.

"Yes," I answered. "You look to me like a very proud 'cock of the roost,' as though all these people in the square belong to you, and as you put your foot down on every stone, as though every stone belongs to you."

He seemed to follow my words very closely, but I knew that whatever he understood, he understood through means other than words. And then I said—and I spaced my words and said them slowly—"Are you an artist, too?"

"Yes, but I only draw flowers." And he gently took my book and pencil from me and delicately drew the outline of a flower on the page. I could tell he was an artist from the way he related one line to another, from the sensitive consideration of the space between the lines, and from the gradual synthesis of the whole page so that it spelled flower. "Do you know what flower I am drawing?"

"No, I don't," I said.

"It is a Guatemalan flower, we have many here, and in its center are little beads of many colors and when I sometimes carve this in wood, then I find little stones of different colors and then I stick them in." He smiled at me and added, "And then I sell them to the tourists."

I looked up from the drawing. "And what else do you do?"

"I am the blacksmith for the village and all around here."

A small boy came up and pushed his way through the crowd and shook the man teasingly by the shoulder.

"Hello, brother," he said in Spanish, and all the children laughed.

"What are they laughing at?" I asked.

He waved his arms now in a warm embracing gesture. "Why, I am courting his sister so he calls me brother."

His eyes travelled now to the figure of a timid young Indian girl walking across the square. Her eyes were cast down, but I could feel that she was quite aware of us. He called out to her softly in an Indian dialect, but it would have been the same in any language. His tone was mocking, affectionate, beguiling, cocky. Just before she passed from view, she turned her head shyly and murmured something.

"Good," he said, "good." And the children laughed knowingly.

"What is good?" I asked.

"Well, I said yes. Do you know the joke about the ducks? How many feet has a duck?"

"No, I don't," I answered.

"A duck has as many feet as he has wives."

"How many feet do you have then?" I asked.

He didn't answer but leaned towards me. "I like American women." And he looked at me questioningly and repeated, "I really do. I like Americans."

"Oh, but I suppose they are harder to get along with, more complicated."

He looked more closely at me now. "Are you married?"

"My husband is dead." It seemed strange to me

to say the words so matter-of-factly. I looked out
over the marketplace and kept talking. It was not
so hard to go on talking to someone who might not
quite understand the words. "That incense over
there in the marketplace, suspended, hanging,
belonging to nothing and still a part of everything,
touching people and seeing them, but never a part
of them—that's how I feel."

"How long has he been dead?" he asked.

"A year," I answered.

"I suppose now you will marry a millionaire." I
felt startled. I looked at him, but his eyes were
kind and reaching out. It was odd that he should
say that, but it was as though he wanted
something nice to happen to me and thought the
best thing an American could be would be a
millionaire.

"A millionaire," I repeated. "He wouldn't have to
be a millionaire, just somebody nice."

He smiled then, and put his hand on his chest.
"That is good, that is good." And there was a long
pause. "Do you think I am nice? I am not a
millionaire, but do you think I am nice?" He
stretched out his hand. I took it. It was warm and
strong and comforting.

I suddenly envied him his freedom, his
ability to take a moment, a chance encounter, to
make something of it if he chose or nothing if he
chose: his ability to offer himself freely to the
accidents of life. Surely that must be the way to
be. I suddenly felt as tight and prim as the two
schoolteachers I had left behind me at the hotel.

His hand closed more strongly on mine. Here

was a gesture to which, if I responded, might carry me from the world of not feeling into the world of feeling once again.

He was reaching out now for my thoughts. "Is it that you still miss your husband?"

"That would be an easy answer," I said. "But it really wouldn't be quite true." And once again I felt safe to talk. "It isn't my husband or the memory of him that stands over me, a ghost-like guardian that says no. A love affair with you—and that is what we are talking about—would be like taking a walk through an unknown forest to capture something I had never seen. It could happen that I would find a rare and beautiful flower, or it could happen that I would find a bitter, difficult, strangling root, but I would have to be strong enough and brave enough to face the dangers and the uncertainties. And should I be lucky enough to find a rare and beautiful thing, then I would have to bring it back and fit it into a mundane, formal scheme of living, of eating and drinking, of getting up and going to bed, of wearing the right clothes and seeing the right people. And then if I hadn't quite killed it and destroyed it, well . . . " And I looked down at his shabby blue pants and his not quite clean but strong hands.

"You mean you do not like me?" he said. "Is that what you mean?"

"I guess I don't quite know what I mean." And I suddenly felt a desire for reassurance, a desire to reestablish my identity. I opened my handbag and took out my mirror and combed my hair hurriedly and fingered my passport as I put the mirror back in my bag.

"I have to go now," I said, and I picked up my sketch book.

"You will need pictures of the marketplace and the church if you are going to make paintings. I have some. I'll bring them to the hotel." And now his tone was very soft, and some of the pride seemed to have gone out of him.

"That would be nice," I answered, and I got up and walked across the square down the small alleyway that led to the hotel. A few scraggly children followed me and stopped at the entrance to the hotel. I pulled the cord on the heavy wooden door with its iron bolts, and the door opened and closed behind me. The marketplace had disappeared. I was back now in the sanctuary of the American tourist.

I went into the bar and found my schoolteacher acquaintances. There was Viola who was big and blowzy and good-natured, and who must have seemed to her students like a Mae West lost in an arithmetic class. Sitting beside her drinking a martini was Marianne, a German woman professor who always marched and never walked, and who seemed to be carrying an invisible knapsack on her back. But I was glad to seem them. They were kind and good company.

"Where have you been, Tina?" Marianne asked.

"You missed a wonderful Protestant missionary," said Viola. "He arrived with fifty other Protestant missionaries, and he was visibly shaken by the carryings-on in the Indian church this morning."

I said slowly, "I don't know that I missed so much. I had a proposal from the village blacksmith, and I am considering it."

"Oh, you are not, Tina," said Marianne, sounding shocked.

"I guess not," I answered. "I haven't any horses."

The manager walked into the bar and over to me.

"There's a man outside. He says he has some pictures for you."

"Have him come in," I said.

"I'm sorry, Miss, but natives from the village are not allowed in the hotel."

"All right," I said. "I'll come out."

I went out and found him standing there, and he looked as a man must look who has had a door slammed in his face. I thought: How quickly can the figure of a man be changed by a sharp blow of humiliation.

The manager stood nearby watching, and I saw the blacksmith for a moment with the sharp eyes of the manager: "Here is only a poor vendor of postcards."

"Hello," I said.

"Here are your cards." His eyes did not seek my face; it was as though he had lost his eyes.

I took the postcards. "Thanks. Thanks a lot." I hesitated for a moment. I saw the manager still watching me. My hand fumbled to my purse, then I dropped it quickly, and turned and walked back into the hotel.

21

When the phone rang that day in 1959, I was in the studio working on a mosaic, feeling that instant pleasure one can feel when looking at the juxtaposition of two brilliant colors. I felt angry at the interruption, and I played with the idea of letting the phone ring, but decided against it.

When I picked it up, I heard my Aunt Rachel's voice, all the way from Paris! "Your mother has had a heart attack. She would like to see you. When can you come?"

"As soon as I can get a flight," I said. "I'll let you know when I'm arriving. How is she?"

"She's not in pain, but she is very weak."

After calling the airlines, I went upstairs to pack my bag. In a few hours, I would be on the airplane; and in a few more hours, I would be at my mother's bedside.

As I packed, thoughts harried me. I knew my mother was dying, and I was overwhelmed with a deep sense of guilt, not because she was dying, but because I had done so little to make her life fuller and happier. After my father's death, she had lived alone for awhile. She longed for a romantic sexual relationship, but after her experience with my father, she was deathly afraid of men. Whenever she was with a man, she was awkward and not appealing.

I was newly married then, had a child, and I was too full of my own problems to be able to help her. She had never lacked for anything material, and my father had left her with more than ample funds. But she had always lacked all the satisfactions that come with life achievements. Still she had always been adventurous, open to new ideas and new solutions to old problems.

All her life, my mother kept looking for a religion that could give her something to live by, and she would go from one religion to another. At the time of my father's death, the Soviet Union was a new country with a new life under communism. She went to the U.S.S.R. alone and came back a fervent communist, preaching communism to anyone who would listen.

In 1940, my aunt's son and husband died within weeks of each other. Rachel stretched her arms across the Atlantic and beckoned my mother to her. This was the worst possible thing for my mother. She was just beginning to spread her wings.

My mother was a lovely, but timid and weak person. Rachel was proud and dominant with no patience for weakness. She loved my mother but had no respect for her. In the fifteen years the two of them lived together, my mother's decisions of what she wanted to do were always overrun by my aunt. And so my mother had no respect for herself and would always concede to my aunt's decisions.

Thinking about all this as I packed, I felt a familiar wave of anger toward my aunt.

When I arrived in Paris, I saw that my mother had had her bed moved to the little sitting room where there was a window that looked out on Paris. She motioned to the window and said, "I wish I were a bird and could fly out of that window and never come back."

After several weeks, I returned to California because it seemed she was going to linger. She died two weeks after I left.

My mother left money to both of my sons. Terry had gone away and bought a house, but Denis stayed with me in the Coldwater Canyon house. We settled down to a pleasant life: our going out to dinner once or twice a week and on the nights we weren't together, his taking out his girlfriends and my organizing a sketch class or going to a movie with a friend. It gave me a secure feeling knowing Denis was there.

But one night at a restaurant, Denis said to me, "Ma, I'd rather be with you than anybody." I felt the same way, but his voicing it made me feel an element of guilt. Was I keeping him from realizing a life that would include a wife and children? I felt that the only way I could make him go out and actively seek a life would be if I found a husband.

Howard Warshaw and I were very close. He and his wife Helen had divorced, and I'd see him two or three times a week. But when he made a pass, I rebuffed him—partly because I was never in love with him, but I was also wary of him because he wasn't a good person in relation to women. He had treated Helen badly. She was a very modest, quiet person, but quite a good painter. Howard had been jealous of her—he didn't want her to paint and wouldn't buy her brushes or paints or canvas. Howard had also had a love affair with his best friend's wife. It was really pretty scandalous, and many people were mad at him for it. Once I went to a gallery with him, and his teacher, Rico, was there. When he saw Howard, he said to him, "You get out of town."

I went out a few times with a cinematographer named Floyd Crosby who had a crush on me, but I wasn't interested. He later went on to win an Academy Award for his work and to father David Crosby of the rock group Crosby, Stills and Nash.

I took a short story class at UCLA from the critic Robert Kirsch. He and I became good friends, but that never led to anything more.

And then I met Charlie.

I knew his wife Pat Carey from the Jepson School of Art. She was a painter, and she came to the house once when I'd invited various artists over. Although she and Charlie were getting a divorce, he had come to pick her up. That chance meeting was to determine the next twenty-five years of my life.

So there was Charlie, standing at my door: blonde, good-looking, a Mr. America with a nice smile, graceful gestures, and his arms stretched out in a welcoming gesture. He seemed a possible choice, and I encouraged him. "Maybe," I thought, "maybe I'll find shelter there and relief from the sorrow of being without Eric."

Charlie Carey

After I started going with him, I told Denis it would be better if he would move out and give Charlie a chance. Denis looked at me with such sad eyes, but I stuck to my idea that we should have separate lives. Looking back and seeing the bad choice Denis made in choosing a wife and the bad choice I made in choosing a husband, I can't help thinking we would have been better off living as mother and son. At least we knew who we were; there wasn't any question or mystery.

Too bad we don't have the power to undo events, put back time, have a chance to try it all over again; but we don't, and we have to live and take the consequences of our choices.

I would have been pleased to go on with Charlie without marriage, as friends and lovers, but he wanted marriage. His company, The Rand Corporation, were a conservative bunch. It was all right to have an affair, a relationship, but it had to have a time limit attached to it. I had to make a decision: marriage or finis.

My analyst was firmly opposed to marriage. "This is your time to be free, to have affairs, to discover yourself. Why tie yourself down? No, you do not have my blessing."

But marriage has always seemed to me to be a blessed state: solid, respectable, even noble and dignified—two people walking hand in hand, side by side. So days after Charlie received his divorce decree, we went off to Yuma, Arizona, where we were married by a lean, cowboy-type minister. We returned the next day to announce our marriage to Charlie's ex-wife and children, who dissolved into tears and beating of breasts, and to my sons and friends, none of whom was very joyful, but neither were they very sad.

And thus we started out on our married life.

But we quickly discovered that we had two different agendas going into the marriage. Charlie wanted a house and a good person that would be a haven for his two children; and he wanted an exciting sex life not limited to one person. I wanted a companion who would help me in the projects that I would embark on and who would provide me with an interesting social life filled with meeting people and making friends. Neither of us got what we wanted.

When I married Charlie, it was like stepping onto a stage with a whole new set of characters, no rehearsal and no learned lines. Charlie would come through the door, hold out his arms and look at me and make me feel, "There is where I belong." Just behind him were the great loves in his life: Sheila and T.C., his two daughters whom he absolutely adored. T.C., a very small, gentle, and sweet child of two and a half with enormous brown eyes that looked at me questioningly, but with no bad feelings for me. And holding her hand was Sheila: a ten-year-old beauty with flaming red hair, white skin, and dark eyes, who bristled like a cat when she saw me. She was unnaturally attached to her father. She hated her mother and she hated me. When she looked at me, hostility covered her like a flaming blanket. I knew I was in trouble as soon as I met her, but I didn't know how much. I learned though: whenever there was an opportunity to make life difficult for me, she seized upon it and used it with precision.

That entrance was a kind of symbolic push-pull

that was to be my atmosphere from then on. "Come," said Charlie; "Go away," said Sheila.

And then on that stage was Pat, dominating in the shadows, her voice constantly on the telephone when the children were visiting, telling me what to do and me taking it to mean, all she has is complaints about how I was treating them.

Charlie went down every weekend to bring back the children, and the whole weekend was a constant struggle of Sheila trying to find out what I wanted and to defeat my getting it. If I were to suggest they wear one thing, I would be promptly contradicted by Sheila who would choose something else. I learned to pick out first what I didn't like, which allowed Sheila to produce a garment that I did like.

Upstairs in our big bedroom we could almost forgot Sheila.

"I do love you," he'd say.

"And I you."

"What about Sheila?" he'd ask.

"Sheila? She's all right."

"She's never had good treatment. You must be kind to her."

"It's not easy when she looks at me with those dark eyes filled with hate. Why does she hate me?"

"Why ask questions for which you know the answer."

"Because I've taken her father."

Charlie would gave a big sigh, and we'd sink back on the soft pillows. At least the next few hours could be peaceful if not happy.

Next morning my pleasure in the roomy silent house would be broken by Sheila's strident demand: "Why do you live in such a big house?" She'd wave her spoon covered with milk and cereal, and the cereal and milk would fly through the air.

I'd want to say, "For God's sakes, Sheila, don't be such a slob."

Instead I'd said, "I like big houses. I like big gardens and big trees and a big swimming pool. I hope you will grow to like them, too."

Sheila would bang her spoon down: "No, I won't. Are we going to spend every weekend here?"

"I don't know."

"There's nothing to do," she'd whine.

Charlie would say in a cheerful, hopeful voice: "We can drive out today to the beach the way we used to. Would you like to swim?"

"We don't have suits, but mother says you're rich and you can buy us anything we ask for."

My dog, Gus, would come into the room.

"Even the dog is big—"

I'd get up and go into the kitchen. I'd had enough; I wanted to break the dishes over her head. Gus would follow me, we'd go upstairs, I'd put on my bathing suit and go down and jump into the pool where the water could surround me and where for a few minutes I could forget . . .

Water was lovely and dogs were wonderful.

Later, Charlie would said, "You don't understand."

I wouldn't answer. I should have, but I didn't. "Silence and sweetness," that was me—while I was trying to make up my mind. I knew it was a mess. I was balancing out the mess against possible good times.

Weekends seemed to have the longest days of

the week. Three or four times the phone would ring. Three or four times it would be Pat. Sometimes the phone wouldn't even ring, and Sheila would come stomping over and say, "Mother wants to talk to you."

I'd pick up the phone and she'd say, "Why are my children so unhappy up there? What are you doing to them?"

"Beating them," I would answer.

"I don't think that's very funny. Tell Charlie to bring them home."

"Here, you can talk to him."

Charlie would say, "What do you want? Don't be ridiculous." And the two girls would stand by, tears in their eyes.

"Let's go out for lunch," I'd said cheerfully. "Where would you like to go?"

"Let's go to a Mexican restaurant."

"You know Tina hates Mexican food," Charlie would say.

"But I like Mexican food. So does T.C."

"Do you mind?" asked Charlie.

How could I? I had learned early that no matter what Sheila said or did I must never correct her. Once she'd taken a red hot pan from the stove and put it on the mahogany piano stool. When I let out a cry and seized the pan, Sheila burst into tears. Charlie rushed over with anger in his face.

"You frightened her!" He embraced Sheila, whose sobs got louder and louder. "Never yell at Sheila. She's very sensitive. Her mother always yelled at her."

Instead of standing up for what was right, I took the pan back to the kitchen and did not return. Inside of me was a whirlwind of anger: *I hate them* all. I wish a pack of wild dogs would arrive and kill them all. It is hopeless trying to create a soft and lovable atmosphere, an atmosphere that would be fun and enjoyable. This is like an orchard filled with bitter fruit. How can I keep Charlie and get rid of the kids? I can't. I've got to accept that. Maybe I could be absent for the weekends or Charlie could take them somewhere else, anywhere else, and I could have my sons here and my friends and resurrect the old days of Eric and the boys. 'You can't go home again.' Thomas Wolfe was right. Where can I go? I'm tired. This is my third marriage. Another divorce? Again an empty house? Look again for another husband?

Back at the analyst's.

His thin profile quivered with distaste. "I told you not to get married."

"You were right."

He said, "Well, you made your bed. Now lie in it."

He said: "Try to adjust. His children seem to be a very important factor in his life."

He said: "You should be calm. They won't be there forever.

And he said: "You're the adult; you should be in charge."

I'd see a picture of me holding reins of a wild horse. "How? Their father is always on their side, never on mine. No one is on my team. I'm standing all alone."

"We are all, all alone always—"

Devastating feelings would sweep over me like horses with iron hooves. What a stupid man! A picture of his wife of forty years would come before me—I had seen them walking side by side, two old sturdy oaks. I would never be a sturdy oak with Charlie. Sooner or later we would walk separately, on two sidewalks with a road between us.

Much later, I learned how to deal with Sheila: meekness and sweetness were not in the recipe.

She once threw something out the car window. I stopped the car. "Please get out and pick that up."

She didn't answer, simply sat stiffly with her hands in her lap.

I started yelling at her. "If you can't behave decently, you don't have to come up here weekends. You can stay at your house, and your father can go see you there. I don't want you here making my life miserable. Now get out and pick up that garbage you threw out or never come here again."

She got out and picked it up. Her eyes looked dark and frightened. I had her on the run.

"You hate me, don't you?" she said.

"I'm sick of being nice to you and your being horrible to me. I'm not going to be nice to you anymore. If you don't want to come here, don't. Stay home with your mother. Your father can go to see you there. I don't want you here."

She clammed up.

So be it, I thought, and I felt frightened, thinking about what I had said and done. But after that, she behaved better. Her loud angry outbursts disappeared and turned into quiet sullenness, which was easier to bear. We never became friends, but at least we were silent enemies, which was a relief.

The weekdays weren't so bad, but Charlie never really enjoyed them.

He made a fuss over the servants.

"No one at Rand has servants. You should learn to cook like the other wives."

So I learned to cook.

He wanted me to fire the servants.

"But why? I can afford to have servants."

"Well, not when I am in the house. They can clean and then go home."

The honeymoon was soon up. Dinner was something for him to get through. Then he began not coming home for dinner. Women began calling the house. I would eavesdrop on the calls, but I never forced any objection. Why not? I suppose because I didn't want to admit that the marriage was a mistake. I didn't want to fight. I wanted everything to be calm and peaceful, loving and warm.

It wasn't.

During my first year of marriage to Charlie, I lapsed into a depression. The phone calls from women kept on coming. I'd stand before the half-opened bedroom door, my arm raised as if to knock, stopped in midair. A half-opened door was surely an invitation to come in. A closed door is like putting up a "do not disturb" sign or else it says, "Give warning by knocking"; but a half-opened door is at least a half invitation to enter, to bear witness.

I'd let my arm fall back to my side. I knew without looking what I would see and hear. Charlie, my husband, lying on an unmade bed, a telephone held tight to his ear, his face suffused, bathed in a sexual aura, his voice low and wooing, saying almost unintelligible words, more like the sounds of an animal pleading. He was talking to a woman. Fear and anger gripped me. They gave me an identity as emotions give people their identity: they made me an "intruder," an "outsider."

Again: Keep on that smiling face.

I withdrew and looked around to see what was left of my old life. I wasn't used to being treated like this. Eric and the boys were always tender and fun-loving with me, and we had been surrounded by a group of friends whom we loved and who loved us. Now my husband, Eric, was dead. My two sons had gotten married. And the new people I was surrounded with were either this hostile family or the rather formal people that Charlie worked with at The Rand Corporation, a prestigious Think Tank with famous deep-think persons in it. We were invited to many dinner parties that should have been fascinating since the men were all possessed of state secrets, but everyone was very tightlipped and the conversations seemed to be restricted to talk about famous wines and famous restaurants. It was so different from my life with Eric when famous people like Piatagorsky came to play bridge and when Eric was visited by philosophers from UCLA or USC and they had illuminating discussions and when the boys would wander in and out, bringing friends, boyfriends, girlfriends, problems and solutions.

I decided if I were to recreate my own life within this limiting framework of my marriage, I needed my own project, something that would consume my time and energy entirely for at least a year if not more—something that would take me away from the petty, useless bickering.

22

I decided my next project would be a film on George Grosz. I had his book called *Interregnum*, which contained drawings that chronicled the periods between World War I and the rise of Hitler in Germany. I thought I would base the main part of the film on these drawings.

Since I had never made a film before I called up a friend of mine, Mort Rabinowitz, who was a production designer at MGM and asked him if he would be interested. He gave me a big yes.

Mort came over, and we laid all the drawings on the floor. We saw that they did make an historical sequence. Mort went ahead and made a story board.

The next thing was to get permission from Grosz. I called my old friend Lester to ask if he knew where I could find him.

"Sure," he said. "He's still teaching at the Art Students League, but he's thinking of going back to Germany now that Hitler's gone and the war is over." I hung up and called Charlie and told him that I wanted to go New York to see Grosz and get his permission to make a movie about him. Charlie had no objection, which didn't surprise me. I knew he was involved with a fat young woman who thought he was God—

I found myself in the cafeteria at the Art Students League sitting across from Grosz. He looked older and more tired—not well at all—and he seemed discouraged about life in general. But his smile was still benign and kind.

"So you want to make a film?" he asked.

"Yes."

He took a clean paper napkin and wrote on it: "OK, Altina — You can make a film." He signed it with his usual signature: George Grosz over a curving line and two dots. That was my contract.

I kissed him. "Thank you," I said, and I thought, "Now at least I have something to do, something to live for."

It took up my next year and a half.

We first shot a segment from the story board in eight millimeter film, and it looked pretty good. Slowly the project began to come together.

I got hold of George Grosz's book *A Big No and a Little Yes* and decided to take the narration from it. I got an out-of-work actor, Mark Ramsey, to comb through the book and find the appropriate material.

Mark, Mort, and I worked in conjunction.

From eight millimeter, we went to sixteen millimeter. We took extensive liberties with the drawings: sometimes only using sections, sometimes turning black into white, sometimes altering the drawings to animate them.

When the shooting was completed, I decided that instead of using music of the between-the-

Wars time, I'd look for a composer of modern music who would express the spirit and feelings of the drawings. I found a young composer, Paul Glass. For the narration, I decided I wanted someone who had lived in that tortured era. Lotte Lenya had, and she agreed to do the voice for no fee.

After the story board was completed, I spent four months with Mark charting the time and noting every move of the camera so that all that my son Terry, who photographed it, would have to do was follow the instructions. As a result of this careful planning, no editing was necessary.

Making *Interregnum* absorbed my days completely. My nights were filled with Rand-related social engagements, where the women were relegated to corner positions away from the men and any interesting conversation.

On *Interregnum*'s completion I took it to the Museum of Modern Art, but they turned it down because they felt we had violated the drawings. A few years and many awards later, they took it into their film library, as did the Hirshhorn Museum.

Interregnum received an Academy Award nomination, the coveted Golden Lion at the Venice Film Festival, the first prize at the Boston film festival, and many other prizes at other festivals.

It was a good project. The only problem was I thought if I gave Charlie credit on the film, he would be grateful and maybe begin to love me. How stupid can you be?

George Grosz never got to see the film. He and

his wife had returned to Germany, where he'd become widely acclaimed. He was very popular, and he took to spending much time in beer halls. He'd come home drunk more nights that not. One night, he fell down the steps as he came in. His wife didn't bother to get up because she was fed up with his drinking. He'd suffered a concussion, though, and by the morning he was dead.

Exhilarated by the success of the *Interregnum*, I was feeling pretty cocky. I must be damn smart, I thought, to get all these prizes for my first film, especially because I had had no education or experience in filmmaking. My head was pretty swelled up. I'll make another, I decided.

I walked into a bookshop looking for material, and I found a book called *March to Freedom* by Martin Luther King, Jr. It was the story of the Montgomery Bus Boycott.

This is it, I thought. I found it. I had found my subject and my hero. I knew I was in the presence of another great man. George Grosz and King worked in different mediums—one an artist, one a preacher—but they both were working against cruelty and injustice. In that way, they were brothers, and I wanted to be part of their fight for justice. I didn't have the talents of either one, but in my way I wanted to help.

I contacted a book agent, a woman, who contacted Dr. King and asked for a year-long exclusive option on movie rights. He granted this to us, and he seemed pleased with the idea.

My friends in the theater recommended James

Baldwin for the screenplay. At the time, he was free and also short on money; he would probably have done it. I read some of his work and was not impressed, so I didn't ask him. I'm sorry now.

I read the writings of many black writers and found one named John Killens whose writing seemed passionate and nervy. I contacted him in New York and asked him if he would be interested. "Yes!" he said.

I told him I would fly to New York and meet him at the Algonquin Hotel in a week.

We spent several hours together that day. He was a small man, lively with a good sense of humor. He wore a very small fedora on his head that made him look silly. We got along very well, and he agreed to come out to the Coast and stay in our guest house for a month or six weeks to write the screenplay.

The work went along very well. When John had completed the script, I contacted Dr. King and told him I'd like to come and show it to him. He agreed. He was in Atlanta at the time.

I knew I couldn't—or I thought I couldn't—go to see Dr. King alone. In those days, people didn't seem to be impressed with a woman alone. For instance, a woman who went into a fancy restaurant alone would probably be told, "Sorry, you have no reservation; we're booked." Two women or three was a little better, but the table they would be given was always the least desirable.

So I talked Charlie into going to Atlanta with me, but that entailed taking Sheila, who refused to stay home with her mother. Unfortunately, she was her usual disagreeable self.

We decided to go by train so that we could see as much of the country as possible. We took along a movie camera.

"This is my beautiful daughter," Charlie would say to everyone we met.

"Ah, yes," I would say out loud. "Oh shit," I would say inside.

When we arrived in Atlanta, whose streets all seemed to be named after flowers, I was struck by the bad situation that the Negroes were in. They were called Negroes or colored then. The term black was not yet used as that was before the "Black is Beautiful" slogan became popular.

The feeling against black people at that time was very strong. The black ghetto had only dirt roads unlike the rest of the city, and a motorcycle policeman was stationed at the entrance where the road changed from asphalt to dirt.

On the train to Atlanta, a white man was talking to a colored girl, and the man seated next to me said in a disgusted tone, "Those niggers, they are getting in everywhere." He looked at me closely, then he looked at my blonde, blue-eyed husband, and then back at me. "What descent are you?" he asked.

I knew the next worst thing to being black was being Jewish. "Turkish and Jewish," I said.

"Oh well," he said with a smile of forgiveness, "You are married to an All-American," and he let it go at that.

In Atlanta, all the help in the hotel was black. As soon as we told the maid that we were looking for Dr. King, the doors of the black world opened for us and we were given help wherever we went. The blacks became very friendly to us and took us as one of their own.

We went to see Dr. King who lived in a neat small house with his beautiful wife Coretta and their two children. He was a warm and welcoming man. He took the script and invited us to go to Montgomery on Sunday where he would preach the sermon in his father's church.

In Montgomery, we climbed the steps of the Capitol. Everything was marble white. I stood high up on the steps, looking down, and in the distant corner below was a small church. A white man came and stood beside me. "What are you looking for?" he asked.

I pointed to the little church. "What is that?"

"That is that nigger's church, and believe me, we'll get him." I felt the hate in his words and a chill ran through me.

Being in Dr. Martin Luther King, Sr.'s Savior Church in Montgomery and hearing the choir singing made any setting I had around me unimportant to the event. The glory of those voices, the spectacle of those black faces with their sorrow and passion and tenderness—

My other experiences in churches had been with pale, white protestant churches: cold and formal and unfeeling or with feelings so deeply buried that they seemed to be unfeeling.

Here, emotion was flowing deep and free and when Dr. King, Jr. spoke from the pulpit, the words streamed out and lighted up the faces of the congregation. It made all white churches seem so pallid by contrast.

Dr. King, Jr. told the congregation about the screenplay, which he had read the night before. He said he had been deeply moved by it and looked forward to the movie.

"It was brought to me by these people sitting down there beside you." They all turned and looked at us, and when the sermon was over they surrounded us and embraced us. It was one of the most moving experiences I have ever had.

Dr. King was very busy, and he left right after the service to go to a meeting of the Southern Christian Leadership Conference. Before I had embarked on this project, I had sent him a letter and a contribution to his organization. He sent us a letter in thanks, which I still have today.

We left Montgomery the next day, travelling up the coast in search of money and support. We approached the well-to-do black families without success.

Before we left Alabama, we had made a point of meeting Rosa Parks who had started the boycott of the buses by refusing to sit in the back of the bus. She was a quiet, impressive woman. We also met Abernathy, King's right-hand man, and we taped an interview with him.

When we got home, there was a telegram from de Sica, the Italian director of *Bicycle Thief*, saying that he would be interested in directing the film. I was thrilled: We had an excellent script, Dr. King's blessings, and now the interest of one of the best directors. All we needed was the money.

I wrote to Nat King Cole, but couldn't get any help from him.

I contacted a liberal lawyer who people said would help me, but when he heard that I had planned to name names and tell of the atrocities that had been committed by the police chief and his dogs, the lawyer said, "I cannot recommend to any of my clients that they invest in this project. They would be sued for millions of dollars and subjected to mistreatment."

And so it went. There was just too much fear. It seemed like people were afraid of getting involved with a dangerous and unpopular cause. Maybe it was a project ahead of its time.

So: no money, no film. An aborted project—

When I was not able to put the film together, I reached a low spot in my life. I was very ill with pneumonia, and for six weeks lay in bed.

Then Florence Rosten entered my life. I had seen her at social events, so I knew who she was when she called me and said, "Get off your ass. There's work to be done. My friend Dr. Ferguson is heading up an experimental mental health center in downtown Los Angeles, a halfway house. He's a psychiatrist—very forward looking. They need volunteers. We can work as art therapists, and maybe he'll let us put some art on his walls."

I didn't hesitate. We went down in her VW Bug,

and forever after I have loved Bugs.

I met Dr. Ferguson, a tall, goodlooking Irish man with red hair and a love of women.

"Well, girls," he said, waving his arms at the vast expanse of white walls in the three huge rooms and the hall. "Here are the walls, and they're all yours. You can paint anything you want on them, and the more clients you involve in the work, the better."

I felt it was the greatest gift anyone had ever given me.

"Come on, kid," Florence said. "Let's get to work." Her shiny face was beautiful, and I felt a great thrust of love go out to her.

And so for the next four or five years my days took a structure: I would get up at eight a.m., jump into the pool to feel fully awake, make breakfast, take a quick look at the clock: "Florence will be here at ten." Make my bed—that was an inflexible rule: never to come back to an unmade bed. I'd dress and begin to say goodbye to my beloved shepherd dog, Gus. Florence would arrive, parking her Bug in the space vacated by Charlie. I'd walk out of the house without locking any doors—it was before theft days. We'd pop into my olive-green station wagon and be on our way through the ugly streets of Los Angeles until we arrived at an equally ugly stucco building on Normandy at Santa Monica, which must have housed a small factory at one time. We'd go through the doors and greet Bob Ben Ali, a 300-pound Arab who led psychodramas once a week and who manned the desk. We always thought of him as a nice fellow. Later on it was shown that he had kept written records of all the activities of the doctors working there and had turned them over to the authorities. In retrospect he did seem like a "slimy fellow"— too agreeable.

The walls of the whole front hall was covered with the mural we had painted when we first came to work at the center. It was based on a contemporary play called *Where have Monday, Tuesday gone?*—fitting, we thought, as so many of the people who came there had mislaid some of the days of their lives. It was quite a good mural.

Into the center's main room: filled as usual with people as yet undecided as to what our program might be for the day.

Dr. Ferguson had established this experimental center for outpatients with a view to trying new ways to help mentally disturbed people. We had psychodrama, dance therapy, daily discussions, political happenings, and for Florence and myself, art. People arrived on their own steam at eight-thirty in the morning and left on their own steam at four-thirty. "Clients" they were called, but I've always hated that word. It seems so commercial, like shoppers at Macy's Department Store. Humans or patients is better.

Every morning when we got to the center, Dr. Ferguson would greet us with a big kiss on the mouth. I didn't like it, but it went with the territory. Otherwise, he was okay, and Florence liked him.

First thing in the morning, without any

leadership, the patients would sit in a big circle and so would we. A discussion would start, usually about current events in their lives.

Someone might say: "I met a poltergeist this morning on the bus." He'd be very upset and wouldn't want to sit down.

And then would come the discussion:

"How did he get on the bus? Did he have any money?"

"Don't be silly. Poltergeists don't need any money. A poltergeist is a ghost."

And that would end that exchange.

Sometimes, there were direct attacks by one person against the other. There would be screaming and yelling and fist shaking. There was only one rule at the center: "No physical violence." Once someone threw a paper cup, and he was expelled from the circle.

This process let off a lot of steam and was actually a good way to start the day.

In the beginning, I was somewhat afraid of the patients. I thought in terms of "we" and "they." But as soon as I had made friends with some of them, that wore off. Still some of their responses startled me—like once I greeted a patient with, "Hi, how are you today?" and he looked at me in anger and said, "How dare you ask me that? Next think you'll be wanting is to jump into bed with me."

Once we saw the day's schedule, Florence and I made up our minds as to what our activities would be. We never missed Ben Ali's weekly psychodrama, which would be based on the inner life and problems of one of the patients. This was played on a circular platform with three levels in the main room. If one of the patients wanted, for instance, to have a family problem worked out, he'd go up on stage and give the problem. Ben Ali would then outline it, and the patient would chose from the audience someone resembling each family member—father, mother, brother, wife—needed to act out the outline given by Ben Ali. Then each of the stand-ins would be positioned by the patient on the stage, using the three levels to get the right degree of closeness or distance. Then under Ben Ali's guidance, the problem would be acted out.

Ben Ali was an extraordinary director, and his psychodramas with real situations and real people as actors were dynamic and moving. I remember one of the psychodramas vividly: a young woman admitted that she had killed her child. Was it true? Would Ben Ali have to report it? What to do? Things like that sort of shook you. Once you've seen psychodramas, it makes commercial theatre seem very pallid by comparison.

Florence and I also enjoyed the dance class that was geared to promoting trust. Patients would dance with their eyes blindfolded, and a "guardian" would follow behind them like a shadow. At various moments, patients were instructed to fall backwards, relying on their guardian to catch them.

We'd set time aside each day to paint as well. It was thrilling to do whatever we wanted on those walls. I think that's when I began to paint my kind of painting, for better or for worse. We did about five murals in that one building. One we did with twenty-three patients. I divided the area up into squares and gave each patient a square so that it wouldn't be too much of a disaster.

At the end of each day, Florence and I would pack up, and on the way home, we'd market for dinner, usually for five or six people. Cook, eat, drink, have lively conversation, wash dishes, straighten up the house, look at late news, and then to bed and sleep.

Those years we volunteered at the center were good years. We painted the five murals there and a few more in other hospitals and such, including a fifty-two-foot mural at Synanon, the drug rehabilitation center in Santa Monica. Everybody was very nice to me. They used to call me Michelangelo. And even though I don't feel I did any work worth preserving, I learned a lot. I learned the techniques of mural painting and of handling big spaces. It was quite thrilling and exciting. I also learned an awful lot from the discussion circles and the psychodramas. I had been rather a repressed person; I never really expressed what I felt. And at the center, I began to learn to express myself—not only artistically but verbally.

Even after we stopped volunteering at the center, Florence's presence made my life full, active, and rewarding. There were some dark spots with Charlie, but having Florence in my life got me through all the troubled times.

There was never anything sexual about my

relationship with Florence. It was pure love and friendship: "I will be there when you need me; I will be there for increasing your enjoyment and pleasure in living. We will paint together, cook together, give parties together, invent ideas and carry them out together." I would wake up in the morning with a new idea and grab the phone. "What do you think, Florence?"

We'd talk while the sleeping body of my husband on the bed beside me was dreaming his own dreams, planning his own plans, deciding what lies he would invent to tell me if he had a plan to be with someone. I still felt a little pang when he would dish out those lies to me, but less and less as time went by. I needed an escort and he was it. He was a good driver, and he would take me places that I was not able to drive myself.

My real life, my good life, my honest life, was from nine a.m. until the evening. I had a friend. She had the same sense of adventure and same interest in discovering the world every day that I had. She had a marvelous sense of humor that lit up every event.

We were always inventing things. Some succeeded and others failed. Once we made a felt picture, cut it up into pieces, and made it into a kit: a "make it yourself" picture. We got a distributor who sent it out at the Christmas season. We made a few pennies, and we sent it to our friends for Christmas.

Florence's presence in my life enabled me to be more myself, and I think it was the same for her.

During my lifetime, different people have

applied different labels to me in conversation. Most of these I rejected, thinking, "That's how they think from their point of view: This label they are assigning me is simply a reflection of themselves; I have just cast a slight shadow on their mirrors, and they have bent their heads and come out with that sign of recognition of my presence."

But, sometimes, at an expected moment from an unexpected person can come a description that seems to fit.

That happened once when I was sitting between a statistician and a police commissioner waiting for their comments on a short film that my husband Charlie and I had made following the Watts riots.

Watts had become a current topic of interest and conversation, and the white community had become aware that there was a seething mass of black humanity that lived in that area and that did not like whites. So a group of us "advanced" white people decided to go down to Watts and face up to the blacks and find out what they thought of us. We met them in a garage space overwhelmingly crowded with blacks. For the first time I experienced the feeling of being one of a few solitary whites in an ocean of black faces. They made room for us towards the front of the group, and then let us have it. It was in the days when the words like shit and bullshit and asshole still had their strong ability to sting and make you feel insulted, not having been watered down by constant overuse.

So there we were: my husband, Charlie, who was a science writer, my friend, Gerry Newmark, who was a psychologist who advised business corporations on how to get the cooperation of their employees, and myself, who was an artist muralist around town and who worked as a volunteer art therapist in mental hospitals. We'd decided to make a film showing blacks how they could better their lot by developing cottage industries for making toys, clothes, etc., and how young companies could distribute the goods and advertise them as coming from black industries . . .

We'd made the film, and we'd shown it to this elite group of intellectuals, among them the president of the University of Chicago, a statistician from Rand, and various others who did not venture down into the black barrio but who were very skilled about figuring out with pencil and paper what was going on down there.

After seeing *Operation Boot Strap*, the statistician turned to me and said, "You are a romantic, aren't you?" I felt he had put his finger on what motivated me, which was something I had always wondered about.

As a child, I never wanted to be a female. I used to stand in front of the full-length mirror in my mother's bathroom and close my eyes for ten seconds. "When I open them," I'd think, "God will have performed a miracle, and I will have become a boy. God will do this for me because I have always tried hard to be good."

I had a boy's suit that I wore to act in our plays. Since there was a shortage of boy actors, I got to be the hero in the play. It combined two things I badly wanted to be: a boy and a hero. Two impossible goals. But isn't that what makes a romantic?

I looked at the statistician, and I thought, "You're all right. You're not just the bunch of figures that I thought you were at first. You beamed right into me."

And that's what Florence's presence in my life released. With her, I could be what I was.

When Nixon took office, he called Charlie's boss, Fred Ikle, to Washington, D.C., to head up Arms Control. Ikle asked Charlie to come with him, so in 1973, we left California.

They had found us a nice house with a big garden that belonged to the Biddles. Soon though, we found a coop apartment on Connecticut Avenue that we wanted to buy. VIPs filled the building: admirals, judges, generals. It was a very snobbish group. They interviewed us first at a cocktail party before we were allowed to buy the apartment. Then there were the rules and regulations we were supposed to abide by: no shorts were allowed, baby carriages had to be taken up and down in the dog elevator, etc. Most of the time we ignored the rules, which meant we were periodically caught by the person who was in charge of running the building.

I had my studio in the apartment where I sculpted. A few years before while we were still in California, I had come across a picture by the great French photographer Cartier Bresson. It was of a group of chairs whose last occupants had left them angled towards and at each other. They were so expressive of the feelings, of the conversations that

Lovers Chair
Carousel Bench
Serenity Bench

Indian Family Bench
Tino & Altina

Lovers Chair
Mother Earth Father Sky Bench
Pagliacci Bench

had passed between the people who had left them that the thought came to me to transform them into humanistic forms, into chairs and benches that were at the same time people. Clare Luce Booth, who'd been one of the first to buy my Harlequin glasses was also one of the first to buy one of my *Chairacters*. There must have been some affinity between what I did and what she liked.

I had some success with my *Chairacters* in California. One of my benches was featured on the cover of *The Los Angeles Times* magazine. In Washington, my benches were accepted and publicized. I became a success, but Charlie became a failure. The change in the administration lost him his job, and for the seventeen years we stayed in Washington, he never found another.

23

The years with Charlie were like weather: It's cold, it's hot, it's windy, it's wet, it's damp, it's dry, it's icy, it's humid, it's piercing, it's becalmed, it's slippery, it's fetid, it's tempestuous, it's snowy, it's rainy, it's lightning.

Sometime after the first few months, the war between us began. Before that, we were too busy getting acquainted, feeling out the soft spots, the hard spots, the fun spots between us, wondering if we would make it, then working out our individual wishes and destinies, side by side and further and further apart until it finally came to a parting of the ways.

Charlie and I were married for twenty-four years—the longest marriage I had, and the phoniest. I was never really terribly in love with him, but he was very good-looking, seemed like a nice person. I never really tried to have a rich marriage. That's a lie; I did try. I hear myself in the early years talking to myself in the upstairs bedroom: "I think he has a potential. I think if we travelled and he could see the world, it would open his eyes and he wouldn't be so tied to just taking the kids for pony rides on Sunday or taking his mother for dinner at some dumb restaurant where they served American, Yankee Doodle Dandy food." But everything we did that was a little out of the ordinary was only used by him to make conversation to impress someone at the office. Outside of the really deep love he had for his children, he was uniquely devoted to wanting to impress the people at the think tank where he worked. Those people who were also involved with impressing each other and jockeying around for position and nodding their heads wisely about all the government secrets they knew that didn't allow them to complete sentences—everything was too classified to mention. Although one part of me liked these people, the other part of me steadily grew to hate them more and more. It was all so frustratingly mysterious.

There were moments in the company of other people where we were playing the parts of the happily married couple, and for those moments, we actually believed it ourselves.

"Why do you insist on fooling yourself?" my psychologist friend Gerry Newmark would ask me.

"What are you talking about?"

"You know what I'm talking about—"

And I would concede. "Because I have to keep the boat from sinking . . . "

Gerry would shake his head and say, "When you're ready to talk, I am here and ready to listen."

At the base of my fear of losing Charlie was the disgrace of a divorce and of being alone without the structure that married life provided. Being married was like a construction that I lived in: I didn't have to keep making urgent decisions; my time was planned and I could live in the boxes of that plan. Nine to six belongs to me, and six to nine belongs to doing what married people do: have dinner, see friends, sleep together, wake up and start all over.

It has a rhythm. When you are single, it's decisions, decisions: Whom shall I go out with tonight? It sucks up too much energy that could be better spent painting, sculpting, exploring. I felt freer when I was married and more tied down when I was free. How crazy can a person think? That's how crazy I was thinking.

What about the incessant war that went on between me and Charlie? What about this "big wall of forgiveness" I erected between us? "You can't hurt me," I was saying. But I kept looking thinner and more miserable and more strained. "You are like a child kicking his mother: you can't hurt me. I am bigger and smarter and better than you are. You don't have anything you really like to do—that's why you loll around with these women. Well, perhaps they give you admiration and self-respect that I can't give you because I don't have it to give you. I feel I am married to a 'thin man' made up to look like a big man—not my kind of man. So, in a way, I don't resent your having women. Everyone has to have something to give themselves satisfaction. I can't give it to you, but I forgive you. I know that it is pretty insulting to be forgiven because it implies that you have sinned, but benevolent me: I forgive you."

Then one day, rising above this underneath conversation, came a dart like a sharp arrow that splintered my "wall of forgiveness."

"You can't buy me, nor my children," he said as he sat on the edge of my bed and looked down at me.

I threw the covers aside. I got up. "What makes you think I want to buy you? You don't look like such a bargain to me, nor do your children."

"I was just kidding."

"Kidding? You're a liar. That came straight from your heart. Maybe it's time . . . " I left the sentence unfinished.

"Yes," Charlie said. "It's time to go out for a walk."

"Okay, why not? Let's walk across the bridge." Symbolic, maybe.

On the other side, we sat in a small cafe and drank cafe au lait and ate sweet rolls. I watched as couples crossed the bridge, some of them clinging to each other as though happy to be together.

When the time came to pay the bill, Charlie said, "Would you? I don't have any change."

"This goes along with my buying you—and your willingness to be bought?"

"Can't you forget that I said that?"

"No, I don't think I can."

In my head, I could hear my father's voice: "They will all want to marry you for your money."

"No, no," I would protest. "Women who have no money get married. Money can't be what a man marries a woman for."

But when Charlie had said that out loud, he had hit a bull's eye that produced cracks in the "wall of forgiveness." It was crumbling, and it was only a question of time.

I paused at the half-opened door as I had so many times over the years. Why shouldn't I plunge into the room and demand that he stop talking to the owner of that sweet-talking voice that I'd heard on the extension, that voice that gave me such a sickening rumble at the pit of my stomach?

For years, my philosophy had been: Ignorance is Bliss. As long as the voices were not talking directly to me, a space was left in which it was possible to pretend that the voice and its owner didn't really exist, possible to keep my image of my marital life wrapped around me like a cocoon that defied the entrance of any foreign creature, that made it possible for me to exist and behave.

I remembered that I had left something cooking on the stove—his dinner. That was important: not to let something burn, not to interrupt the regularity of eating, sleeping, talking, planning the activities of the day or evening. Maybe I'd say to him, "Shall we go to a movie? Or perhaps take a walk? Or go to that little cafe across the bridge and have dinner and forget about cooking?" In the soft night, the park with its abundance of trees that stretched under the bridge would look beautiful. Perhaps if we could look at something beautiful together, it would help things. Things? What things? No, it was feelings, not things that might take the sharp edges off our words, those barbs whenever we spoke, the hidden stings . . .

As I stood in the kitchen, the apartment stretched behind me, the studio with my unfinished sculpture, the living room that needed to be straightened up and set in order. The girl wouldn't be in to clean for another three days. There were so many things to be attended to. That was what life was really all about—the unread newspaper still folded and unopened lying on the kitchen table waiting to tell me what was going on in the real world outside. I turned the gas down, enjoying the delicious aroma that came from the meat, onions, and carrots as they blended together. I let them continue to cook; after all, we might decide to eat at home. I turned back and walked to the half-opened door. Instead of knocking as I always had before, I moved the fingers of my hand gently so they made a small tapping noise on the door as I took a hesitant step into the room.

It was as I knew it would be: Charlie lying on his unmade bed, the telephone pressed to his ear. He looked up at me, startled. I had never come into his room before without knocking, without asking permission. He stopped talking, turned his head, and looked directly at me. "I'll call you back," he said into the telephone. And then to me, in a matter-of-fact voice, he said, "I was talking briefly to Ruth." Whenever he felt guilty about something he would insert the word "briefly" as though the shortness of the act would mitigate its being wrong.

I wished for the courage to grab the telephone and smash it down on his head. For a split second in my brain I could see his face gashed, perhaps bleeding against the white of the pillow, then the phone falling to the floor and that sweet, sickening voice calling out, "Hello, hello? Are you there darling?" That voice disappearing with the telephone into the tufts of the carpet.

Charlie rose in the rumpled bed and leaned his head against the wall behind him. "What can I do for you?"

Those words brought an image to mind: my standing in front of his desk, waiting to be given permission to speak.

"Please come in and sit down," he said, waving me towards a chair near the bookcase.

I passed my hand over the books. "Books are my friends," I thought. My hand stopped at a book in a red and black paper binding. I pulled it out. *Blood and Money.* I remembered it. It was a "page turner."

I said aloud to Charlie, "This is a good book. Did you read it?"

"You didn't come here to talk about books, did you?"

"No. I got a message for you from Gordon. He called from his office at the World Bank and said they have an opening there. He'd like to make an appointment for you with the head of personnel."

I watched his face as I spoke. It began to look flushed and angry. The skin seemed to rise up pink around his nose and eyes, to vibrate in a way, and his mouth formed a twisted downward line.

"You don't care, do you, what job I take, as long as I take a 'job.' Nine to five! You think: He'll be occupied and out of my way. Then he'll come home, and we'll listen to the news and then eat dinner. You know how I feel here? As though I were in jail."

Now we're getting to the heart of it, I thought. If you are in jail, then I am the jailer. I looked at the book I held in my lap, stroking its glossy cover. "I love books that are page turners. Once you start reading them, you are immersed in the world they create and your own world stands on the side, waiting until you're done and only then does it call you back."

"What's wrong with your world?" asked Charlie. His face was filled with reproach, tinged with dislike. "It seems to me you have pretty much everything the way you want it."

"What's wrong with my world? What's wrong with my world? What's right with it? What's right with it? I have a husband who has no job and who doesn't bother to look for one, who lies on his bed all day, reading *The New York Times*, masturbating and talking to his mistress who's 3000 miles away. Where do I fit in?"

As I listened to the words stabbing the air, my voice frightened me. It sounded like the croak of an ugly hen.

"So what if I was masturbating."

"I think it's disgusting."

"Disgusting?" He got up off the bed, and stood over me, and his bigness drew from me the same response I had always felt.

"Why don't we introduce a new character into this equation?" he said. "How about: 'Truth.' It's been absent for a long time. You don't satisfy me sexually. So this is what I do. Don't you ever masturbate?"

I was silent for a minute, and then I decided to welcome the new character Truth.

"Yes, I do sometimes when I am looking at some handsome guy on the T.V., but I don't make a career of it. I only do it occasionally, late at night, when you're not lying on the bed next to me."

I was standing up now, challenging Charlie, and more than that, challenging my great fear, the fear that was always there: the fear of abandonment, the fear of being alone. All this time I had kept Truth at a distance, hoping that ignoring its presence would keep me from being abandoned. I would tolerate almost any abuse to keep from being alone. That fear of the void, the deep throb of being alone.

I felt the apartment behind me. All its activities: shopping for food, making of meals, getting new recipes, trying to be funny and cheerful. All this had been allowed to stand for a good marriage.

Truth had been missing. I had felt that its absence had warded off my being abandoned, but in that moment, I knew I had been wrong. Despair permeated my being with the realization.

I carefully placed the book back into the space where it belonged. I pushed it in carefully so that its back was even with all the backs of all the other books. So much for that: at least that had been regulated and put in place. I turned and left the room and went into my studio.

I looked at the piece that I was working on—a man and a woman, attached back to back. The man, with a sullen face, was looking into the distance. The woman held a large bird in her hands, its beak touching her half-opened mouth as if she were telling it her secrets. I looked at the sculpture long and carefully, turning its pedestal slowly round and round, and in that looking, I realized what I had known all along: that the man was Charlie and that I was the woman. That was why I had placed them so. They had reached that position of non-communication, back-to-back, but still fused together. My sculpture, I thought, speaks the Truth that I had been afraid to speak.

I picked up a small saw and began cutting the face of the man in half. As I did this I felt a sense of bitter satisfaction flow through me.

But it was not enough. I went over to the wall where my tools were hanging, picked out a hammer with a steel head, and began smashing the face with fury and anger. The pieces fell on the floor all around me.

I sat down on the small child's chair that I kept for working on the lower parts of my sculptures—a little chair of dark wood with a woven string seat that I had picked up in Greece. It had come a long way to help a sculptor view her art work. It was one of the objects that I treasured, one of the many objects strewn around the studio that were my valuables. "One man's junk is another man's treasure." Where had I heard that? It was true. Next to a small plaster skeleton from which I had learned anatomy was the head of a Greek boy with his pure profile and full lips and next to that a bronze of a Rodin head, beautiful in any position. These were all mine: to hold, to finger, to fondle.

On the wall, the self-portrait of my first lover in Paris to remind me of him and his studio at the head of a rickety staircase where I would climb up daily and where there was only a charcoal stove to keep us warm.

I studied the sculpture, turning it on its pedestal. That looks good, I thought. That flat form, coinciding with the sharp features of the other side. Far better than leaving it just an ordinary usual face.

But the mutilated face seemed to say back to me, "Come on! You did to me what you wanted to do to Charlie. Cut me, gashed me, punished me for being enraptured by that sweet-talking voice and the girlish giggle. Cut him down, cut him back, destroy him, throw him away."

"Oh, shut up," I said back to the face. "Don't be absurd." I picked up a piece of sand paper and began sanding the places where I had cut until the surface was smooth and shining white. Then I gradually moved to other parts of the piece. My smoothing strokes went over the carved wings of the bird. A wise bird. You are my talent; you are what I communicate with; you are my identity. I am a sculptor, not a jailer. You are what gives me my urge to survive, what gives me pleasure and hope for the future. No one can take away from my hands the ability to make things, to make something that has never existed before, to make these special shapes and forms. Even my tired muscles and fingers give me a certain satisfaction. My hands and abilities absorb and possess me, cancel out place or time, allow me to work without the feeling of time pursuing, problems interfering; a true flow into the rhythmic development and progress of the forms as they emerge into being.

Through the open door, I saw Charlie coming towards me. Surprise crossed his face as he looked at the mutilated head on the man. He took a step into the room and said, "I have decided to go to California. There's a conference on ecology that I very much want to attend."

I stood quietly. We exchanged talking glances. Mine was saying, "You want to go to California to be with your lover." His was saying, "We both know I am going to California to be with Ruth. What are you going to do about it?"

I heard a voice coming out of me saying, "If you go to California, you don't have to come back anymore."

His eyes jumped as though an electric current had passed through them. They looked suspended. "Are you serious?" he asked.

"Yes, I am. I've decided to live for a change with this character called Truth and follow where it leads me."

He turned and left the room.

I thought, "Can it be true what I just said? A declaration of independence. I am ready, even if I am not ready—"

Turning back to my work, I took up the steady rhythm of sanding. It was dark outside, now dark inside too.

Back in my room, I lay on my bed and flipped on the television: Come in, news. Tell me of all the horrible things that are happening. See if I care. It will help to pass the time.

South African police beating with sticks on blacks appeared on the screen. I flipped to another channel: an old classic movie, Cary Grant and Audrey Hepburn. Shiny and beautiful, that's the way things should be: funny, light, witty, and graceful. I heard a sound—Charlie standing at the door.

"I've decided not to go. When are we having dinner?"

Surprise, pleasure, despair. Who had won? Who had lost? I felt a sense of relief that nothing big, nothing drastic was about to happen; then a sense of disappointment as though I had been robbed of a new excitement, a new experience. I had to turn back on the road I had just forged ahead on, had to find my way back to the old situation. Why? Give it another try? Why? Why? Making beds, cooking and keeping house, and filling barren moments with small pleasures. That would be the fabric of my life once again. Maybe I could try harder to reach out, to try to find out if there was any feeling left between us. But I knew it would only be a few hours or at most a few days before that sweet, sickening voice with its girlish giggle would be heard once again on the telephone.

I pushed it from my mind. I said, "Do you want to go to that little restaurant across the bridge?"

In 1980, I went to New York for a show of my *Chairacters* in a gallery on Madison Avenue and 70th Street. Charlie came to "help" me. The show had good attendance, but not good sales. Charlie

Girl Chair
Cleopatra Bench
Altina & Freddy

went back to Washington.

From there I went into Art Expo, which was at the Coliseum on West 59th Street in New York City and showed works of artists from all over the world. The show lasted a week, with about 25,000 visitors coming through. I sold about twenty pieces to people from around the world and got good critical reviews, but it was a very wearying experience as I had to be there from early morning until night.

When the Art Expo closed, I went back to Washington. Early the next morning, the phone rang and when I picked it up, I heard that sickly sweet voice once again, asking for Charlie.

"Who is calling?" I asked.

"Ruth Baker," she said.

I heard Charlie pick up the receiver in the other room. I said to Ruth: "If you want him, you can have him with my compliments."

"I thought you were madly in love with Charlie," she said.

"No, I am not. I don't even like him. So take him." Then I yelled into the phone, "Charlie, are you there? Tell her she can have you." Two phones clicked, and I was the only one left on the line. I heard the front door bang, and I knew Charlie had gone out in the street to call her up, to reassure her.

When he came back, he came into my room and sat on the edge of the bed. Before he could speak, I said, "I want a divorce. I've had enough of this mess."

The corners of his mouth turned down as they

always did when he was in distress. "Why? I love you, Tina, and I always will."

"I can do without that kind of love," I said. "I'm going to get that Japanese girl lawyer, and she will contact you about the divorce."

He looked at me, his eyes blank and unbelieving.

"I'm not kidding. I want you to leave. Go to your lover in California. Take a suitcase for now, and I will send you the rest of your things later.

He went down to the storage where we kept our luggage and came back with a brand new suitcase that I had just bought.

"Hey," I said. "That's my new suitcase. You can't take that."

"Are you going to be that way?"

"Yes, this is the new Tina, not the old 'I'll take anything without objecting' Tina."

Later I went to the door with him, and as I watched his figure walking down the hall, carrying his own old suitcase, I could feel the great pain gripping me.

I turned back and walked through the door and into the open mouth of my great fear: Abandonment. I could feel it swallow me up. I had been abandoned. I would live alone, surrounded by empty walls, my own voice echoing through the silence. The apartment would seem vast and empty. I would lie on my bed for awhile and cry and cry.

24

After Charlie left, I thought I would be very depressed and sad, but surprisingly I felt as if a load had fallen off my back. I looked at myself in the mirror, and a lot of the strain that I had been seeing in my face had disappeared.

I discovered some of the positive qualities of living alone: I could yell if I wanted to, to talk out loud and say things that I would have been afraid to say in the presence of another person; I could do exactly whatever I wanted to do, when I wanted to do it, without asking for permission or approval; I could run or dance or do whatever I was moved to do—I was free! I wondered if there existed any companion in the world with whom one could feel so absolutely free. Probably not.

But then I met Tino.

When Tino came into my life in 1980, I was working on a full-scale bench of two lovers with their heads inclined towards each other. I first worked the core in styrofoam, which is light and easily cut; then built up the form's composition in plaster; and then added the details. The lovers were human size, but some of the people of my

Chairacters were larger than life. When *The Lovers* was complete, I would send it to the studio and factory in California, where they made molds and then produced fiberglass casts that were the finished product.

I was working towards a show that would happen in the spring, only six months away. My assistant, a young sculptor named Brian Kirk, was leaving because he wanted a job that paid him more money so he could get married.

I needed a strong assistant because sculpture is hard work—pieces to lift, heavy materials to move—and I needed someone with some artistic know-how. I asked at the Corcoran Art School, where I'd been taking classes, and then I asked Gladys, my friend and masseuse, who had just come back from Cuba and had brought her sister and brother and his friend back with her.

President Carter had sent word to Castro that he would allow into the United States any Cubans who wanted to leave and whom Castro didn't want: 100,000 Cubans came.

Gladys, who is a very courageous and, even, I might say, a heroic person, went to Miami, bought a boat, and hired a crew to go to Cuba to pick up members of her family. The boat proved unseaworthy, and they were escorted back by the U.S. Coast Guard.

She had spent most of her money, but she collected some more from the sale of her and her friends' jewelry. This time, she rented a thirty-five foot motorboat that came with an American captain and crewman. After having its seaworthiness checked, she once again set out for Cuba.

The bay at Havana was full of rescue boats. The procedure was to go in to the harbor, register at a dock, giving your name and the names of the people you wanted to pick up. She did this, and then she went back into the harbor, anchored down, and waited to be called.

She waited three weeks, going in twice a week for food. Finally her name was called. They went in to the dock and picked up her brother Fernando, her sister Ophelia, and their friend Celestino Miranda. To get her own family, though, Gladys had also to take the prisoners and mentally disturbed people that the Cuban officials jammed onto her small boat.

Crossing ninety miles of choppy seas in an overloaded boat, the people on board were sick, screaming, hoping and praying they'd reach the U.S. Finally after nine hours, they saw the shores of Key West. The Coast Guard helped them unload, and they went through customs and to the doctors.

They were met by a friend of Gladys', who arranged their flight tickets to Washington D.C. There they moved into Gladys' apartment at the Watergate in Virginia.

Tino had left Cuba with his hat, his shorts, his shirt, and his shoes. Everything else had been taken from him. Gladys bought him clothes and a wristwatch, which he still wears.

Fernando and Tino both got jobs in a restaurant

Fernando

in Washington, Bojangles—Tino as a chef and Fernando as a busboy.

When I asked Gladys if she knew anybody who could help me, she said, "Yes. Celestino Miranda. He can do anything and everything, and he is a fine man."

Saturday at nine, the doorbell rang. I opened the door, and I looked up at Tino. He had a beautiful, dark, and kind face, and he wore a funny little hat. Inexplicably, I had a feeling of comfort and reassurance when I saw him. His hand as he shook mine was large and strong, but sensitive.

"Come in," I said.

He spoke no English. I spoke a little Spanish, enough to be able to tell him what I wanted and what I needed. I had learned the language from my parents, who spoke an old dialect because they were of Sephardic Jewish stock that had been driven out of Spain in the 15th century.

We went into the studio. Besides *The Lovers*, I was working on a large six-foot figure with his arms stretched out, covering it with large pieces of brilliant-colored mosaics. Surprisingly, Tino picked it up, and I could see he had very strong and knowledgeable hands.

We introduced ourselves, and I asked, "Have you done any sculpture before?"

"Some," he said, "but I have made many things."

He explained that because of his chef's job, he could only come to help me on Saturdays and Sundays.

I wished he could come every day. Still two

days a week was certainly better than none.

Working with Tino was so smooth and easy—and fun. He was fast and accurate and handled clay and other materials very well. He was also extremely helpful and had many good ideas and suggestions that I could use. I began to look forward to his coming. We seemed to understand each other and work well together, and I felt very close to and at ease with him. I looked up into his face one day, and I think I knew then that we would have a good and deep relationship.

Summer was coming on. I had bought a house in Santa Fe where I expected to spend the summer. I decided to ask Tino if he would like come there and work in the studio and help in the house. He agreed. He said he would have to give the restaurant a month's notice so that they could get someone else.

I liked it that he was concerned about doing the right thing.

So I decided to go ahead in May, and he would come in June. I felt quite happy with the idea that he would be in Santa Fe and that I would not be living in a new unknown house, facing an unknown future, alone.

I had exchanged a house I had on the beach in Oxnard, California, for the Santa Fe house, which was owned by a woman architect. As the house in Oxnard was worth $50,000 more than the Santa Fe house, I had gotten some money I could use to do some remodeling. The architect agreed to stay in the house until May and to supervise the work, which helped me very much. When I arrived, there was no need for any further building.

Florence and I had picked out the house together. It had been hard being separated—with her still in California and me in Washington D.C.—and the house was a way we could spend at least the summer months together. But Florence would not be coming: even though she was only fifty-one, her heavy smoking had caught up with her and she'd died of lung cancer in April. This was a great and sad blow to me. She'd been my closest friend for twenty years.

I'd flown out to see her twice. The last time, she was in the hospital. I'd sit by her bed and hold her hand and talk of what we'd do that summer in Santa Fe. It was hard for me to believe that she would die, but she did. She died a week after the last time I saw her.

I think of 1981 as being the best and the worst year of my life. The best being Tino becoming a part of my life, and the worst being the loss of my dearest and best friend. For those twenty years, I had had the experience of friendship: a deep, abiding, rewarding friendship that lasted until the day she died. She'd said to me, "I have never loved anyone as much as I love you." I felt the same way.

Brian said he would drive with me to Santa Fe and help me get settled. When I told him I appreciated his coming, he turned his frank, open face to me and said, "We are soul mates. You have taught me a lot about sculpture."

I was surprised. "I have? I think you are a much better sculptor than I am."

"I didn't like leaving you, but you know I had to make more money. I think, though, that this fellow Tino will work out well for you. I like the way he handles materials. He has a kind of magic touch. When he touches earth, flowers spring out; when he touches clay, it takes shape."

"He has a lovely nature too," I said. "I would think that he would be hard and bitter after the way his father abandoned the family. How he was taken out of school, deprived of an education, and put to work when he was twelve.

"Have you seen his hands? Some of the fingers are without nails, because he was physically abused. And yet he handles everything with such care and delicacy."

We finally reached the house in Santa Fe. It was empty except for two beds, and 110 boxes waiting to be unpacked.

I walked around the house and then outdoors.

There was a lovely blue pool with a Jacuzzi attached and a large open space spreading out from the pool that was covered with gray stones like a Japanese garden. Big packing crates containing some of my *Chairacter* benches stood around the back yard. There was a lot of work to be done to make this place a home. But at that moment, I could think of only one thing—to stretch out on the bed and sleep.

Next morning we stared at the 110 boxes. What to unpack first? Luckily we'd marked them. We found the crucial ones: pots and pans, towels, and sheets. We cooked our first meal and took our first swim.

"Before we do anything else, Brian, let's go and buy some outdoor furniture so we can sit in the sun and enjoy this blue sky and the mountains."

The people in the stores were helpful and friendly. If they didn't have what you wanted, they told you where to go to get it. There didn't seem to be the feeling of competition between stores that existed in the big cities. We bought a round table and four chairs and two chaise lounges, and they looked fine by the pool.

The furniture from the Oxnard house stood in packing crates. We began prying them open and placing the furniture around the house. And then we unpacked the rest of the 100-plus boxes. Slowly the house began to look livable.

Charlie came "to help," and Brian left.

"I'll miss you," I said to Brian. "I hope you're going to be happy."

"Well, you know I'm not crazy to get married, but Mary Lou is going to have the kid."

"I don't like women who do that to fence in a guy to marry them."

"Oldest trick in the book. Still, I like kids," he said, and he was gone.

It didn't surprise me that Charlie was disappointed that I hadn't put his name down as co-owner even though we were divorced. All he ever seemed to think about was money—but money that he could get without working. Working wasn't on his list of desirable things to do.

He spent all his time reading the newspaper and worrying about the world situations.

June came. The phone rang, and it was Tino in Albuquerque. Charlie and I went to meet him. He had a small suitcase and a bewildered look.

We drove the fifty miles in silence. When we got to the house, he asked to use the phone. He called our mutual friend Gladys.

"I don't know where I am, in the middle of the mountains. It all looks a little like Cuba."

He told me later that Gladys had said to him, "Don't worry. Trust Tina."

I showed Tino his room and bath, and he seemed reassured. I showed him the studio and a bench of an Indian family that I had started.

He offered to cook dinner, and we cooked together.

In a few days Charlie left, and then the situation eased.

Tino and I began to have fun.

"I'll teach you how to drive," I told Tino. "We'll get a driving teacher."

His face lit up.

I started working with Tino on the Indian Family Bench. He did the back of the Indian, his big braid that hung down. He was as talented as Brian and as hard working. Tino taught me Spanish, and I taught him how to drive a car.

I was lucky. A Santa Fe gallery owner Elaine Horwitch saw and liked my work, and I became a member of her gallery. She promised me a show the next year. So now I had two galleries: Touchstone in Washington and Elaine Horwitch in Santa Fe.

Touchstone was a cooperative gallery, where a group of artists had joined together to show and help each other. We had a very able director, which is something cooperative galleries need as artists rarely make good directors. It was always fun to go to Touchstone. It was like a second home, and fellow artists were all generous in sharing their knowledge with each other.

Elaine Horwitch was a very prestigious commercial gallery. But I didn't know any of the other artists unless by chance I happened to meet them at an opening.

With Tino, I had a platonic, close working relationship. It seemed very calm and peaceful after the turbulence of the past year. I sort of wished it could go on forever, without any big decisions to make.

My son Denis came down. He was divorced at the time. He and I went on a trip to Carlsbad Caverns, and we were both so impressed by it. Those stalactites and stalagmites, sculptures of nature that excelled anything made by man.

Denis seemed to like Tino in a friendly way.

Terry and his Chinese-American wife Freida and their two small children came to visit.

"Do you think," Freida asked Terry, "that there is anything between Tino and your mother?"

"Oh no," Terry said. "Ma is like that. She makes many platonic male friends who are devoted to her and she to them."

Freida didn't answer.

The little girls loved Tino and he them. Tino seemed to be weaving his way into my life and the life of my family.

But the summer came to an end, and October opened over us with its crisp sunny blue days. My show at Touchstone would open at the end of October. Tino and I left for Albuquerque at four a.m. one morning in a taxi loaded with our luggage. I had found someone to take care of and live in the house for the winter.

I sat close to Tino with my arm through his. I knew when we got back to Washington, there would be decisions to make. I dreaded going to an empty apartment and Tino's going to live in an apartment that Fernando had taken with his mother, whom he had brought over.

That night in Washington I felt so lonely. The next morning Tino arrived, and I went over and kissed him.

He told Fernando, "Tina kissed me with a kiss that was more than a friendship kiss." He was right. The next day when he came, we went into the bedroom and made love. Our new relationship had started. We both were very happy, and every day the happiness grew.

Gradually the idea of getting married came into being, and one night while doing the dishes after dinner, we decided to.

He had told me a week before that he had never

been married, but had a son with a woman with whom he had lived for three years. She had been a bad mother and an unfaithful partner, so he had taken his son to his mother, who was bringing him up. I was pleased that he had never been married.

We began to plan our wedding. We would only have people of whom we were very fond.

I invited my friend who lived upstairs with her husband who was a general in the Air Force, and I invited the doorman who had been the first person to welcome us in Washington. Gladys, Jo my sculpture friend, Brian, Fernando, his mother, an Italian couple who had collected many of my chairs. In total, there were no more than thirty-five at our wedding, but they were a wonderful range of people.

I asked Schmutzhart, my sculpture teacher at Corcoran who was an ordained minister, if he would marry us. He was an Austrian and one of my favorite people. He bought an Alpine suit for the ceremony. He was married at the time to a beautiful woman from Thailand, who was also a sculptor.

Gladys brought us a wonderful three-tiered cake from a French bakery. Tino and Fernando cooked us a feast, meat stuffed with hard boiled eggs, four or five salads. The long table was covered with wonderful food. We had champagne and music and we all danced!

Tino looked very handsome. He bought himself a tan suit and cut his hair in a kind of bob. This was my fourth wedding and my happiest one.

I had a very successful show at Touchstone and

Tino was working on his own pieces to submit to Touchstone to become a member.

We worked hard all winter and planned a trip to Spain in the spring.

My marriage didn't sit well with the snobbiest people in my building, but I couldn't have cared less. I knew I had married a wonderful man, and after fifteen years, I am of the same opinion. He is thoughtful, kind, unselfish.

Our honeymoon in Spain was wonderful. Because of Franco and his dictatorship, I had never been there before. But now he was gone, and the monarchy had been restored and Spain was democratic and liberal.

We found a wonderful man called Fruto who had a taxi, and we hired him and his taxi to drive us all over Spain. He carried the picture of a beautiful girlfriend in the front of his cab.

25

Sometimes I see flashing in front of me the image of a matchmaker. "Matchmaker, matchmaker, make me a match." She is a thin woman in a pointed hat. She holds a pencil with a sharp point, and she has a long list on white paper in front of her. Male. Female. She matches them up in a sort of conventional, accepted way. He should be a few years older than she. They should be the same religion, nationality, education, etc. Then she came to my name and Tino's. All wrong, all wrong. Almost nothing as it should be.

She was older than he. They were different religions: he was Catholic, she was Jewish. They were of different nationalities: he was Cuban, she was American. They were of different classes: he had to begin work when he was twelve to support his mother because his father had deserted them and gone to Venezuela with another woman; she'd had private schools, plenty of money, first-class travel all over Europe. He had worked cutting sugar cane. She never worked but had people working for her.

The matchmaker was tired. What if she did tie up these two? Then she could go home. She would send those lists to the higher up matchmaker and hope for the best.

Florence had come for a visit in 1980. After spending time with me and Tino in the studio, she said to me, "You need someone like Tino, but with more education."

It was true that Tino didn't have much education. He had been only a boy when his father had abandoned him and his mother and his five brothers and sisters to leave the country with his mistress. They had been left destitute, and Tino had been obliged to leave school to help his mother support the family. They moved in with his aunt as his father had sold their house, leaving them homeless. There seemed to be no laws in Cuba to protect women or families. Tino took work wherever it was offered, and he and his mother had pulled the family through very difficult years.

There are different kinds of education, though: school education and life education. Both Charlie and Bidge had had plenty of college diplomas signed by distinguished citizens, but those diplomas had not done much towards educating them in interpersonal relationships or in how to treat a woman. Tino's hard-life education had taught him values that were basic. He was stern in his judgments of people and put sincerity and truth high up in his operating philosophy.

I knew that if I were to make a long-term alliance with Tino, there would be gaps in it that could not be filled. Discussions about books and ideas, a lot of informal exchanges that one takes for granted with people of one's own background. I knew that much of my social life would go down the drain. With Charlie I had been half of a desirable social couple with many more invitations than we could accept. With Tino these invitations would no longer exist.

But Tino had a thoughtfulness and consideration towards me. He was also strong and decisive in his actions. He was courageous. He was manly. He was very talented and creative and always full of ideas about things he wanted to make and projects he wanted to do. In that way, we were very much alike.

And he had a lot in common with my father who was also an immigrant with little education, but with an innate business sense so that in a country like the U.S., in the early years of this century, he had been able to carve out a fortune for himself.

The three important men in my life were all immigrants, two were refugees. I have tremendous admiration and respect for people who leave their country to go to a new country and make a new life. I think it takes a lot of guts and a lot of courage, which is something I admire. As Walpole said, "It's not life that counts, it's the courage you bring to it." I really believe that. I think in life you get knocked down very often, and when you get knocked down, you have to get up. And even though you just crawl for a while, you finally get back on your feet. You have to do things. Even though you do those things without grace and without style, the important thing is to do them.

I decided I wanted to spend my time with a man, rather than a façade of a man. And so I chose Tino—

I have never regretted it.

Jeremy
Jessica & Brittany
Peter

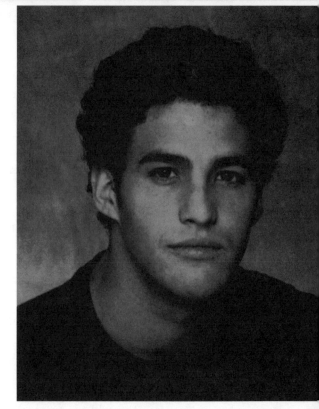

Victoria
Dalton
Juliette

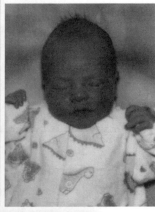

On December 11, 1987, my son Denis died. The last time I spoke to him was that afternoon. I had called him the night before to tell him I was thinking of moving to California. He was calling back to say that he hadn't returned the call that evening because it was too late—12:30.

"What were you doing out so late?" I said, kidding him.

"It was 12:30 your time only 9:30 mine," he said, and we both laughed because I was treating him as though he were once again sixteen and had to answer to his mother.

Then I told him about moving, and he answered in his usual cheery way: "That's good, Ma. You've had the Washington experience, and now it's time to come home."

And next the horrible phone call from Terry: "I don't know how to tell you. Denis died."

"How, how, how?"

"In his sleep."

Terry told me Denis had had trouble with his asthma, and the doctor gave him some strong medication, which they found in the bottle by his bed.

His wife Sherri who was away at school had been trying to reach him, and after she got no response all morning, she finally called Jim and asked him to go and find out if Denis was all right. Jim had a key, and he went in and found Denis in his bed. He had died in his sleep.

Denis' funeral was very hard. We rented a limousine to take us—Terry and his wife Freida;

their children, Jessica and Brittany; my niece Laurette; and me. We drove from Los Angeles to San Diego. When we arrived at the funeral parlor, Sherri was standing on the steps, dressed in black, with a soft black hat shading her eyes. Her face was swollen from crying. Beside her stood Denis' children, Victoria, Julie, and Peter. Denis' friend Bob Lee stood beside her. Sherri hugged me and her big body folded around me like soft comforting pillows. She wanted me to go in and see Denis, but I resisted. How could I go to see my son lying in a box, cold and dead?

After a few minutes standing next to the room where Denis was lying, I felt I was abandoning him. I went in, but I still couldn't find the courage or whatever it takes to walk across the room, lean over, and look at him. In the back of my mind I knew that if I was to survive, I had to avoid great shocks.

The wife of one of Denis' friends came over and told me that during a party once they had each described the kind of a funeral they would like to have. She said Denis had said he wanted a Dixieland band and afterwards chili con carne. And so it was when we went out to the Glen Abbey Memorial Park in San Diego. There were four men playing Dixieland music. It looked strange and very touching to me to see the men with their trumpets in their funny hats playing "When the Saints Come Marching In" as the coffin was being carried to the holder above the grave. Denis' son Peter, Tino, Denis' friends David Steinman and Bob

Lee, Jim and Terry were the coffin bearers. Still I didn't really feel that Denis was imprisoned in that box. It was still a joke.

Charlie had come, and he embraced me and started crying and didn't stop. I felt he loved and wanted me more than at any time during our marriage. I felt very sorry for him, and he felt sorry, too. All the hostility that Tino felt for him disappeared. The question came to my mind: Had he truly changed, or if we were back together, would he once again revert to his old ways? I think he really had changed, and I felt sorry.

Terry and Denis had been estranged for years, but I felt as though it had evaporated and he and Denis were together as they had been when they were nineteen or twenty. I also felt his feeling for me had been cleansed and we were as before his ten-year marriage to his first wife, where all his emotions had become distorted and not understandable. The great shock of Denis' death had made us more honest and direct.

Sheila was there with her son Anson. Knowing the story of his infatuation with Hitler and how he pasted Hitler's picture on the walls of his room, I suppose he reminded me of the boy in Brecht's play, *The Enemy of the People.* He seemed strange and turned inward and his face was not clear and clean.

Bidge's sisters Mary Lou and Janet were there. They went back further than anyone. They were both dear and sweet, gentle and fine.

Not long after Denis' death, Tino's doctor

became worried about a growth in his gut. He wanted to do exploratory surgery to rule out cancer.

When they wheeled Tino down the shiny green antiseptic hospital hall to the operating room and he disappeared, I stood as though all that lived inside of me had gone with him, and I was left standing like an empty, stiff, discarded sack. Would anyone notice that I was no longer a human being, but only a void surrounded by skin? I must have looked the same to the nurse who came over and put her arm around me.

"Come, my dear," she said. "We'll go back to the room now, and wait there. He'll be all right. Dr. Golden is a wonderful surgeon."

I wanted to hiss into her face: "What do you mean he'll be all right? They are going to cut into him, a knife held in their gloved hands like a scene from T.V., to find to ask to probe, what is this growth that the x-ray showed? Is it good, is it bad, is it the dreaded word cancer? Our whole future could hang on this word."

"How large is it?" I'd asked the x-ray man.

He put his hands together, fingers touching as though around a globe.

"Like . . . like a grapefruit?"

He nodded, his eyes sorrowful, unhappy. Thank you, I'd thought, for your sorrow.

I followed the nurse back into the room. I found I had difficulty in swallowing. I concentrated on that. "If I can't swallow, I will die." Death is a solution to too great misery, of course.

I found a chair to sit in. I looked at the clock up on the wall: It was 7:30 a.m. I must find something to look at, I thought. It was imperative if I wanted to survive the waiting time. I must keep from screaming and yelling. Why? What difference would it make? Someone would probably just walk in the room with a syringe full of dope, burying it in my arm, and smothering my screams and yells.

"Quiet now," they would say. "No more protests please. Be a good soldier."

It must have been my shock and fatigue, but as I sat in the chair, I seemed to go into a trance, a kind of sleep. With a shock, I felt a hand on my shoulder shaking me gently. A voice pierced my consciousness. "Mrs. Miranda." I knew it must be the surgeon. I could see his legs in front of me. I was afraid to raise my eyes to his face because I was afraid to read a bad message there.

I heard myself say yes with a questioning rise in my voice.

His voice went on steadily. "We did exploratory and his lungs, liver, pancreas and stomach are clear." He paused and the pause seemed interminable. "The tumor is attached to his small intestine, and I believe it is cancerous."

"No, I don't believe it." My voice was strident, full of anger and tears. Until a week ago, he was fine. How could it be? How could it be? I could feel my fists banging on an imaginary wall, protesting. I stood up and faced the doctor.

"Are you sure? Are you sure?"

"No," he said quietly. "But I'm pretty sure. I could lie to you, but I won't."

My mind was searching for an exit from hell. "Did you take it out? Did you get rid of it?"

There was a long pause before he spoke. "No, I made the decision not to. There are ways to cure it. Aggressive chemotherapy. Surgery would have left him an intestinal cripple for the rest of his life."

He turned now and started to leave the room. I ran after him. "Where's Tino?"

"He's still in intensive care. He will be back here in an hour."

He was gone.

I felt intensely bitter again. I had difficulty swallowing and the sweat came out all over me. I wished that my mother were alive. I wished for someone bigger and stronger than me that I could rest my head against and cry. But there was no one.

There was a year of chemotherapy when Tino would come back from a treatment shaken and nauseated and lie on the couch for hours, wrapped in a red velvet blanket. I would read to him, play classical music for him. He was courageous, a fighter. His hair all fell out. From being manly handsome to the point that women would openly embrace him in a crowd, his figure grew large and bloated from the drugs. He was no longer beautiful. We got him a big hat that he would wear when we went out to restaurants for a change of atmosphere.

He had all sorts of minor ailments. His feet were so sore he could not walk, and Fernando would sit on the bed and massage them for hours. Once Tino had fungus in his throat and lost his voice. That was the most desperate moment when he looked at me with his brown eyes so sad, appealing with a look that you sometimes see in the eyes of an animal.

Fernando is very religious, and he burned many candles in the church for Tino, each one with a separate prayer and a promise of something he would do if the prayer were answered. He and Fernando were friends: there was no limit to what Fernando would do for him. And I felt the same.

Slowly Tino got better. His tumor was reduced, and then came the report from the doctor. "You are free of cancer—for now. Let's be glad and thankful."

We had been going back and forth from Washington, D.C., to New Mexico, but in 1989, we decided to keep the D.C. apartment, but to make our year-round home in Santa Fe. After living for a year with what, I thought, was the knowledge that Tino was cured and that we could resume our life of working in Art and living with nature and travelling, a report came that doomed us once again to blackness and endness—Tino's cancer had recurred. I called Dr. Monzak in Washington and told him. "It's hopeless," he said. The only possibility he could extend for Tino was a bone marrow transplant, but I knew that, in and of itself, was a very serious and dangerous procedure.

Dr. Bogart, our cancer doctor in Santa Fe, thought it would be better to try a eight-month course of chemotherapy. She said in her gentle way, "Hopefully it will work."

All I could think was: "If Tino dies, I will kill myself." There was a lot of talk going on about the right to die. I bought a book, *Final Exit*, that told how to do it. How many pills to take and how to take them. Sure, but where would I get the pills? I didn't know anyone who would give them to me. When Florence was afflicted with lung cancer, I didn't want her to suffer and I asked a friend of mine, a physician, if he would help me get some drugs. He was very angry at me. How could I ask him for such a thing?

What was there to get so angry about?

Why is suicide considered a crime?

I remembered a case of a man who had been sentenced to death. He tried suicide and failed. He was rushed to the hospital, given exquisite care and he recovered so that he would be good and healthy when they put him to death to satisfy the law.

How best to kill myself? I didn't want to live without Tino. Pills? Not available to me. Drive the car into the garage, close the doors, and let the engine run? That should be a good way out. I remembered a friend of mine, an industrial designer, who had received a national design award the same year I had. When he knew his wife had terminal cancer, they committed suicide together in their car, inhaling carbon monoxide. And there was another friend and his wife who committed suicide by sitting on the couch and drinking poison. What kind? I never knew. There never were sufficient details.

But while I was thinking of suicide, Tino was taking another tack entirely. We had bought some additional land adjacent to our house. He sowed some of it with seeds—corn, beans, tomatoes—and on the rest of the land, he began building shelters for animals. "I may have cancer," he would say, "but I don't intend to die of it. The way I see it, the cancer is walking behind me, and I will attend to it when I have to, but I am in front, and I have a lot of things to do." So he learned of a man who lived thirty miles away who raised strange and exotic animals, and he discovered companies that would send him catalogs of rare and unusual animals. The animals started to arrive: four Afghan sheep, guinea hens, Angora rabbits. Tino spent hours in the Food Bin buying animal food, and he and a small squat Indian called Eloy built shelters for the animals. By this time, I also was involved. We got a fake windmill and put it up so the place really began to look like a farm. It already smelled like a farm and sounded like a farm. The neighbors would come and lean on the newly built fence and stare and ask all sorts of questions about the animals. The councilman from the district stopped by and said he wanted to meet the man who cared so much about the earth that he wanted to bring it back to life. I wrote an article about Tino's fight with cancer and about the farm he'd created; it was published in *The Santa Fe Reporter.*

Time passed. The chemotherapy prescribed by

Dr. Bogart was working, and Tino seemed to be hanging in there and getting better. At the end of the eight months, he tested normal, and we went around with thanks and prayers in our hearts. I forgot about suicide, but I put the book up on a shelf in the bedroom: Final Exit.

Dr. Bogart was a wonderful person and a wonderful doctor. To the dismay of her patients, she decided to give up her practice and go into painting and being an artist.

I have always been a believer in the "quality" of time rather than the "quantity" although I resent the way modern phraseology has a way of wringing poetry out of words leaving them with basic stark labels that could be pinned on a dress put on a department store counter to be sold at lower prices.

When I was thirty, I was faced with the possibility of spending six months with Eric who was expected to die in that time or twenty years with someone of lesser quality. I chose the husband for six months for I knew that in the years that possibly stretched ahead of me when I might be lying in bed alone in the night, it would be important to me to remember how I had watched his hands move over the piano keys and how I had heard the notes with their delicate fluctuation— sound used as no one else I had ever heard except perhaps for the greatest pianists like Horowitz. I knew those memories could sustain me through dark hours and assure me that my experience would rank among the best so that it became an integral part of me and my every day living.

I'm not a believer that "less is more." I firmly believe that more is more. I once saw a show of "minimal painting" at the Pasadena Museum. In a room with blank white walls stood a guard. He was neatly dressed in blue with a gun by his side and a face of such pained blank boredom that my feelings went out to him. I felt like holding his hand to give him a feeling that he existed.

"Do you see anything?" I asked him.

"Well," he answered slowly and carefully, "if you go up very close and you look very hard, you will see tic-tac-toes drawn in pale gray pencil."

This struck me as patently absurd—to have a fully armed guard with a gun policing four blank walls.

When I go to a museum, I want the walls to thunder out at me. I want to see El Greco's with their fury and anger and whites, blacks, and grays. Or Velasquez with his velvets and sensuality. Paintings with their almost total recall of life that is pulsing all around us outside these museum's walls—that's what I want to see.

Now fifteen years later, my marriage to Tino seems sunny and warm and bright. When I wake up at six o'clock, he leans over and kisses me. "Good morning sweetheart. I am going now to feed the animals. You can sleep some more."

When I get up a few hours later, I find him at the dining room table reading the newspaper. He looks up and says, "It's nice to see you again."

Altina & Tino

So it's sweet and it's funny.

We live on a dirt road only about two miles from the center of Santa Fe. As you approach the farm, you can see the dark fence that embraces and surrounds it and leads you up the hill. Then you see the land that Tino has planted and the rustic shelters that he has built for the different animals—Archie, the big white turkey who follows you up and down the little mounds and pecks at you with his strange red drooping beak; the guinea hens who delicately make their way between the rows of vegetables where they nest, laying their eggs; the golden pheasant who startles with his glint.

On one side of the road live the "Latinos" with their hand-built stone fences and with their venerable old New Mexico names: Sandoval, Vigil, Gonzales, Montoya. And on the other side, a mixture of couples: Anglo and Hispanic, Anglo and Indian. And then there are the dogs. Dogs, dogs, and dogs. Our dogs and everybody else's.

I still miss my friends in Washington, D.C. I miss the museums and the art shows. But I do love Santa Fe. It is an experience much closer to living with nature. When it rains, I can see it from every window. When the wind blows, I see it in all the trees. There is so much sky here, not just Washington's little pieces seen from small windows in big concrete buildings.

I lead a quite different and limited life now. My eyesight is failing, and my ears are no longer sharp. My energy is at low ebb. I used to pack the activities of one day into what takes me a week. Now my days are at a very slow tempo. I do more looking into the past, evaluating what my behavior was then. I study fewer things, but more deeply, less like riding a brightly colored moving carousel, more like a slow walk under the shade of trees. I do not have the swarms of friends coming and going as I once had, but I have Tino who surrounds me with his love and Fernando who cares for both of us. This is a lot, and I am grateful for it every day of my life.

My deepest thanks to my editor, Colleen Mariah Rae, whose excellent work and good counsel never failed me.

My loving thanks to Victoria Sanders whose keen intelligence has always guided me.

And thanks to my lovely friend Rose Mary Stearns for reading to me the proofs of this book.